Light Rains
Sometimes
Fall

Light Rains Sometimes Fall

A British Year Through
Japan's 72 Seasons

Lev Parikian

Elliott&Thompson

First published 2021 by
Elliott and Thompson Limited
2 John Street
London WC1N 2ES
www.eandtbooks.com

ISBN: 978-1-78396-577-9

9 8 7 6 5 4 3 2 1

A catalogue record for this book is available from
the British Library.

Typesetting by Marie Doherty
Printed by CPI Group (UK) Ltd, Croydon, CR0 4YY

CONTENTS

Contents

INTRODUCTION

There are many ways to divide a year.

Head for either pole and you'll experience two seasons: Dark and Light. In the tropics it's a similar story: Wet and Dry. And wherever you are, focusing on the hours of daylight will give you Days Getting Shorter and Days Getting Longer.

Add an intermediary season and you have three, whether it's Thailand's Cold, Hot and Rainy, or the West African Wet, Dry and Harmattan – this last named after the dusty trade wind typical of that region between November and March. The Rule of Three would also be familiar to the Ancient Egyptians, who knew *Akhet* (Inundation), *Peret* (Emergence) and *Shemu* (Harvest).

Four is what we're used to. Spring, summer, autumn, winter – so entrenched in our consciousness as 'the seasons' that we forget they really apply only to the temperate parts of our planet. And even then they don't quite cover it. Just ask Kurt Vonnegut, who reckoned the eastern seaboard of America had six: the usual four, plus 'locking' (November and December) and 'unlocking' (March and April).

You'll find variations on that theme everywhere. Little additions to the 'pattern of four', taking local conditions into account. The Hindu calendar has six seasons, or *ritu*, including the monsoon and a two-part winter. The Gulumoerrgin language group in Australia's Northern Territories divides the year into seven, their loose criteria based partly on the local climate and partly on natural phenomena such as the laying of goose eggs. And the Sami people of Swedish Lapland interleave the regular seasons with bridging periods – spring–winter (*gidádálvve*), spring–summer (*gidágiesse*), autumn–summer (*tjaktjagiesse*), and autumn–winter (*tjaktjadálvve*).

Perhaps the most extreme example is the Ancient Japanese calendar. Four seasons, each divided into six, with each of those twenty-four subdivisions (*sekki*) in turn divided further into three, for a total of seventy-two microseasons (*kō*). Five days each, with the occasional six-dayer to even it up.

The word 'ancient' is doing a lot of work. It carries associations of tradition and wisdom, while at the same time being conveniently unspecific. In this case it harks back to the sixth century, when the system of twenty-four solar terms – based on the lunisolar calendar – reached Japan from China, by way of Korea.

The calendar was rewritten and adapted for the Japanese climate in 1684 by Shibukawa Shunkai, the Edo period's first official astronomer. The microseasons referred to in this book were established in 1874, the year after Japan adopted the Gregorian calendar.

At the heart of each large season are the solstices and equinoxes – *shunbun* (vernal equinox), *geshi* (summer solstice), *shūbun* (autumnal equinox) and *tōji* (winter solstice). The beginnings of each season are also marked – *risshun* (beginning of spring), *rikka* (beginning of summer), *risshū* (beginning of autumn) and *rittō* (beginning of winter). In between, the names are dominated by the weather – rainwater, small heat, frost descent, large snow and so on.

It's in the names of the seventy-two microseasons that we see elements specific to Japan's island climate. They also reflect the importance of agriculture and the natural cycles of plants and animals in centuries past. The microseasons have haiku-like names – 'east wind melts the ice', 'frogs start singing', 'cotton flowers bloom' – each one a marker of a small bit of progress through the year. They're rooted in the rhythms of the land, but they also reflect what we intuitively know: the little changes of an ever-evolving cycle require finer definition than the broad sweep of spring, summer, autumn, winter. We all know the difference between the first flush of spring in March – daffodils, cherry blossom, great tits testing their voices – and its maturity in May – swallows, wisteria, butterflies on the wing. Officially, they're the same season. Reality and our own observations tell a different story. Big rhythms encompass small, and the simple act of acknowledging them leads to a greater connection with the natural world, which, as we all know, is a Good Thing.

How, then, do these seventy-two microseasons relate to the passing of the year in twenty-first-century suburban London, where I live? Well, in many ways they don't. While Great Britain and Japan are both island networks, there the similarities end. Different geology, different climates, different fauna and flora. And while we in Britain like to think we're fond of nature, our relationship with it lacks the formality and ritualisation captured in such uniquely Japanese concepts as *momijigari* – making special journeys in autumn to see the turning of the leaves – or *hanami* – the viewing of cherry or plum blossoms in spring. And despite the recent popularity of *shinrin-yoku*, or 'forest bathing', the average down-to-earth Brit would most likely prefer to call it 'going for a walk in the woods'.

But the beauty of this way of dividing the year is that it can be applied almost anywhere. For Japan's lotus blossom, praying mantis and bear, we have bramble, woodlouse and urban fox. And while the precise rhythms of the year will vary according to geography – and have recently been affected by the vagaries of climate change – the microseasons act as an incentive to look more consistently at the slow evolution of the natural world around us.

I am not naturally organised – although I do recognise that enviable quality when I see it – so the neatness of this system is alluring. It acknowledges the broader seasons, admits the narrowing down to more specific periods, and then nails each little moment to its own tiny mast. Big, medium, small. And there's something enticing about the convenience of putting each little bundle of five days into its own box: 'dragonflies lay eggs on water', 'starling hullabaloo', or 'maple reaches peak of glory'.

But nature is messier than that. It defies our attempts to impose order on it – just talk to any taxonomist struggling with the continual reassessment of what constitutes a species, or to a gardener doing battle with mare's tail or bindweed. It sprawls, encroaches, spills all over itself, its many tendrils inextricably intertwined. So, much as I'd like each season to have its own distinctive character, conveniently clicking from one to the next at midnight every five days, reality has other ideas. Nature doesn't roll up its sleeves on 20 June and say, 'Right, naff off, spring – it's summertime.' It rolls and waves, ebbs and flows, the distinctions often too blurred for us to notice. So I became curious about the idea of these miniature compartmentalisations, and whether this detailed dissection of the seasons was in fact valid and useful. Would it be helpful to look at nature through this lens?

Yes, it turns out.

For one thing, paying attention to the natural world for at least one day out of every five ensured I didn't inadvertently lose my connection with it. And limiting my observations to a small area I already knew – our garden, the streets around our house, the local cemetery where I take my regular exercise, the nearby common and its associated small wood – made me look again and more closely at the familiar, the everyday, the easily overlooked.

I also humbly submit that it's a worthwhile thing for anyone to do, wherever they live. It's likely that if you've bought this book you're already engaged with the natural world to some extent, but as a population we have become estranged from the rhythms of nature – so much so that expressions such as 'grain in ear' will at best be recognised as a nostalgic reference to the past, at worst misunderstood completely as some sort of bizarre instruction.

This disconnection from nature, it hardly needs overstating, has played a large part in getting us to Where We Are Now.* All the more reason, then, to find new ways of paying attention, and to give the natural world the respect it so desperately needs. The first step is to acknowledge that it's all around us, wherever we are, and – crucially – that we are part of it. We're all in the same boat together – perhaps it would be a good idea to get to know our fellow passengers that bit better. You might not know the name of that yellow flower or the butterfly that's just flitted through the garden or the bird that keeps on diving out of sight, but no matter. It's the noticing that counts.

---

* Do I need to elaborate on the many ways in which we have failed our planet, and the catastrophic situation we find ourselves in? The question is rhetorical.

1

CLEAR LIGHT SHINES
THROUGH MIST

4–8 February

Beginning of spring (*Risshun,* 立春)
East wind melts the ice
(*Harukaze kōri o toku,* 東風解凍)

When does spring start, really? With the first chiffchaff, its two-note song pinging down from the canopy? Daffodils, their taut blooms unfolding in a blaze of yellow? A woodpecker drumming, rhubarb emerging, crocuses, wild garlic, lesser celandine?

Or is it something in the air, an indefinable quality, a vibrancy you feel the moment you set foot outside? There's warmth, yes, but it's not just about temperature. Not to get fanciful, but you could almost swear the air itself is quivering with the springness of spring. And when you step out it's on your cheek, tickling the nape, lifting the spirits, the growth of everything surging through the ether.

Whatever it is, we're not there yet. Not by a long way. The sun is bright, the snowdrops quiver, blackthorn blossom sprays its light amid the gloom, but these are merely harbingers. Spring is round the corner, but the corner is long.

Each of the big seasons of the traditional Japanese calendar starts at the midpoint between equinox and solstice. It's as good a place to start as any, but even though it says 'beginning of spring' and 'east wind melts the ice', this year's reality begs to differ. There is no ice to melt. Not in West Norwood. Not in 2020. But there is chill. In the air, on the pavements, dusting the leaves of dormant plants. These early-February days hold memories of past winters, the thermometer hovering just above zero, the sun low and bright. A time of walks and anticipation.

False spring.

Some years, winter delivers a bitter rebuke, just in case you were getting smug – a late snowstorm, bud-nipping frosts. This year it is rain. Much, much rain.

I survey the garden and its neighbours from the safety of my office. Standard strips lined up side by side, and backing on to more of the same. There are trees to break up the monotony. A large cedar of Lebanon two doors down, its angular shape sadly truncated by surgery; behind it a tall, looming cypress, its denuded tip a favourite perching point for a variety of birds; to the left, more lone trees, thrusting rudely up above the suburban sprawl.

Look beyond and there is a gentle rise, streets populated with lines of houses, a repeating tessellation of London brick. On a good day, with the sun slanting on them from a certain angle, I can see in them – I admit it takes a small leap of the imagination – the contours of a Tuscan hillside town, a configuration of straight lines and angles and light and shade and warmth that does pleasing things to the brain.

As I say, a leap of imagination. But where would we be without it?

The garden is showing signs of emerging from winter. The hazel on the left has offered a welcome patch of brightness among the general drab for a couple of weeks, but now the catkins have passed the luminous-yellow phase and have an air of self-pity. Their work will soon be done, pollen scattered on the breeze, leaves emerging, the business of slow and steady growth under way.

Beneath them, a scattering of pale pink cyclamen, their propensity for self-seeding resulting in a mild spot of lawn encroachment. Next to them, a patch of snowdrops, in their prime, their milky blooms hanging slightly open, like fairground grabbers.

The garden is soft underfoot, unwelcoming. To venture into it too often would make it a quagmire. Instead, I take to the streets. Left out of the door, down the hill past the bus garage, up again – shutting out the rumble of traffic, weaving through oncoming pedestrians and ignoring the temptations of the excellent Italian deli. The manic tinkle of a goldfinch from the trees by the bridge accompanies me past the station, fading as I go down the hill, past the bare horse chestnut standing sentinel at the church gates, across the road and into the cemetery.

The path splits near the entrance. You can take the big loop, or you can get distracted by the crossing paths.

I get distracted. It's easy enough, today. There's a clarity to the early-morning light. Low sun angles through the mist, lending the scene an other-worldly feeling, as if sent to lift you from the doldrums.

This place, one of the 'Magnificent Seven' (large, private cemeteries established across London in the 1830s), was built by people with a respect – awe, even – for death. Monuments abound, and family vaults. There is statuary galore – stone angels draped over slabs in poses of anguish, or holding one finger up in the air, like a cricket umpire delivering their final adjudication. There are well-established trees: willows, planes, oaks, sycamores, a dying ash, others whose names I don't yet know. There are areas left untended, tangled undergrowth and fallen trees combining to give the cemetery a welcome feel of wildness. There is a crematorium at the top of the hill, its post-war architecture lending a faintly municipal air to that part of the site. Today, there is a magnificent, rude energy in the air. These sunny late-winter days seem to bring it out. The birds of early spring – dunnocks, great tits, goldcrests, wrens – are shouting, their libidos awakening like a teenager's.

They're accompanied by splashes of bright colour among the drab and soggy, standing out with remarkable freshness, enhanced by the cold winter light. Euphorbia's two-tone greens; the bright red of rowan berries – all the more dramatic against the ice-blue sky; a dogwood, its long, slender branches hooping upwards, zinging yellow as if illuminated from within.

I don't know what makes me look up. There's no warning *gronk*. A disturbance in the ether, perhaps. It's only there for a few seconds, its familiar quasi-goose-like silhouette jarring in this place. A cormorant, flying busily somewhere, gone behind the treeline almost before I've had a chance to register it. I find joy in the familiar, but surprises can be good too. I will remember it: that time I saw the cormorant over the cemetery.

2

DUNNOCK SONG DEFIES
TRAFFIC NOISE

9–13 February

Beginning of spring (*Risshun*, 立春)
Bush warblers start singing in the mountains
(*Kōō kenkan su*, 黄鶯睍睆)

The weather changes overnight. A switch flick, conveniently marking the new season. Everything is different. The barometer plunges; the wind picks up. Rain – wild, unfettered, destructive – batters the country into submission. A quashing of hope, a reminder of our abject weakness in the face of nature's doodah.

Storm Ciara is in town.

There is a grim fascination to storms. I watch Ciara's progress on an app, the pretty green swirls intensifying to orange where the wind is strongest. It's easy and safe to monitor it on a screen but the reality is devastating. She leaves behind her widespread flooding and millions of pounds of damage. Living halfway up a hill in a big city, we're protected from the depredations, can see it out in comfort and warmth without worrying about the aftermath. Hunkered down in my office, I nonetheless eye the rattling fence panels with mild concern.

The next day, a small squadron of goldfinches appears briefly on the silver birches flanking the gravelled parking area in front of the house, drawn by the seed heads. They've been regular and welcome visitors recently. Not the twenty-strong flock that illuminated our winter dusks two years ago, but a loyal band of four, their chattering energy a constant boon. Bounce in, plunder, bounce out: irrepressible, uplifting.

I venture out. The wind comes in gusts, as if still itching for a fight. The sky is half and half: lucid blue overlaid with fast-moving fluffies.

My walk past the bus garage is interrupted by a loud scrabbling song. A dunnock, brazenly advertising its availability for early-season shagging. A defiant 'Business as Usual' sign to the world.

They're early singers, dunnocks. They don't quite match robins and wrens, which sing through the winter, but if you hear an indeterminate jumble of birdsong in January – some would call it a mindless jangling – it's likely to be a dunnock, and by early February it's a constant. The bush warbler, a semi-migratory bird that moves from mountains to city when spring arrives, has been a staple seasonal marker in Japanese culture for over a thousand years. The dunnock finds its place in our culture not in poetry but in the wealth of folk names – more than fifty of them, including 'shuffle-wing', 'hedge Betty' and 'winter nightingale'. 'Dunnock song defies traffic noise' might be less poetic than 'bush warblers start singing in the mountains', but it's accurate and feels appropriate.

I stop for a moment. This is not a place for natural lingering. An intersection of roads, the air constantly assaulted by traffic noise. But there is some relief from the unremitting cacophony. A community planting scheme has brought a transformation. The low walls and borders skirting the bus garage have been planted up, a large banner displays a Carol Ann Duffy poem about bees, the red-brick walls bear the words of Alfred, Lord Tennyson behind sprightly fruit trees and low shrubbery. It makes a difference, and this dunnock seems to want to make it its home. It perches on a low shrub, belting out its song above the din of the blessed, cursed, infernal internal combustion engine. It waits for a bus to pass, then flits across the road and over the brick wall behind me, scant respecter of the Green Cross Code.

I continue. Corner shop, cafe, pub, church. Roar of motorbike. Scatter of pigeon.

In the cemetery, Ciara's detritus is everywhere: branches scattered higgledy-piggledy across paths, benches upended, pools of water gathering in hollows. Runnels stream down the sides of the path, diverted by gatherings of twigs, mud and leaves. A scattering of earthworms, washed onto the path by the storm, stranded, but working their way gamely back to safety. I stop to pick one up and rehouse it on the verge. It shows its gratitude by shrinking to a fraction of its former length and making little exploratory wrigglings on the mud. When I return twenty minutes later, it's gone, burrowed down into the earth to work its aerating magic.

The aftermath has a certain peace to it, despite the gusting winds. There is a pause, a recalibration, as if the world just needs a cup of tea and a bit of a sit-down before getting back to it. The sun, low in the sky, combines with the backdrop of grey clouds to do magical things to the light, kisses the treetops with a glimmer of burnished gold.

But now the wind is up again, and fast clouds roll in. A brief, drenching squall. I attempt the 'it's only weather' attitude towards showers. It half works, but chill and damp undermine optimism. I slow my pace, and my eye is caught by another piece of luminosity. Moss on a gravestone, usually dull green, caught a glancing blow by the sun. Up close, it turns into a magic garden, yellowy fronds frizzing upwards on the slenderest of stalks, bronzed tips slightly curled. Further on, a desiccated umbellifer leaf hangs loose, twirling in the reduced breeze, its veining a grid map of delicacy bound together with sturdy, elegant arteries. Small details, rewarding close examination.

Two trees have succumbed to the wind. They weren't large – eight metres or so – and their slender trunks perhaps belie a fundamental weakness. Standing alone, away from the protection of their colleagues, their root systems weakened by the relentless rain of January, they were no match for the indiscriminate violence of the storm. They are a forlorn sight, measuring their length on the ground, lying across graves, the randomness of physics no respecter of personal feelings. Trapped underneath one tree is a clump of vivid colours: yellow, red, pink. Fabric flowers, impervious to seasons, their grinning artificial brightness incongruous against the spillikin tangle of the dead tree's branches.

In an ideal world these trees would be left where they fall, would provide a home for countless little bugs and fungi, would decay naturally over months and years. But they will be removed, tidied up, their root holes filled, and we'll carry on as if they were never there.

3

RAIN SOMETIMES TURNS TO HAIL

14–18 February

Beginning of spring (*Risshun,* 立春)

Fish emerge from the ice
(*Uo kōri o izuru,* 魚上氷)

This is not a season to be trusted. You pull back the curtains to clear skies, but check the forecast and there's treachery afoot: rain, wind, squally nonsense set to ruin your afternoon.

According to the Japanese calendar, fish emerge from the ice, then duck back down again sharpish if they've got any sense.

What I'd like is a proper cold spell. Frost and ice and maybe snow. But instead we get unsettling wind and spirit-sapping rain. February, the shortest and longest month.

For some reason I stop on my way out. There's no flash of colour to catch my eye, nor a particular movement, but some instinct makes me look at the wisteria to the right of the front door, its branches twining up from the knobbly base. Despite their slenderness they give the impression of age, a wizened aspect in stark contrast with the fresh whitewash of the wall behind them.

In a couple of months they will throw out frothing cascades of lilac-coloured blooms, the epitome of suburban horticultural splendour, framing the windows in a way satisfying to the eye, if a mite hackneyed to some tastes.

But I love wisteria. Partly because it's one of the ones I know. But it's also that delicate colour, and the impression of light and air the blooms give when in full spate. A champagne plant.

At this stage it's no more than the merest hint of growth, the tiniest, most tentative toe in the freezing swimming pool. From the rough branch comes a hard, dry twig, and from the twig the darkly curled beginnings of a leaf, and cradled in that growth is a morsel of palest yellow, so embryonic it looks ready to duck back in at any moment.

It's the last day of the *sekki* ('beginning of spring'). However tiny it may be, the wisteria bud has appeared just in time.

We have peregrines.

These words, unimaginable for a Londoner forty years ago, put a spring in the step. The post-war slump in their population, driven by increased pesticide use, has largely been redressed, and now they're a common sight in city centres. Every outing to West Norwood *ville* brings the possibility of an encounter. Reason enough to venture outside in unpleasant conditions.

A peregrine's natural nesting habitat is a cliff face. And London abounds with them. Charing Cross Hospital, Tate Modern, and now our local church. The male* flies up into the belfry as I pass. Its

---

* Smaller than the female, as is often the way with falcons and hawks.

partner steps aside to let it in, maybe passing comment as she does so on her spouse's failure to bring breakfast.

Over the road, through the gates, traffic noise receding as I make my way into the cemetery. A goldcrest welcomes me with a short burst of its thin, piping song from a yew tree to my right. To the left, a robin's shivering ribbon of song adds cheer. From somewhere, a wren, loud and sharp. And up ahead, a patch of grass becomes birds, a flurry of wings alerting me to their presence as they fly up with a chorus of *tseeps*. Always busy, always on the move.

Redwings. Ten, fifteen – no, twenty at least.

They're a reassuring presence through the winter, arriving from Scandinavia sometime in October in search of milder weather and a steady food supply. The mysteries of birds are many and unfathomable, but migration is surely chief among them. When I think of it – whether it's the winter journeys undertaken to escape the harsh north, or the long haul from Africa in search of an abundance of insects – my mind fills with questions. How do they know when to leave? How do they know where to go? How does a tidgy thing like a redwing, twenty centimetres from stem to stern, fly all the way from northern Scandinavia to West Norwood without keeling over and dying?

Not all of them do. But if death is a possibility over the roiling seas, it's a certainty in the frozen north, so over they come. They'll gravitate towards their favoured foods: red berries such as hawthorn in the first instance, then earthworms and other wriggling grubbers for the second half of winter. A cold patch in early spring – like the Beast from the East of 2018 – might send them to gardens in search of handouts, and the alert and sympathetic gardener will oblige by throwing out an apple or two.

They're our smallest thrush, with a keen look enhanced by a creamy stripe above the eye. The red of the name – a soft red, the same as the bricks of the old library over the way – always seems to me to be under the wing rather than on it. But 'red armpit'* would be less appealing.

I stop, let them settle. Do not disturb. They're flighty, keeping me at a distance. Fifteen metres or so, no more. Then, without prompting, they're up and away, over my head, to another part of the cemetery, and as I crane my neck round and up to watch them pass, suddenly it's not the birds I notice. By stealth, the last vestiges of blue sky have been engulfed by thick, dark clouds. Clouds of menace. Clouds of trouble. Clouds wanted in twenty-six states. And a relatively rare phenomenon – a drop in temperature so swift you actually feel it as it happens. From 'pleasantly mild for the time of year' to 'someone's just bundled me into an industrial freezer' in ten seconds flat.

It starts as rain – heavy, fat, splashing drops blattering down like clumsy fingers on a piano keyboard. And now hail, the closest thing we've had to a wintry shower in months. They're not big stones, no more than grains really. But I'm in the middle of them, which isn't the position you'd choose when it comes to hailstones. They're not big enough to hurt, and they're gone in a couple of minutes, but file them under 'inconvenient'.

'There's no such thing as bad weather,' Alfred Wainwright once said. 'Only unsuitable clothing.' He was right, I suppose. Although possibly also a trifle smug.

---

* Or even, strictly speaking, 'red wingpit'.

4

WOODPECKERS START DRUMMING

19–23 February

Rainwater (*Usui,* 雨水)
Rain moistens the soil
(*Tsuchi no shō uruoi okoru,* 土脉潤起)

The man – slim, dark, somehow forlorn – cuts a resigned figure as he ploughs his way gamely through the sodden grass in the cemetery. In his left hand he holds a piece of paper. In his right, daffodils, yellow buds peeping out from their wrapping. He stops, consults the piece of paper, looks vaguely around, finds his bearings, sets off again.

The brightness of daffodils is an antidote to the weather. There has been rain – moistening the soil in accordance with the name of the season – but if these days have a defining feature, it's the wind.

It keeps me awake one night, rattling the windows, howling around the eaves. I'm all in favour of a light breeze ruffling my collar on a warm spring day, but this is something else. Turbulent, untamed, unsettling.

The complete absence of the sun for the first four days only intensifies the need for cheer. The clouds vary from highish to very low, but not once do they part to give us a glimpse of blue sky. The weather feels stuck, swirling around in a frustrated vortex of its own making. What it needs is a nudge, and eventually it gets it, the fifth day of the season dawning brighter, warmer. But not, it turns out, drier.

The drizzle footles in half-heartedly mid-morning, not even having the grace to be proper rain. Dingy, dismal, soul-sapping. For once, though, my keen weather eye coincides with an accurate forecast and I'm out early, entering the cemetery as the gates open, my arrival coinciding with Daffodil Guy's.

His offering is mirrored by clumps of daffodils on the ground. The prevailing atmosphere might make humans hunch into their raincoats, but the daffodils haven't got the message. They're relentlessly upbeat, jauntiness in flower form.

It's easy to be sniffy about daffodils, with their ubiquity and obviousness, but today their yellow trumpets are the fillip I need. Besides, it's not their fault they're popular. They never hurt anyone.*

My preference has always been for the more delicate members of the narcissus family, those bonsai-like offerings that add cheer to a small terrace pot. And if I see one of the two-tone varieties, I think of the wild daffodil, supplanted to such an extent by the cultivated form that if we were to encounter one, we'd be unlikely either to recognise or appreciate it.

---

* Unless they mistakenly bought them thinking they were shallots and sliced and fried them to include in a casserole, but in those cases I have to say my sympathy remains entirely with the daffodils.

But I'd be lying if I said I was immune to the allure of a tightly furled bunch of daffs wrapped in florist's paper. An offering of friendship, or a token of self-care. Something to brighten the kitchen on a drear February day. A couple of quid well spent.

I leave them and walk up the hill. The snowdrops on the left, so perfect just a few days ago, are on the wane, their petals splayed like the legs of a drunk on the sofa at 2 a.m. Some plants age gracefully, their retreat undergone without fanfare. But these have given up on appearances, the recent battering stripping away their delicacy and neatness.

A sound. Faint and distant, almost an illusion. I stop and tilt my head,* hoping it will come again. After a few seconds it does. *Duuurrrrr*. Instant uplift.

Great spotted woodpeckers are common enough, and increasingly regular visitors to garden feeders, but even a distant aural encounter with one counts as an event. Perhaps it's their colouring, the pied and barred plumage offset by vivid red on the nape[†] and vent; perhaps it's their extraordinary ability to move round a tree trunk with no apparent effort, side-slipping without visible propulsion; perhaps it's simply because they're bigger than the feeder regulars, so when they appear it feels like an exotic visitation. Whatever the reason, whenever I hear their short, sharp *chik* my head snaps up and I start scanning the trunks of nearby trees. And their drumming in the dying stages of winter is a marker of transition to the next stage. Today it's even more welcome than usual.

---

* This, I am told, is the best way to locate the source of a mystery sound. The idea is that you're trying to replicate the hearing system of an owl, which has one ear higher than the other.

† In the male, at least. The female's head is black.

The gentle charms of the woodpecker's drumming are over-shadowed by the dramatic sight that confronts me as I turn the corner.

It's the splash of white against the dark grass that draws my attention. And then I see the still figure hunched over it, wary, alert, alive to the possibility of disturbance.

I keep my distance.

Bloodthirsty creature that I am, I wish I had seen the kill. A peregrine stooping on its prey is famously one of the most dramatic sights in nature, and I'm a strong believer in the importance of embracing all aspects of the natural world without queasiness or revulsion.

No matter how clean the initial strike, the aftermath is messy. Feathers strew the grass. A few of them swirl up in a gust of wind as the peregrine goes about its business.

The identification of dead birds from a distant glimpse of their disfigured corpses isn't my forte, but I lay myself a quiet wager that the bird in the peregrine's clutches is a black-headed gull. The white feathers point towards gull rather than pigeon, and while a peregrine might easily have the capacity to take out a herring gull, the smaller black-headed seems a more likely target.

Gulls are increasingly regular in towns. I saw one the day before, flying low the wrong way down a one-way street, in defiance of convention and traffic regulations. If this is the same bird, it's had a swift and brutal comeuppance for its flagrant disregard for the law.

The peregrine takes things slowly. Constant vigilance is its watchword. It plucks at its prey, then looks up to check the coast is clear. It has a good meal, and is keen not to give it up. But before long two carrion crows enter the scene. Jaunty walk, itching for a rumble. The peregrine grabs what's left of the gull and flies off, trailing feathers in its wake. An unspecified organ dangles by a thread of what I assume is intestine.

The man is still there as I complete the loop. Standing alone by the grave, his slender frame silhouetted against the plain brick wall behind.

5

CROCUSES EMERGE
FROM DAMP SOIL

24–29 February

Rainwater (*Usui,* 雨水)

Mist starts to linger
(*Kasumi hajimete tanabiku,* 霞始靆)

We will have mist. Perhaps not the mist of Japanese art, cloaking the mountains and forests with mystical softness; nor even the mist of haiku, rooting the reader in a specific part of the year, enabling the poet to invoke vivid scenes with maximum economy.

But there will be mornings when its soft evanescence descends, making everything 10 per cent more attractive before gradually lifting to ease you into the day.

These are not those mornings.

There is wind. Whippy, bone-chilling.

There is cold. Heating-and-duvet cold.

There is rain. Not a benevolent hair-frizzing mizzle, but sharp spikes on the skin.

All in all, a disincentive for activity. My instinct is to hunker down, an instinct not shared by two feral pigeons, which swoop in mid-morning and walk around the garden, apparently impervious to the elements. Their strutting action – head going back and forth in counterpoint to the body – is a technique to help them build a more complete view of the world, a compensation for the immobility of their eyes in their skulls, but it somehow gives them a comical air, an impression only reinforced by the staring madness in the eyes themselves.

It's easy enough to dismiss these birds as 'rats with wings', but if we hate them for their ubiquity, adaptive success and propensity to make life unpleasant for species that want to share their space, then maybe that's just because they're stealing our shtick.

I like to spring to their defence, pointing out the attractiveness of the green and purple iridescence on their necks, or their aerial ability. Watch, without prejudice, a feral pigeon fly – fast, manoeuvrable, wings held in a sharp 'V' as they come into land with unerring accuracy – and maybe, just maybe, you'll watch through different eyes.

Slice it whichever way you like, the garden remains uninviting, the soil damp and squidgy. But there is hope in it. Crocuses, beloved as early harbingers of spring, stand out, a little pool of brightness in a sea of drab. That combination of rich purple and zinging orange is an antidote to gloom.

I'm also buoyed by the gradual increase of light. The slow playing-out of the year's rhythms, gradual lengthenings and short-enings, is mostly imperceptible, but sometimes the hours of daylight seem to take an abrupt leap, and spring is suddenly a touchable prospect. Sunrise is now before seven; sunset after half past five. It feels like a watershed of sorts. And with the passing of this arbitrary marker comes a renewed sense of anticipation.

The blackbird plays its part. Early mornings and I are not natural friends, but from time to time I snap awake at 4.48 a.m., fully alert and ready for the day. And in spring, there's the blackbird waiting for me, somewhere over the road. If I have the energy I get up and sit outside, at the back of the house, swaddled in jumpers and clasping a cup of coffee, listening to the world waking up.

I do not have the energy. Not on this occasion. But when the time comes I take myself out and roam the streets, and the blackbird's still there. Its clear, mellow song cuts through the traffic, offering a counterpoint to the relentless background thrum of the city.

This urban environment, dominated by man-made materials, can seem bereft of nature. Concrete, tarmac, stone, brick, metal, glass, plastic. No space for greenery. Yet everywhere it seizes opportunities where it can find them, even in the busiest places. Opposite the station, above a cafe, down that little alley. Plants poking up in the gaps between paving slabs, a straggly flower sticking out from a ledge at the top of the pub building. Remove all human activity and you would quickly see to what extent our mere presence suppresses the natural world. This thought is both dispiriting and heartening. Dispiriting because it's a damning indictment of human beings in general, but heartening because it's also testament to nature's resilience.

The skies clear. The wind is cold enough to warrant three layers, but at least there is sun.

A three-way wren-song battle plays out around me, punctuated by the *chips* of a great spotted woodpecker. Robins sing loud. Three goldfinches bounce over. Blue tits and great tits provide a constant backdrop of twitters and shrieks. A wood pigeon flies out with a clatter of wings – recognisable from that sound alone. A jay flies off to the left, its white rump, splayed wings and slight pot belly catching the eye. A parakeet gives a small, half-hearted squawk as I pass. Carrion crows patrol the paths, always on the lookout for scraps. A fox scampers out in front of me and I nearly lose my balance.

Adventure everywhere.

The clear skies can't last. Already the wind is doing its work, bringing in more unsettled weather, the sky darkening ominously behind me.

I beat the rain home by a few seconds. It blatters the terrace in a way that makes me glad I'm not a flagstone. A short shower, but heavy, passing through quickly.

Then, out of the flux, a miracle.

The sky, like Gaul, is divided into three parts. Behind and to the right, clear blue; ahead and to the left, receding dark clouds illuminated by low sunlight. And bridging the gap, in accordance with the laws of physics, a rainbow.

My fascination for rainbows is almost primitive. I can sympathise with early cultures around the world that built legends around their miraculous appearance in the sky. In Japanese mythology a rainbow was seen as the Floating Bridge of Heaven, on which the creators of the world, Izanagi and Izanami, descended to create order from chaos – an interpretation that has its attractions. No matter how clearly I hold the science in my head, with its reflections and refractions and dispersal of light through water droplets and visible light spectrums and all of that, they still seem like evidence of a benevolent god, a god who knows what we like and is minded, just occasionally, to indulge us when we need it most.

This one is a cracker, vibrant against the dark clouds behind, and allowing me to forget for a moment the bland urban landscape below it. While I know the bands are in fact a continuous spectrum, my brain tells me they're clearly defined. The colours are intense, sharpened by the last remnants of fine mist in the air. It's the kind of rainbow that instantly has you looking for its ghostly reflected twin just above.

And so it comes to pass. The second, outer rainbow is less intense, as they always are, and not quite complete. Childlike, I will its two ends to meet in the middle. If only wishing made it so.

But with the nearly double rainbow comes that special light, of low sun slanting across a city against a backdrop of dark clouds, illuminating the landscape in previously unconsidered ways, and with that illumination comes a lightening of the spirit, a quelling of turbulence, and a warm glow to counteract the chill.

6

BLACKTHORN SHEDS BLOSSOM

1–5 March

Rainwater (*Usui*, 雨水)
Grass sprouts, trees bud
(*Sōmoku mebae izuru*, 草木萌動)

The sunshine was an aberration. Back comes the damp with a vengeance.

On the first day it takes the form of a mist-like mizzle, the kind of saturation that almost doesn't qualify as rain. 'Soft', some would call it. But there's nothing soft about the accompanying chill. It's not measurable by thermometer alone – just a feeling.

The garden birds seem unaffected. The lone dunnock forever busy around the base of the lavender; the coal tit smash-and-grabbing from the feeder – spry, alert, whizz, gone; the invisible wren, offering the merest snatch of song.

And then on day three the weather takes the gloves off and lays about it with the abandon of a saloon bar fighter with a chair leg. Grass sprouts, trees bud, then rain bastards them into submission.

I'm open to the pleasures of rain. Often I embrace it. But its extent, variety and sheer relentlessness in recent weeks has worn me down, and this is the final straw. It turns out that what we thought was rain wasn't rain at all. It was merely the preparation for rain. This is rain designed to bring on impromptu Gene Kelly impersonations; rain to give you a true and first-hand understanding of the word 'drench'; rain to make you shout, 'Oh, fuck *off*.'

We are now in the realms of content usually reserved for subscribers.

And it all kicks off during my daily walk. Of course it does. After a few minutes it ceases to be a walk, turning instead into an upright swim. Bedraggled, I troop disconsolately home, where I squeeze myself out and settle in for an evening's gentle steaming.

This saturation makes the next morning's blue skies all the more welcome. The few clouds aren't about to deliver watery misery – they're high and fluffy, chivvied across the sky by a stiff breeze that makes walking faster not a choice but an imperative. At times the wind feels as if it might settle into some warmth, but then a gust puts me right and I hunch deeper into my coat. After yesterday's downpour the ground on the common is boggier than I fancy, parts of it churned up by the footfall like a recreation-ground goalmouth, so I give it a miss in favour of the semi-formal gardens of the Rookery, where the paths are reassuringly firm, and the shelter of the walls and hedges gives respite from the elements.

A few days ago, the blackthorn blossom was so full of life it felt permanent. Now the tree has shed almost all of it, like an impatient Jenga player saying, 'Ah, sod it', and sending the blocks tumbling down in a heap. The discarded leaves surround the tree, a snowy smattering on the floor, pretty in the sunlight.

Out of the familiar soundscape comes a distinctive *pock*. I look up, more in hope than expectation, and almost by accident see the dumpy shape of a nuthatch fly over, its silhouette enhanced by what I presume is a nut in its beak. Awakened, my ears pick out a series of sounds. Chip of woodpecker, squeal of blackbird, wail of child, chuckle of father.

The light has a vividness lacking in recent days. It catches the plumage of a blue tit, makes the colours sing. The bird is perched on a nearby bush, apparently having a good swear at the world, and I'm close enough to catch the belligerent glint in its eye. It fixes me with a glare, tells me to fuck off, and then it's away, bouncing out of my sight.

I relish the blue tit. It's a common species, ubiquitous almost, but still fascinating, and this specimen, vivid of appearance and character, is somehow memorable.

But, unlike what I see next, it's not unusual.

I nearly don't see it at all. And, having seen it, I nearly dismiss it.

It's sitting at the top of the cedar of Lebanon. This is a magnificent behemoth of a tree, all height and darkness and dramatically fingered branches reaching all around.

At its top, peeking out from behind a cone, an unusual bird. Unusual for my patch, at least.

I've never been a great one for rarities. Certainly not to the level of driving across the country at the mention of a dusky thrush, or whatever the latest arrival to our shores is, swept across the Atlantic only to make landfall and find itself staring into a hundred implacable telescope and telephoto lenses.

But that doesn't mean I'm averse to the unusual.

I notice the bird not because I'm looking for a bird in the tree, but because I'm looking in general. The act of noticing, once undertaken, makes you realise how little of your life you've spent looking – really looking. And it's an addictive process. It can take the form of examining something familiar in great detail. Or it can take the form of seeking out the hidden, the out-of-the-way.

In this case it manifests itself as a sort of background 'always on'. And when you're familiar with an area, the unfamiliar sticks out, rings little bells in the back of your head.

At first I think it's a pigeon, but then my unconscious looker says, 'No, that's not right, it's not plump enough.' Then it reckons it might be a mistle thrush, which would be a fine thing in itself, but no, not quite right. And then, in the instant between raising my binoculars and holding them to my eyes, the word 'kestrel' jumps into my head.

In fact it's more like: 'KESTREL!'

Because I haven't seen a kestrel here before. So this sighting is at least a moderately sized deal.

Through the binoculars I can see its short, hooked beak, the slender yellow eye ring, the pale grey on its crown, the streaking on its front.

It's seen me, of course. That's the rule of thumb. When you see any bird, and in particular a bird of prey, with their enhanced optical capacity, it will already have seen you some time ago.

I will it to stay in place a bit longer. When you have something unusual, you don't want the encounter to end.

Willpower isn't enough. It's off, flying its nimble kestrel flight – definitely not a mistle thrush, how could I have been so stupid? – over the white garden and away behind the wood, leaving me with the memory of it to accompany me home.

7

BIRDSONG FILLS THE AIR

6–10 March

Insects awaken (*Keichitsu,* 啓蟄)

Hibernating insects surface
(*Sugomori mushito o hiraku,* 蟄虫啓戸)

There must be something in the air.

Perhaps it's simply that, for once, it's not raining; perhaps, despite my perception that it remains two-jumper weather, there's a hint of apricity* not detectable by mere humans; perhaps the birds are taking their cue from the awakening insects.

Whatever the trigger, the air is suddenly full of song.

A lot of it, I realise, is song thrushes. They get going early in the singing season, and it doesn't take many of them to stir up a racket. The volume and timbre of a song thrush's song – loud and full – is ear-catching. And when you have two of them giving it large from

---

* This obsolete word, meaning 'the warmth of the sun on a winter's day', has been brought back into use recently by esteemed word-wrangler Susie Dent. And a good job too.

opposing trees, it takes an act of defiance not to listen. Bold and strident, but not without melodious qualities, they're at it hammer and tongs from somewhere off to my right as I enter the cemetery. It prompts me to take the less trodden, anticlockwise loop, and soon enough I find the first of them, somewhere high in a large plane tree.

Some of the phrases sound as if it's whistling to get your attention; others – fluting, mellifluous – as if it's got stuck on the first two notes while trying to learn a blackbird's song; one phrase is a poor imitation of a green woodpecker's laugh. The phrases are all short, and they are all repeated.

'That's the wise thrush; he sings each song twice over.'*

Which is all very well, but sometimes you want to say, 'Yes, heard you the first time.'

It's easy enough to be caught up in the thrush's song. It drowns out most other things. But there are gaps, and in the gaps I hear a thin, piping voice. It's familiar to me, and is nowadays invariably accompanied by a small pulse of relief. I can still hear it. Decrepitude is held at bay for the moment.

The goldcrest's song is high. Our hearing range contracts as we get older. The conclusion is inevitable: at some point I'll lose the ability to hear it. But not yet.

Audible it might be, but it keeps itself hidden. Every time I hear one I embark on a mission to find the source, a mission often doomed to failure. Goldcrests (tidgy) like to hang around in conifers (untidgy), with predictable frustrations for the searcher. Part of the knack – goldcrests being notorious flitters – is to expand your

* Robert Browning, 'Home-Thoughts, From Abroad', to save you looking it up.

peripheral vision and set the sensors to detect the merest hint of movement. Most often all you'll be able to say is that you saw the twitch of foliage where you thought a goldcrest might have been, but it's an engaging enough pursuit. After an enjoyable but fruitless five minutes, accompanied throughout by the goldcrest's chirpy song, I throw in the towel and move on.

I might not have found the goldcrest, but the act of searching is a reminder to look up, which, in the age of abject slavery to the rectangle of misery we like to call our 'phone', amounts to an expression of individuality. Rebellion, almost. And it stands me in good stead at the end of the same day, when I take myself to the other end of my patch for a related but different birdsong experience. If the battle of the repeating song thrushes in broad daylight was arresting to the ear, there's a different quality to the crepuscular blackbird duel.

There's an other-worldliness to these moments when day yields to dusk. A world of shadows and unknowns, scarier in its way than total darkness. The moon, one day off fullness, illuminates a passing cloud from behind – stock horror-film footage lacking only a howling wolf. The soundtrack is rather more reassuring. Robins provide silvery backing, but the main attraction is the blackbirds, giving forth their famous song from the treetops.

From where I stand – just off the path so as not to impede passing dog-walkers – I can hear four of them. Two are distant, adding a sense of depth to the aural spectacle. But two are close, equidistant on each side of me, the nuances of their throaty offerings clearly audible. It's territorial advertisement, establishing credentials early in the season, all in the interest of procreation and survival for the individual and the species. But as I listen to them toss their songs back and forth, each waiting for the other to finish before starting its own refrain, it's tempting to liken them to a pair of jazz musicians. Play, listen, respond, adapt, develop. Here's a nice idea. Ah yes, and how about this? Nice, nice, and then of course there's this.

In half an hour or so these birds, and the robins with them, will fall silent, or will downgrade their vocalisations to repeated, nervous chipping sounds – checking the locks before lights out, imagining a burglar behind every leaf. But this is the golden moment, and for ten minutes I stand and bathe in it.

A chill wind ruffles the branches of the trees in the wood behind me. It is cold. I am wearing, as so often, one layer too few. Forever destined to misjudge clothing.

A disturbance, a wrong shadow, large, moving just above the treeline, then merging with it. A known unknown. Something different for a second, now gone. I replay the moment in my head, move towards the spot, searching the dark outline of the trees for irregularities.

And there it is. A conifer, its branches darkly outlined against the dusky sky, has an addition. An addition with a gracefully curved S-bend neck and dagger bill, incongruously perched on the top. Old scraggle-beard, that beaky reminder of the dinosaur ancestry of all birds. Pterodactyl in a grey shawl.

A heron. My first for this place.

Maybe it's a regular here. Or maybe it's just stopped off because it knows there's a carp in the little pond just the other side of the fence. Maybe there won't be a carp in there for long.

It's mesmerising in its stillness, a reminder that good things can happen if we slow down, or even stop completely. And if I shut out the joggers and dog-walkers and the background hum of modern life, and concentrate very hard, I can just about touch the idea of going back to a time when these birds lived in a different, human-free world.

I stay for a few more minutes, until the chipping of the robins and blackbirds has quietened and the heron's outline is swallowed by darkness.

8

CROWS START BUILDING NESTS

11–15 March

Insects awaken (*Keichitsu,* 啓蟄)
First peach blossoms (*Momo hajimete saku,* 桃始笑)

If our garden has an equivalent to the Japanese peach blossoms, it's the three columnar fruit trees arranged in a line along the right-hand fence. Apple, pear, cherry. The pear in the middle makes the first move, tentative buds poking through. In the corner, a josta-berry bush* does the same, and on the other side of the garden the flowering shrubs match them step for step, clematis and hydrangea showing strong early-season form. The soft, furry roundness of the buds, showing a hint of the creamy white that will dominate their particular corners of the garden in weeks to come, contrasts with the spiky dark green of the accompanying leaves. For now there is still more twig than bud, but it's only a matter of time.

---

* Given to us by musical friends and fellow allotmenteers, this is (so I'm told) basically a posh gooseberry. This information has made me more aware than ever before of the social hierarchy in soft fruit.

At the front of the house, a magnolia buds shyly, as if unwilling to commit itself until certain it's safe. Just the one bloom for the moment. Wouldn't want to overdo it. On the other side, under the silver birch, not flamboyant but there if you look, the plants I've always called 'that nice little flower' open up to the world. Rigorous research* reveals them to be *Pachysandra terminalis*. They're unshowy, but they have their place, and it's good to appreciate the easily overlooked.

These slight but perceptible changes are accompanied by an increase in temperature, the kind that spurs you to go out coatless, a decision you regret just when you're too far from home to rectify it.

And by 'you' I do of course mean 'I'.

Dismayed by my inability to gauge temperature – a fifty-five-year learning project still not bearing fruit – I nonetheless plough on, picking up the pace to try to offset the chill.

Down the hill. Up again. Hello, peregrine.

My peregrine hit rate has been high lately. They've developed a pleasing habit of going for a little fly just as I pass the church. Today the bird's timing is perfect. A little call – *kii-kii-kii-kii* – to catch the attention, then launch, dip down, flapflapflap gli–i–i–ide.

I think, for the millionth time, how much fun it must be to fly. The freedom. The views. The whooshing sound in your ears.[†] And even if my instinctive reaction to aeroplane journeys is 'AAAGGGHHH, WHAT ARE WE DOING? THIS IS MADNESS', it usually morphs quickly enough to 'Ooh, look at the pretty clouds',

---

* I ask my wife, a garden designer by profession. She knows everything.

[†] I don't suppose birds do get a whooshing sound in their ears when they fly, probably because their ears are neatly protected by feathers. But how do we know?

once we're airborne. No doubt the avian response, given that the air is their milieu, is less neurotic.

The peregrine's flight – fast, loose, shallow of beat – contrasts with that of the carrion crow rowing gamely through the air over my head as I enter the cemetery. Not that crows fly with difficulty – far from it, as anyone who has seen their playful tumbling display will testify – just that they often give the impression of flying into a gentle headwind.

The magnolia at the entrance is at least two weeks ahead of ours. Its curled petals, edges pink-tinged, are beginning to fall. Early, my instinct says, but without the authority of one who knows. Further on, there's a nondescript, medium-height evergreen of the kind I can never quite place. Uniformly green last week, it now puts out tiny, startling lipstick-pink buds on the tips of its brush-like leaves, as if very lightly paint-dipped.

These changes catch the eye, but there's something subtler going on, something I can't put my finger on. I walk around vaguely, not quite knowing what I'm looking for, just aware of an indefinable difference in the air. I try to picture what this place looked like last week, and after a minute I realise what it is.

It's the trees.

For the first time, after weeks of small, individual changes – a blackthorn blossoming here, a magnolia in flower there – the burgeoning is almost universal. And crucially it's visible from a distance. The Edward Scissorhands appearance of the treetops, sharp fingers reaching for the sky, is softened by a light green tinge.

As I admire the stately shape of an old oak, another carrion crow flies past, a large twig in its beak. Another small marker in the year's progress: project 'crows making nests' under way.

It's a reminder not to overlook these abundant, everyday birds. I see them all the time – here, over the house, up at the woods. They walk that strutty walk – confident, slightly spivvish, eyeing you up with a view to relieving you of your wallet.

Indulging a flight of fancy, I imagine the antithesis. What if they were endangered? What if there were just a single bird left, continuing its life without knowing it was the last carrion crow on earth?

It is, admittedly, difficult to imagine the carrion crow going extinct. While it's not universally popular, especially among those who revile its habit of predating eggs and young birds, prospects of its being hounded to oblivion are remote. Corvids are famously intelligent, problem-solving birds. They exploit feeding and breeding opportunities; they learn and adapt. You'll see crows with chips in their beaks; you might also see them dropping molluscs or nuts from a great height to smash them open. You wouldn't bet against them perpetrating a basic phishing scam against the elderly.

But plenty of species go extinct without our even being aware they existed, and among the many to have departed this earth on our watch, you can count several whose place on it seemed permanent.*

So I look closely at the crow, taking in its complete blackness, the gloss of its plumage untinged by the purple sheen of its close congener, the rook. I admire the stout curve of its bill, the dark of its eye, the absence of distinguishing features.

---

* At this point it's obligatory to mention the passenger pigeon, the most dramatic example of species eradication at human hands, from an estimated global population of 3 billion to extinction in less than a century.

I do this occasionally, looking at something as if for the first time. It's a way of finding beauty and interest in the mundane, learning to appreciate the things that form the backdrop to everyday life. And if it serves as a reminder of the fragility of all life on earth, including ours, then that's no bad thing.

9

CHERRY BLOSSOMS
IN FULL BLOOM

16–20 March

Insects awaken (*Keichitsu,* 啓蟄)
Caterpillars become butterflies
(*Namushi chō to naru,* 菜虫化蝶)

There is a place, not far from here, where magic happens. It's a brief, evanescent kind of magic, but if you can catch it, the rewards are plentiful.

One cherry tree in blossom offers a splash of prettiness; thirty of them qualifies as a spectacular, the clouds of pink-tinged white irresistibly festive. The transience of the blooms – a reminder, if ever we needed it, of the impermanence and fragility of life – is part of the attraction. Constant beauty becomes wallpaper; give it to us for just a few days and it becomes a special treat.

It's not strictly on my patch, but it's within walking distance, and a street full of Yoshino cherry trees is enticing enough for me to alter my normal walking routine.

The importance of cherry blossom in Japanese culture can

hardly be overstated. The ritual of *hanami* (flower-viewing) has been around for over a thousand years, finding its expression not just as a group activity, but as a pivotal theme in poetry and art. While it started as an activity for the aristocracy and military elite, it spread to the common people around the sixteenth century, and remains popular today, most often taking the form of group picnics in parks where the trees are common. And while other flowers – particularly plum blossom – have their place, it's the cherries that have become symbolic of the Japanese relationship with nature. So entrenched is *hanami* in the Japanese consciousness that the progress of the flowering – *sakura zensen*, or 'cherry blossom front', based on fifty-nine sample trees – is monitored and reported by meteorological agencies in daily bulletins.

I like this. I like that an aspect of nature is so deeply instilled in a country's make-up that it features in news reports. And I like that after many centuries this activity still maintains a toehold in the lives of ordinary people. And while *hanami* – along with its siblings *momijigari* (leaf-viewing) and *tsukimi* (moon-viewing) – aren't necessarily representative of the average twenty-first-century Japanese citizen's own daily relationship with nature, they endure, and we have no real equivalent in Western culture.

Activities or lifestyle philosophies appropriated from other cultures – take your pick from *hygge, lagom, ikigai, ubuntu** and quite a few more – have taken hold in the British psyche over the last few years. No doubt one aspect of their popularity is the opportunism of

---

* Here's an extremely brief and certainly inadequate encapsulation of these lifestyle concepts: 'warm, convivial togetherness' (Denmark/Norway), 'just the right amount' (Sweden/Norway), 'a sense of purpose in life' (Japan), 'humanity towards others' (southern Africa).

marketing people trying to outdo each other to find the next trend. But there's more to it than that. Perhaps these activities or philosophies somehow represent a better way of doing things, a better way of living, that for whatever reason we don't think we can find in ourselves.

It's not that we don't have our own forms of stress relief, but maybe we undervalue the importance of 'having a sit-down and a nice cup of tea' or 'going for a bit of a ramble', thinking they don't quite do the job.

My solution – going for a bit of a ramble to do some flower-viewing while drinking a nice cup of tea – feels like a lifestyle trend just waiting to sweep the nation.

There are many attractions to my local area. Walking down the high street on a busy weekday morning isn't one of them. Buses, cars and lorries are enthusiastic participants in a pollution-belching competition, and my fellow pedestrians take no prisoners as they vie with each other for limited pavement space. I'm just about to duck down a side street when through the din I become aware of a familiar tinkling. Soft and distant, its high frequency cutting through the traffic's bass rumble.

There's a goldfinch nearby, and I shan't rest until I've found it.

I scan the upper floors of the high street parade, trying to locate the source of the sound, looking for goldfinch-shaped irregularities on ledges, silhouettes on rooftops. I do the owl-listening trick again, tilting my head one way, then the other. It does the trick, and now I can home in on it, a vibrant little blob two storeys up on the other side of the road, singing to the world about who knows what. I find the goldfinch's song exuberant and uplifting; others think it mindless and inane. Each to their own. Rather that than a busker belting out a shonky version of 'Blowin' in the Wind', in my view.

If I'm aware that I cut a strange figure, standing on the edge of the pavement, looking at a building over the road with my head cocked, I'm secure in the knowledge that this is London: as odd behaviour goes, this doesn't even register.

I have to quell my evangelistic urge on a daily basis. There's nothing so zealous as the recent convert, and the resurgence of my interest in the natural world in middle age has been like a tsunami, engulfing everything and carrying all before it. I see the people walking down the high street, engaged in their daily routine, oblivious to the tinkling songster above their heads, and I want to shout, 'Up there! Just listen to it!'

But while I've become less reticent about sharing my enthusiasm, I also don't want to be known as the local character – 'you know, that weird bird guy' – so I keep my trap shut.

Almost as if it senses my watching it and is suddenly overcome by a paralysing shyness in front of an audience, the goldfinch stops singing and is off, bouncing over my head to pastures new.

The cherry trees do their bit. Looking at their festive pink-and-whiteness against the backdrop of the regularity of the street's houses – all red-bricked, bay-windowed well-to-do-ness – brings a sense of freedom and calm. The ritual of *hanami* was once thought to transfer the life force of the blossoms into the participants, an idea that really doesn't seem all that fanciful. Worth the detour, in the language of the Michelin guide. I'm unsure whether what I'm doing counts as *hanami*, or whether there are vital aspects I'm missing, but it counts as a therapeutic activity, so that's good enough for me.

I'm accompanied, as I make my slow way along the street, by the monotonous song of a great tit, the manic whistlings of a starling and, all too briefly, the fluttering of the year's first butterfly. Big, dark, strong in flight. I lack expertise in butterfly recognition unless they sit for at least five minutes, wings conveniently spread and a purple arrow pointing at them with their name emblazoned in 64-point Helvetica, but nonetheless decide this is a peacock. There is nobody around to contradict me, so what the hell.

The return journey is enlivened by the unexpected sight of four mallards flying – true to type, in formation – fast over the cemetery, as if pursued by a police car. I say 'unexpected' simply because the nearest water is a couple of miles away. Ducks and geese don't figure high on my 'patch sightings' list. They're gone in a flash.

These things – the peacock, the mallards, the goldfinch – last a few seconds at most. The accident of my seeing them is pure happenstance. And while the time frame for the cherry blossoms is wider, the window for enjoying them is nonetheless short.

But the impact of these sightings is disproportionate to the time they last. Each one sticks in the mind in a way the background stuff simply doesn't. Our perception of time is skewed. A moment lingers in the memory; huge uneventful swathes are forgotten.

On the fourth day the weather decides it's winter again. Cold, damp, enthusiasm-quashing. Clouds develop by stealth, bringing with them a depressing dampness, putting a stop to our springtime fun.

True to the vagaries of the passing of time, those two days seem to last about a month.

10

FIRST CHIFFCHAFF SINGS

21–25 March

Spring equinox (*Shunbun,* 春分)
Sparrows start to nest
(*Suzume hajimete sukū,* 雀始巣)

When I was a child, at that stage of illness when you're well enough to be bored beyond belief but not well enough to get back to normal, I played a game. It wasn't as fun a game as 'round the room with feet off the floor', but I didn't yet have the energy for that. I'd read all the books, and didn't have the patience to wait thirty years for the invention of the internet, so this simple game of my own devising had to do.

It went like this.

Opposite my bed of woe was the bedroom window. Six panes. Four central squares flanked by tall rectangles. The game was simple; it consisted of noticing what I could see through each pane.

The natural angle, from the point of view of the languisher, was slightly upwards, towards the sky, but if I stood up on the bed I could see the lawn, and fields beyond.

I developed a scoring system. A completely blank pane, filled only with blue sky, counted as one point. Sky with a bit of cloud was half a point. The merest hint of a tree or grass or wall, or anything that interrupted the purity of the framed view, rendered that pane null and void.

There were variations. One point per tree. A bonus for a bird. And sometimes I reversed it, standing on the bed and counting a pane filled only with grass as a one-pointer.

I played it when I had mumps. I played it when I had chickenpox. I played it, so it seems, often enough for it to take hold in my memory. Even today, when confronted with a wait and a window, it keeps me distracted for a few seconds, makes me look.

I start playing a variant of the game from the terrace outside the back door on day three of this season. Three days after the equinox, three days into Astronomical Spring. It's the day lockdown begins, the day from which we can officially mark the irrevocable changing of all our lives, the day we're all told to stay at home.

In Japan, the equinox (*shunbun no hi*) is a public holiday, a time to get together with your family. There'll be none of that this year.

My day* job† is as a conductor, a role rendered instantly redundant by Covid-19. And while I now have plenty of time to write, I have no attention span with which to do it. But for my day-to-day routine on the patch it's business as usual. I'm already going out once a day to look at the area around my home. The lockdown gives it the official seal of approval.

---

* Evenings, mostly.
† I mean, you can call it a job if you like, but plenty of people will disagree with you.

The effect it has on my mood is another story. Hence the need for calming distractions.

So I find myself scrutinising the view from the terrace even more closely, framing it through an imaginary window and counting the empty squares. I start counting the number of species of fauna and flora I can see without moving, craning my neck to catch a glimpse of the copper beech in the garden five doors down, where the wood pigeons roost. Then I draw the focus narrower, to within the confines of our garden, examining, evaluating and cherishing each last detail, framing it as if I'm a film director, imagining that this is it, this is my view for ever. Encouragement to examine what you have, and to realise just how much there is in it.

We have the garden. An extraordinary, everyday privilege. I feel sheepish about it, thinking of all the people in flats with only a view through a window at the outside world. And that sheepishness, guilt almost, hardens my resolve to appreciate it all the more.

The cycles of life are unaffected. And there are signs of accelerating spring everywhere. The first chiffchaff of the year, the first I've ever encountered from the garden. Its opening *chiff* is faint, almost a mirage, but enough to propel me from the kitchen, binoculars in hand. And there it is, busying around in the cedar two doors down, calling its name. By June I'll be sick of its unvarying monotony, but today it's a tonic.

Even more cheeringly, and in a display of rare synchronicity with the Japanese calendar I vowed to reflect, our house sparrows have upped their feeder-visiting schedule from 'intermittent' to 'regular'. I don't know where they're nesting – somewhere over there, where 'there' is indicated with a vague flap of the hand – but I'm happy beyond expression that they've chosen to grace us with their presence. Strange, perhaps, to be so excited by something so unremarkable, but the fact remains that they're not to be taken for granted. This is the first year we've had them in the garden with any kind of regularity, and I will them to stay, to bring their chirp our way more often.

But the cheer is short-lived. The seismic shock of this wrenching upheaval hits hard and deep, and these days are coloured by the undertow of anxious uncertainty.

Most of all, this feels like a time for thoughtful walks. And when you're limited to one a day, you want to make the most of it. The government guidelines specify 'exercise' as a permitted reason for going outside. I extend its meaning to encompass 'mental health', and stay out as long as I can.

The atmosphere about the place is both hyper-real and unreal at the same time. No cars, few people. The clarity of the air is striking, the view from the hill bringing London to arm's length.

My mind jumps around, concentration impossible, scattergun thoughts everywhere.

Stop.

Breathe.

Listen.

An exercise in concentration, distraction, whatever you like to call it. An exercise in not thinking about The Situation. It's the simplest thing, an examination of silence. Stop for five minutes; write down everything you hear.

I stop by a tree, listen, write:

Great tit (*TEEEEE-chuh TEEEEE-chuh*)
Motorbike, roaring

Footsteps – light, regular

Child – distant, complaining

Blue tit (*TSEE-TSEE-tsabbadabbadabba*)

Dog – small, barking

Police siren, far away

Wind, ocean-like, moving in waves through the
trees

Parakeet, squawking into a wind lull

Boy admonishing dog

Robin – mid-distance, silvery

Tennis ball bouncing

Dog bell jingling

Nuthatch, *pock-pock-pock*ing

Wind in my ears

The rustle of shoulder on tree trunk

Man, whistling 'come here, dog'

My own breathing

Footsteps – irregular, clumping

The *shh shh shh* of my hand as I write in the
notebook

The snap of my glasses as I fold them shut

Silence is a relative term.

11

MOTHS SOMETIMES FLY

26–30 March

Spring equinox (*Shunbun*, 春分)
First cherry blossoms
(*Sakura hajimete saku*, 櫻始開)

I look up by the church. Blue sky, unsullied.

A speck, impossibly high, moving.

Binoculars up. Speck becomes shape, with a distinctive outline. With wings outstretched it rides the thermals like a buzzard, but the peregrine's silhouette is unmistakable.

Their local celebrity status means they have no privacy, and the grapevine tells me they were seen mating last week. So maybe the female is now on eggs – she will have laid two or three, with one-day gaps – and this is the male, getting a bit of well-earned rest. At this distance it's hard to tell.

I've come for another thoughtful walk to the cemetery. It's debatable whether surrounding yourself with the dead in a time of pandemic is good for your mental health – but perhaps it's not a coincidence that I gravitate towards it. Subconscious workings dictating actions.

The warmth of the previous week, the singing chiffchaff, that feeling of surging spring – they feel like false alarms. The regression from spring to winter was marked by a day of wind, cold, rain and about ten minutes of hail – thanks very much, but no. But today is clear and bright, and if the warmth in the air isn't enough to make me jettison the extra layers, it is at least an invitation to get outside.

A goldcrest – *my* goldcrest – sings to me from the conifer by the rose garden. I've heard it six times this year, looked for it six times, failed to see it six times. Hearing the song, on this occasion, is strangely reassuring.

Up by the crematorium I peel off from my usual route onto the grass and towards a bench. It's a tempting bench, facing a cherry tree. Since my visit to Herne Hill, I've noticed cherry blossom everywhere. An isolated tree doesn't have the same impact as an avenue, but this one – variety unknown, at least to me – is showing some good game nonetheless, throwing up not only the obvious clouds from its branches, but also sprouting little clusters from its trunk. These growths are endearing, like tufts of hair on a badly shaved face. And they draw my attention to the tree's distinctive bark, the smoothness interrupted not only by the inevitable gnarly imperfections of any tree of decent age, but also by the distinctive thin horizontal fissures common to many members of the *Prunus* family.

As I sit in quiet contemplation of the world's woes, my eye is caught by a scattery movement.

I'm familiar with scattery movements. They're the bane of my life. Because once you've seen one you're obliged by the laws of nature-watching to see where it takes you, and where it takes you is often peering into a mass of foliage, waiting for it to repeat itself.

So many missed sightings, an unending torrent of non-identifications.

Little scattery movements, in general, mean butterflies. But this has something different to it. I'm familiar with the handful of early-season butterflies on my patch. The pale yellow of a brimstone, the dark shadow of a peacock, the various whites. All butterfly-sized and coloured, even from the merest glimpse.

This is small and brown. This is a moth.

Moth species are overwhelmingly profuse. My *Collins Complete Guide to British Butterflies and Moths* has 318 pages. The first fifty are devoted to butterflies; the rest cover the moths. Ominously, the last nineteen pages are covered by the title 'An Introduction to Micro-Moths'. You mean there are *more*?

The prospect of identifying this nondescript little flutterer is daunting, but I'm keen for something to focus the mind. Keeping a close eye on its flight path, I follow it, and before long it settles obligingly on the side of a gravestone, my view of it unimpeded by undergrowth or foliage.

Normal procedure at this point would be to take some photos with my phone, and work it all out later. But my phone has no battery, and I have no notebook, so I'm forced to resort to memory.

I examine it. The base of its splayed wings forms a broad 'W', their colour running the gamut of shades of brown. Beige, buff, chestnut, sand, a hint of taupe. Russet streaks blurring, morphing to grey at times, moments of black. These subtleties of shading, so easily overlooked, now draw me in as I try to commit them to memory. And as I look more closely, the moth begins to take on the status of 'underrated beauty'. No doubt a seasoned moth-er* would give it a casual glance before turning to more glamorous subjects, but I'm new to this, and easily impressed.

Once I'm sure I have the image in my head, I continue with the walk. Faster, less thoughtful. I'm keen to get to the bottom of the moth.

Browsing a field guide is a calming process. Page after page of moths. Seemingly infinite variations on brown and grey, with the odd eye-catching page of pink or green. A world of its own.

I leaf through the pages. Nope. Nope. Nope. Maybe? Nope. Nope. Aha.

Pugs. Not the dogs. The moths. There are dozens of them. Sloe pug, toadflax pug, slender pug, lead-coloured pug, mottled pug, ochreous pug and many more. Among them – I'm almost certain as I compare the image on the page with the one emblazoned on my cerebral cortex – brindled pug.

It's widespread and common (tick), the larva feeds on oak and hawthorn (tick) and the adult is in flight from April to May (close enough).

A small moment of triumph, only dampened by the caveat that 'many pug species are difficult to identify, with similar and variable wing markings'. If you think bird identification is hard, try moths for size. You'll go running back to birds with open arms.

I ponder this brief encounter for a while. It's vanishingly unlikely that anyone else saw it. But for my presence, it would have joined the roster of the myriad lives that pass without observation or

---

* Someone who studies moths, as distinct from 'mother'. A mother might be a moth-er and vice versa, but omitting the hyphen is a dangerous habit.

comment. Substitute 'if a tree falls in a forest' with 'if a moth lands on a gravestone'.

The moth doesn't care that I observed it. It might have been aware of me as a dimly looming presence, but wasn't bothered enough to fly away. It will continue with its life, blindly pursuing its main purpose: to be a brindled pug, and to play its part in the continued existence of brindled pugs on the planet. But on this clear spring morning it unwittingly made a contribution, however tiny, to the accumulated sum of human joy, so for that reason alone it holds a special place in my heart.

12

GREAT TITS SCOUT FOR NESTING SITES

31 March–4 April

Spring equinox (*Shunbun,* 春分)
Distant thunder
(*Kaminari sunawachi koe o hassu,* 雷乃発声)

They've closed the cemetery.

While this feels like an overreaction to the spread of Covid, indignation would be a waste of precious energy. But I am sad, because I've come to regard it as at least partly mine.

I suspect this is a common reaction. We become proprietorial about our special places. *My* bench – the one with the good view that I always use for a mid-walk breather; *my* oak – the one I sat under on a warm spring afternoon in a better time; *my* fox – the one that trotted across in front of me without so much as a by-your-leave, back when urban foxes were a sighting to cherish.

So while I understand that the cemetery belongs to everyone, and that each of its regular visitors will have their own special spot, I mourn its closing as if I've been denied access to my own garden.

There are places here where the birds live. I like to think I am the only one who knows about them. There's the slope opposite the crematorium, all wonky gravestones and ivy-covered oaks and awkward terrain; there's the bit down the side of the memorial rose garden, where the robin perches on the bench and the invisible goldcrest taunts me from the depths of a yew; there's the Greek enclosure, with its ornate statuary, and a pair of blue tits nesting in the closed mausoleum. My touchstones, a sort of comfort, accrued over multiple visits, each little encounter adding to the strata of fond memory. All, temporarily at least, taken from me.

On the first day of closure I do a circuit of the outside, looking for vantage points from which I might catch a glimpse of what's going on. The long, tall wall down Robson Road – magnificent in its own right, testament to Victorian building quality – has a stretch of solid railings. A small child used to being shoved up a chimney might squeeze through them. But there's little to see, the view blocked by trees whose foliage pokes scrappily through the gaps. And once you reach the end and turn right the roads lead you away from the cemetery's boundaries. Houses, a rubbish dump, an industrial estate. Then right again, up the hill and one more turn and there it is: a length of wall broken up by more railings through which I can survey a limited patch of grass dotted with trees, and look towards the crematorium beyond.

I stand for a while, like a child looking through the playground fence, not allowed to play with the cool kids.

A blackcap sings from a tree to the left, scrappy-voiced, with only the distinctive fluting tones near the end giving a sense of melody. A blackbird bounces towards me, head cocked, then *pock-pock-tskliii-skli-skli-tskliiiii* and away. A green woodpecker calls in the distance. It's a laughing, mocking sound, taunting me from afar. I'm used to not seeing them, but this time it stings more than usual.

It's irrational, this sense of missing out. I'm not locked in my house, and other open spaces are available. I can extend my one permitted daily walk as far as I like. I could, and occasionally do, use it walking the streets, enjoying the strange freedom of being able to stroll down the middle of the road without fear of being run over, pausing occasionally to see what plucky new plant has forced its way up through the cracks in the pavement. And a walk to the common on the third day yields not only a pleasing absence of humans but an even more pleasing abundance of birds: blue tits checking out a nesting hole; a chiffchaff calling its name in a constant, mindless recitation, like a newspaper seller; nuthatches everywhere, *pyoo*-ing and *tuuit*-ing as if they're on commission. And for just a second, in between *pyoo*s, a thin, shivery call from high in the canopy. A treecreeper – small, brown and restless, like a feathered barkmouse. I adjust my hearing level from 'always monitoring' to 'listening really hard', but despite my best efforts it doesn't oblige again.

Maybe I was just imagining it.

A single frosty night is followed by a general warming, and on the fifth day sitting outside is an option. I'm rewarded by an almost constant flow of birds to the feeder. Watching garden birds, we are told, is a healthy, restful activity, and I have no evidence to contradict that assertion. There's a satisfying rhythm to it. Wait in a nearby tree, swoop down, take food, throw some on the ground for no particular reason, return to tree. Repeat.

A glitch in the matrix. A great tit follows the routine but eschews the tree, instead flying up at a sharp angle towards the house. Towards the swift box.

The swifts will arrive in a month or so. If previous years are a template, they will nest in the eaves of the house on the left. They will nest in the eaves of the house on the right. They will nest in the eaves of the house two doors down, and they will nest in the eaves of the house three doors down.

To summarise: the only house whose hospitality they refuse is ours.

This is undoubtedly because the eaves of our house were blocked off by overzealous builders some years ago. But they also shun the swift box we installed by way of compensation. It clings to the wall forlornly, an unloved boxy prefab in a world of shabby-chic cottages and tumbledown shacks. But if the swifts don't fancy it, the great tits clearly do, so our effort hasn't been entirely wasted.

They're good company, these birds, and their constant activity helps keep the blues at bay. The notion is mooted in various quarters that wildlife is growing to fill the gap caused by our enforced absence. People tell me that the birdsong is louder than they've ever heard it.

I don't buy it. It seems more likely to me that these people – many, many people – are simply noticing it for the first time. Spring is springing. Birds start singing. Activity is all around. Take away the shield of traffic noise and it's there in plain hearing. But it was always there. It's pure happenstance that this year spring coincides with a time when everyone's in a mood to be aware of it. Human life is closing in on itself – for everything else it's business as usual.

13

DAWN CHORUS INTENSIFIES

5–9 April

Pure and clear (*Seimei*, 清明)
Swallows return
(*Tsubame kitaru*, 玄鳥至)

Thanks to lockdown, the transition to 'pure and clear' holds surprisingly true. The reduction in traffic leads to a dramatic drop in pollution levels, with visible results. From the hill in our local park I look across London, a stunning panorama taking in the broad sweep from the Post Office Tower to Canary Wharf and beyond. Normally shrouded in a pall of smog, the view is sharp and clear. Unprecedentedly, I can see Alexandra Palace, thirteen miles away on the other side of London.

In another manifestation of synchronicity with the Japanese calendar, the swallows return right on cue. I learn about it, as always, from other people's reports. Swallows don't favour our neck of the woods, generally preferring to hang out in more rural areas. This isn't to say they're completely absent from cities, but I only ever see them when they're passing through. As this usually happens in the classic migration seasons of spring and autumn, I spend my time in these periods almost constantly on the lookout for them, scanning the skies for their distinctive shape – shoulders and streamers – and fast, flitting flight.

No dice.

Other things catch the eye as I potter in the garden enjoying the sunshine. Honesty – the shape of the five on dice – in two colours: purple, slender at the petal base, and white, the veins delicately outlined in fine tracery. Hazel leaves, deeply furrowed. The wisteria moves from furry beginnings to thrusting buds. Tiny leaves on silver birch, fluttering like confetti in the breeze. A peacock butterfly, black shadow on the garden chair, then unfolding to bask – vivid purple with scary eyes on its wings. If necessary, they will enhance this predator deterrent, rubbing their wings together to produce a hissing sound. So much for our image of butterflies as dainty, delicate little things sent to brighten our day with prettiness. They're just as bent on survival as anything else – that's how they've made it this far.

As if to discredit this pragmatic vision of lepidopteran aggression, a pale yellow flutter appears in the corner of my eye, gone as quick as a flash. A brimstone butterfly, one of the pillars of spring.

Dainty. Delicate. Pretty.

Tick one more stage off the list. Spring is very much springing.

It would be pushing it to call the sound that greets me as I skirt the woods 'the dawn chorus'. It's ten o'clock, for one thing – firmly mid-morning. And 'chorus' isn't quite right either, implying as it does a togetherness, a unity of execution. These birds are intent on the same thing, for sure – territorial rights and shagging – but they each plough their own furrow, occupying an individual niche in the soundscape. We're the ones who attach further meaning to it, allowing it to infiltrate our hearts and lift our souls. If so inclined. Some people – often those woken early by a blackbird or the raucous squabblings of herring gulls – complain about it.

Welcome or not, the sound is gradually adding layers of complexity as its mid-spring peak approaches. To the familiar simplicity of great tits (the famous *TEA-cher* call subverted by variations of rhythm and emphasis) and the year-round silver stream of robin song, other species add their voices, each in their own niche.

There's the chiffchaff's two-noter. The sound itself has a banal chirpiness to it – not a thing of great beauty. But hearing it regularly after a layoff of eight months is an undoubted boon.

The blackcap's song is something else. Where the chiffchaff has two notes, the blackcap seems to have two thousand, scattering all over the place in apparently random manner, a mixture of scratchiness and warmth. It's fast too, so often the downfall for human ears trying to fit birdsong into recognisable patterns. No discernible rhythm, no melody, and too rapid for us to process. The poet John Clare called it 'the March nightingale'. In a similar vein, Daines Barrington – one of Gilbert White's regular correspondents – had it as 'Norfolk mock nightingale', which seems unnecessarily dismissive.

I stop and listen. It's no more than two metres away, but on the other side of a tall fence, so it's unaware of my presence and I don't have to worry about disturbing it.

It's a virtuoso display. All blackcap song has a bravura to it, but this one is particularly unrestrained. And somehow it feels richer than the blackcap song I'm used to. After about thirty seconds I realise why. In among the scattery rubble and rich flutings are little

Easter eggs for the quick of ear. Imitations, fragments of song belonging to other birds and purloined for the blackcap's own purposes. What those purposes might be isn't exactly clear to me. Perhaps the variations add complexity to the song, making it more attractive to potential mates. That is often how it works.

The blackcap eventually exhausts its repertoire, and I move on to a different place – the copse at the top of the common, a loose gathering of mixed deciduous trees with a broad central path, leading to an expanse of grass sloping down to the A23 below. Shadows of trees on bare earth. Slanting sun illuminates overflowing bin. Squirrel scampers vertically.

On the scrubby grass by the copse, a pair of mistle thrushes. Brown washed through with grey, blending in well with their surroundings. Scrabble, hop, ear down, jump, scrabble.

I like the mistle thrush. I like that its name in Swedish is *Dubbeltrast* – the double thrush – in recognition of its size; I like its upright bearing, compared to the slouching gait of its smaller cousin, the song thrush; and I love that its folk name in Scotland is 'Big Mavis'.*

One of them flies up into a tree, metres in from the edge of the copse. I watch through binoculars, keen not to invade their personal space. They have an industrious air that says they're not just hanging around amusing themselves.

The second bird flies up, into a different tree. Higher. A lookout point.

---

* It originates, I gather, from the French *mauvis*, meaning 'redwing' – the mistle thrush's smaller cousin.

Back to the first bird, settled now in a crevice a few feet above head height. I note her almost defiant look, the angle of her tail, the glimpse of a cup-shaped structure underneath her.

It's a nest all right. At this time of year it's probably a second brood – they're early nesters, often starting in February. And now I'm nervous, knowing I'll spend the coming weeks visiting this place as often as I can, watching for signs of success and failure. Irrationally, I feel a responsibility towards them, a sense that I must somehow protect them from dog-walkers and carrion crows and random disturbances, from the realities of life in the city. But of course, as in most such matters, I am powerless to intervene.

14

MIGRANT BIRDS ARRIVE
FROM AFRICA

10–14 April

Pure and clear (*Seimei*, 清明)
Wild geese fly north (*Kōgan kaeru*, 鴻雁北)

I'm on the phone when it happens.

I'm on the phone so rarely these days that it feels like the confluence of two extraordinary events, and for the rest of the day, aware that these things happen in threes, I'm on full alert for the tertiary phase.

The phone call is dull, a matter of insurance, and I'm doing what I always do on such occasions – looking out of the office window, thinking about everything except the phone call. The gentleman on the end of the line is nice enough, but it's insurance, and there's a goldfinch on the feeder. No contest.

He's reading me questions; I'm giving automatic answers. Has the value of the house's contents increased in the last year? Has there been any material change in our circumstances? Would I like to pay in full now, or by monthly direct deb—

Fucking hell, what's that?

It's my question, not his. And I don't immediately know the answer. The closest I can get is 'fast small thing, chased by fast larger thing'. Then the small thing banks sharply to the left and the larger thing follows it as if locked in with tractor beams. And then they're gone, and I'm aware of the silence on the other end of the phone.

'Kestrel. I mean, sorry, umm . . . yes. Sorry, got distracted.'

The silence of mild disbelief, nary an instant.

'Which one?'

'Oh. Right. Direct debit, please.'

I wonder if this acrobatic bird is the same preternaturally still one I saw back in early March up at the Rookery. They're not so common in south London. Not unknown, but noteworthy. Worth interrupting a phone call for.

And I will always be enthusiastic about a kestrel, if only to annoy a person I shall refer to as Anonymous Experienced Birder.

Anonymous Experienced Birder once wrote this dismissive phrase on the internet: 'the kind of people who get in a lather about a blackcap or a kestrel'.

That's me.

Getting in a lather about things is what it's all about. If you can't do that – whether you display the lather to the outside world or not – then why are you doing it? You might as well sit at home on the sofa eating cake until you explode.*

Kestrels are miracle birds. The hovering – minute adjustments of wings, tail and body combining to ensure the head remains entirely

---

* I do like cake. And sofas. But variety is important.

still; the eyesight – ultraviolet perception tracking vole's urine trail; the sheer damn kestrelness of it.

And then there's the setting. There is something about an urban bird of prey that quickens the pulse. Think of buzzards soaring over a Welsh valley; golden eagles perched on a Highland crag; marsh harriers quartering a Norfolk reed bed at dusk on a cold winter's night. Raw, rugged, magnificent.

And then you see a kestrel doing a fighter-jet impersonation over a suburban back garden. It's as if Paul Newman dropped in for a cup of tea.

Consider me in a lather.

Outside, away from phone calls, there is warmth. British, low twenties Celsius, that's-quite-enough-for-me-thanks warmth. Three days of it, sun warming the nape. T-shirt. Shorts, even. If you insist.

Growth is everywhere, impossible to track. Peony stems, the dark red of a vintage car, thrust rudely through the soil; a snake's-head fritillary, delicate purple-and-pink chequerboard pattern, droops elegantly; a scrappy yellow plant, name unknown, street fighter written all over it, pushes up between two paving slabs, spreads itself in unruly fashion. Spring feels unstoppable. It'll be warm for the next six months now, surely?

Then the wind swings from west to east, and with it comes the chill. Grey one day, but – glory be! – bright the next. That clarity of light, the absence of oppressive clouds, more even than the temperature, is what I crave. Smile-on-face weather.

I visit the mistle thrushes, proprietary feelings to the fore.

She is there, on the nest. A minute's looking and I find the father, up and to the left, alertness birdified. There is a nobility about him, to my anthropomorphic eyes. Teamwork at play. Everyday, remarkable.

The father flies down in a flurry, as if reacting to the dinner bell. A few seconds of exploration – hop, tilt head, rummage – and a worm dies. My eye is caught by a scrap of movement behind it. Shift focus. A peacock butterfly chasing away an orange-tip. The peacock is brutish next to the smaller insect's delicacy. The orange-tip engages for a few seconds, all flutter and dink, but decides enough is enough and scatters off to forage elsewhere. Some fights aren't worth the candle.

Intent as I am on these dramas of life and death, the soundtrack nearly passes me by. *Rat-a-tat-tat* of wren; *chip* of woodpecker; *tseep* of blue tit.

Something else.

A mournful descending sound, barely detected at first. Then it's repeated. No doubt about it. Willow warbler, fresh from Africa.

If I'd seen it, not heard it, I might have thought it was a chiffchaff. They're tough to distinguish – a question of leg colour, wing feather length, eyebrow prominence. But contrast the songs: chiffchaff's banality versus willow warbler's fluting melancholy. Soft in tone, there's a plaintive quality to the willow warbler's song, often offset with a little skip in the step at the end, a moment of uplift, the unexpected Jaffa Cake hiding beneath the Rich Tea in the biscuit tin of life.

Greenish-brown, or brownish-green – depending on which field guide you read – it's about 12 centimetres long. No more than a scrap of a thing, yet every year it travels all the way from its wintering grounds in sub-Saharan Africa.

The journeys these birds make. Millions of them, criss-crossing the globe. From Africa come warblers, swallows, martins, redstarts, flycatchers, wheatears, whinchats, nightingales, cuckoos, swifts, and on and on. And while they arrive, our winter visitors – redwings, finches, ducks, swans, geese and more – make their way back to their breeding grounds in Scandinavia and beyond.

Many die on the way, succumbing to unfavourable conditions, predation, hunger, exhaustion. But many make it. That's the calculation, at a species level. How many die if they stay where they are versus how many die if they move. Better for the species as a whole to move. So they do, following the routes of their ancestors, using instincts and knowledge we still don't fully understand.

This willow warbler has chosen a tree near me to sing its song: 'Here I am. I made it.' It feels like a benediction.

15

SPRING BUTTERFLIES
ADD COLOUR

15–19 April

Pure and clear (*Seimei*, 清明)
First rainbows (*Niji hajimete arawaru,* 虹始見)

Time passes fast and slow.

Three weeks since lockdown: an eternal moment. In those three weeks there have been hours lasting days, days lasting seconds, a general sense that the space-time continuum isn't all we once thought. Our perception of time is relative, an impression only heightened by The Situation. Without the distraction of gainful employment, I loll. I flummock. I flounder.

Routine becomes central to proceedings. Do these things at this time every day and at least you will have done those things. Not much, but something.

Exercise is key. My daily walk becomes even more essential. Right, up the hill, right again, zigzag of residential streets, squiggle through the estate, cross the main road, down the little track, into the woods, relax.

But nature as therapy doesn't always work. The mind wanders, thinks odd, disturbing, circular thoughts. To keep it on the straight and narrow I set it little tasks, observational homework. Go for a walk and look for square things. Or smooth things. Or green things.

Those are easy enough to find – grass, leaves, bark – and easy enough to photograph and assemble into a collage. Forty-nine green things, in a 7-by-7 grid.

Then – and only then, with the photographs assembled neatly on my computer screen – I start looking. Properly looking. The smooth, hard gleam of the metal tube on the swing chair – dark, almost racing green, morphing shades; the random tangle of lawn grass; the mes-merising geometry of a single leaf, a map of arteries, veins and cells; another leaf, all fur and softness; yet another, bubble-wrap bobble.

Forty-nine photographs; forty-nine shades of green.* Infinite variety in a single colour.

There's a sort of madness to this close examination, but sanity too. A way of distracting oneself from the surreal horror of our new reality, a way of appreciating things in a new light. Finding interest in the banal is a neat trick for your mental health if you can pull it off. No need to wait for wanton beauty to present itself. Just look at the run of the mill.

But when wanton beauty does flutter into your life, it's as well to be prepared.

On day four of this season – a nondescript, kind-of-fine-but-no-more-than-that season – a butterfly lands on the lawn.

I've learned enough about butterflies to divide them, more or less, into seasons. As with many things, our little corner of south

---

* So nearly a worldwide erotica sensation.

London isn't a haven of lepidopteral abundance. Of the sixty or so butterfly species that occur in the UK, I've knowingly seen no more than a dozen on my patch. I suspect there are more, but I lack the knowledge or patience to find them.

Of that handful, some emerge early to brighten up our spring days. And of these, if we have to have a favourite (we don't, but let's just pretend for a second) I will always choose the orange-tip. Perhaps it's because its distinctive colouring – predominantly white with orange tips to its wings – makes it one of the easiest to identify, and therefore one of the first ones I learned. Perhaps it's simply that its colouring is so basic and bright – the work, apparently, of a child with a single orange crayon. Whatever the reasons, the sight of one fluttering low down by the path in the cemetery, near a patch of its preferred cuckoo flower, has become a marker of the year's progress.

But I've never seen one in the garden. Until today.

It just flies in and sits there, calm as you please, unaware of its impact. And I, displaying what I hope is due deference and caution lest it be spooked and fly away, lie down near it.

Some butterflies hold no secrets. Those banes of the gardening community, the two species – large white and small white – commonly lumped together as 'cabbage white', do pretty much what they say on the tin. One is larger than the other, and they are, more or less, white. There are dark spots and wing tips to contend with if you really want to sort them out, and their underwings aren't so much white as the kind of colour Farrow & Ball might call 'Grandmother's Custard', but you know where you are with them. Similarly for brimstone (the male is brimstone yellow, the female more like 'Faded Post-It'), holly blue (it's blue and likes holly) and speckled wood (it's speckled and lives in woods).

But others present one face to the world while concealing another.

The common blue is indeed blue* when seen in flight, or basking with its wings open. Or at least the male is. In the female the blue presents itself only as a faint tinge on predominantly brown wings. And the underwings of both sexes, seen only when they are closed, are beige, with a delicate patchwork of white and black spots and orange teardrops near the edge. Not blue at all.

And so it is with the orange-tip.

In flight, the eponymous wing ends show up clearly enough, an uplifting sight on a spring day. But find it at rest, and, even better, get right up close to it, and the hidden treasure of the underwing reveals itself, a filigree patchwork of mottled camouflage, torn scraps of sage on white. Unexpected subtlety on an apparently plain insect, and, to my eyes at least, astonishingly, strikingly beautiful.

It's spent nine months as a chrysalis, suspended on a stalk, brilliantly disguised in vegetation to evade predation. And now it's sitting on my hand.

We commune. Or at least I commune and it tolerates. Overhead I hear the wing clap of a displaying wood pigeon. Around me in the garden are plants in bloom – vibrant oranges, purples and yellows, all hitting mid-season form. There is no need to do anything. Not just yet. Not while this scrap of spring sits willingly with me, somehow, obscurely, lending meaning to my indolence.

Time passes fast and slow.

---

* Although not, these days, very common.

16

LILY OF THE VALLEY BLOOMS

20–24 April

Grain rains (*Kokuu*, 穀雨)
First reeds sprout
(*Ashi hajimete shōzu*, 葭始生)

I haven't come to a 'special place'. It's not a pilgrimage to a grand sight of nature, a breathtaking spectacle to make you gasp and squeal and upload the video to Twitter in anticipation of viral acclaim. It's just a morning walk in my local woods at the top of Streatham Common. No breaching humpbacked whales, murmurating starlings or rutting deer. Trees. Birds. The odd squirrel. But despite its apparent mundanity, this place will always make things just a bit better. It's infallible like that. And today it gives deep satisfaction.

Whether it's the dappled early-morning light, the strange geometry of the trees, the *shurr* of wind in the canopy, the multiple layers of birdsong accompanied by the soft *flumph* of my shoes on the leaf litter, the gentle rise from the bottom of the wood to the top, the comical sight of a squirrel nearly coming a cropper as it misjudges a branch's load-bearing capacity, or the combination of these things, it's enough to make me forget the harsh realities of all the whatnot in the wotsit.

Perhaps its ordinariness works in its favour. When we seek perfection, it can only disappoint. And while the human urge for discovery makes us susceptible to the lure of the new, sometimes it pays to feel the soothing balm of familiarity. In any case, right now I'm merely satisfied to be alive, awake and functioning well enough to put one foot in front of the other.

The birdsong has layers now. A couple of weeks ago any illusion of complexity was the result of several birds of the same species singing at once. But as the arriving migrants add their voices to the texture, it acquires an intricacy that takes some concentration to unpack.

Preferable, perhaps, to let it wash over me and work its magic without questioning or analysis. Just this once.

But I can't help myself. I've spent ages learning these songs, dammit. So my brain goes to it automatically, unpicking individual voices from the jumble.

Blue tit. Another one. Robin over there, blackbird to the right. Another blackbird, hang on, *two* more. At least three great tits. Chiffchaff *chiffchaff*ing, blackcap behind.

Ooh. Nuthatch.

TREECREEPER.

That shivery sound, conveniently placing itself in the moment's silence.

Birds seen: zero – birds heard: loads. Never has the time spent learning them seemed more worthwhile.

My ear is drawn to the more complicated songs – blackbird, robin, blackcap. Perhaps it's because the songs we find the most fascinating blend the musical – sounds we might recognise as something like music – with the 'other' – sounds that evoke a kind of other-worldliness. One of the reasons we find it difficult to imitate birds is that they have a syrinx while we have a larynx – put simply, this means they can make more than one sound at a time. This unattainability might play its part in our fascination with birdsong. But it also speaks to something primeval in us. They've been our constant companions since we appeared, providing the soundtrack to all human existence. Add to the mix birdsong's association with the coming of spring, with all that means to us – love, growth, rebirth – and it's not difficult to see why we find it so alluring.

Or maybe it just sounds nice.

I've found myself drawn to the mistle thrushes, invested in their future in a way I find difficult to explain. Perhaps it's a manifestation of the prevailing vulnerability in what we are now obliged to call These Unprecedented Times. Perhaps it's just that their progress through this breeding cycle is being played out in public view.

Whatever the reason, I find I can't come to this place without visiting them. I gravitate towards the copse, just to check.

Stand in a certain spot and the nest is clearly visible, if you know where to look. But it's well disguised – ten yards to the left and it disappears behind a tree. The bird's speckled plumage is a natural camouflage against the bosky background, her tail easily mistaken for a branch stump. The tree they've chosen is handy for feeding – just yards from the grassy expanse of the common, an abundant source of the worms and slugs and other wrigglers that are their chosen food source; but with that comes the possibility of disturbance by passing human traffic. Joggers, dog-walkers, buggy-pushers. Urban birds get used to this, but perhaps they'd rather not.

Behind, a blackcap sings. In the distance, a wren. The mistle thrushes remain silent. They have other things to occupy them now.

Back home, an impulse makes me look low down. Sure enough, in the shadow of the wall I see the first stirrings of growth.

The lily of the valley is starting.

They're easy to miss in the shadow of larger, bolder flowers, but when you know, you know, and you monitor their particular spot.

If the delicacy of their appearance – pert hanging jingles on slender stems – isn't enough to set the senses alight, it's worth getting down on your knees. That passer-by casting a sidelong glance as you lower yourself gingerly and place your face on the gravel? Let them think what they will. It's their loss. For they're not the ones who will benefit from that scent, a smell so individual and potent that even seeing a photograph of them will convince me I can feel it in my nostrils, in the same way that I can smell the linseed oil on my childhood cricket bat merely by thinking about it. The power of association. Harness it and you could power the grid.

Lily of the valley's scent is the kind of thing chemists labour for years to recreate. An aroma of intense, deep sweetness, not sickly but green and fresh, very floral, mmm, mmm, yes, and am I getting a hint of lemon? Its strength is out of all proportion to the appearance of the flowers. The scent equivalent of the wren's song.

No doubt there's a formula for it, a string of abbreviations and numbers that a chemist might look at and say, 'Ah yes', and then reel off a word full of things like 'hydroxy' and 'methyl' and 'carboxaldehyde'. But how much more evocative are the words 'lily of the valley'. All the anticipation of spring is held in those quivering jingles.

There's a danger that we forget to notice what is there in front of us. But lily of the valley is an antidote to that. Vibrantly alive, drawing you in with its delicate appearance and arresting aroma, and with a season no longer than a pint of milk's, it's a reminder, more than any mindfulness course, to live in the moment.

17

RAIN REFRESHES
PARCHED GROUND

25–29 April

Grain rains (*Kokuu,* 穀雨)
Last frost, rice seedlings grow
(*Shimo yamite nae izuru,* 霜止出苗)

They've reopened the cemetery. It feels like an exhalation of a breath I didn't know I was holding. As I walk round it for the first time in weeks, I make a conscious effort to slow down, halve the speed, halve it again.

It is gloriously unkempt, the enforced neglect allowing the plants the freedom they require. Despite the lack of rain – three weeks and counting – they thrive.

Slender-stemmed grasses groan under the weight of seeds. Horse chestnut candles blush pink; hawthorn blossom blushes pinker. The paths are decorated with the delicate pollen of the ubiquitous London plane tree. Pretty, festive even, skating across the ground in fleecy bundles – misery on toast for allergy sufferers. A clump of three-cornered garlic* flowers catches my eye. If any plant can be said to droop pertly, it's them. The bright yellow of Oxford ragwort – an opportunist plant, plonking itself down anywhere that'll have it – waves at me from a neglected corner. A smile in flower form. Dandelion heads are at peak fluff. The sight of them always evokes childhood memories – telling the time by counting how many puffs it takes to get rid of all the seeds. I habitually underestimated the strength required – canny dandelion, ensuring that the little seed parachutes are released only by a breeze strong enough to carry them away from the immediate area.

I follow a jay at a distance, picking out its pot-bellied shape as it moves from tree to tree. Ash bark oozes tarry globules – *Daldinia concentrica*, otherwise known as 'King Alfred's Cakes'. Goldcrest sings, great tit insists, blackbird burbles.

It is a good time.

It is, I see from Twitter, the season of obligatory wisteria photographs. Having for the first time in living memory monitored the plant's progress from the earliest budding, I look at the offerings with a slight air of superiority.

'Yes yes, obviously it's gorgeous *now*, but where were you six weeks ago when it all kicked off?'

---

* I am a wildflower ignoramus. I have the names of only the blindingly obvious (dandelion, cow parsley, bramble) ready to go in my head. So when I drop the name of a wild flower casually into the text like this, you can assume it's the result of hours of tortured study or an embarrassed plea to the expert botanists of Twitter.

But I have to admit they're right. The cascade of blooms is irresistibly cheering. And this is the appropriate season for it, conforming with the correct order of things as laid down in the seasonal almanacs of Japanese poetry. I jumped the gun by mentioning that early growth – wisteria's place is after the cherry blossoms are done.

Matching the wisteria, the back garden clematis has finally burst into full and fine array. From a distance, festooned along training wires against the dark green fence, it's a festive sight; up close, it's sensational. Six or seven papery petals, delicately interleaved, now splayed open, revealing a cluster of pale yellow stamens – luminescence against delicacy, a sure-fire winner.

The colours clash slightly with the honesty nearby, the two plants' positions on the broad spectrum of 'white' not quite aligned in sympathy. But to my eyes it's a harmonious clash. There's a contrast of geometry too, the clematis's garland taunting the more structured pyramid of the honesty.

My tour of the estate is interrupted by a squawk and a clatter. Parakeets, incoming. Two of them, landing on the feeders on the terrace. Brash, noisy, unsubtle. One of them is up and away almost immediately, leaving its companion to eye me beadily from its perch. The other feeder swings like a saloon bar's doors when a new gunslinger's in town.

I tolerate the parakeets because of the infrequency of their visits, and their relatively low numbers – even though they're prolific in the general area, the most we've had in the garden is four – while acknowledging that if I lived anywhere near a roost, where they sometimes number in their hundreds, my attitude would be less generous. Originally experienced as a welcome splash of colour, the sight of them has pleased London residents less and less as the years have passed and their numbers increased. The line between 'welcome sighting' and 'bloody vermin' is vague, but their propensity for ruckus-making only adds to public perception of them as a growing pest.

Meanwhile, the great tit – the one with the lighter nape – waits patiently in the tree overhanging our garden fence, dashing down to nab a buggy nibble whenever the coast is clear. It will, by my reckoning, be providing for up to ten hungry mouths any time now. It needs to be in prime condition.

And so the long day wears on. A sunny day, punctuated by the occasional slow rolling of the kind of clouds my cloud-spotting book calls 'Cumulus fractus' but I call 'tiny fluffies'.

It can't last.

It doesn't.

On day four it rains. Proper, pissing, splatting, water-shooting-up-your-trouser-leg-when-you-step-on-a-loose-paving-stone rain. The first in weeks. It's cold too, the sharp drop in temperature recalling those interminable days a couple of months ago when we thought the rain would never stop.

The earth drinks, absorbs, lets out a soothing breath. And now you can almost see the plants growing, filling themselves with much-needed sustenance. Three weeks isn't a drought, but it's quite long enough for the arrival of any form of moisture to be welcomed with open leaves.

We get nearly a day's worth, the onslaught eventually giving way in late afternoon. It leaves behind a persistent, sullen mizzle of the kind you think is going to stop soon but doesn't.

I go out anyway. After rain is a good time to see birds, especially if they've been hunkering down, waiting for it to stop. They need to eat regularly, and wetness, while endurable for most birds, isn't an ideal state for continued well-being. So they find shelter and emerge when the coast is clear.

My reward for suffering the last throes of the rain is a blackcap singing near the cemetery entrance, like a welcoming fanfare. The place is alive with *chirrups* and *tseewits* and *tick-ticks*, as if the birds are checking with each other that it really is safe to emerge. The rain has both refreshed and subdued. The dandelion clocks, perky and ripe twenty-four hours ago, have been battered into extinction. A sycamore has shed its flowers, and now they lie scattered on the ground, their green-yellow mixing with the bedraggled pink of ruined magnolia petals to give the dark asphalt an air of an experimental art project. By contrast the cow parsley has withstood the onslaught and now, apparently growing as I watch, threatens to engulf whole buildings with its fecund burgeoning. And everywhere there's the drip-drip of droplets from leaves. Brush too close and you get a river down your neck.

Twitter has abounded with videos of 'nature healing' because of human absence, many of them spurious. But just for a moment I allow myself to believe it. All is not well with the world – far from it – but for now, in this little corner, rain or shine, there is contentment.

18

FOX CUBS START
TO PLAY

30 April–4 May

Grain rains (*Kokuu,* 穀雨)
Peonies bloom
(*Botan hana saku,* 牡丹華)

It's a vivid memory, the image preserved across two decades, fresh as if it were yesterday. Early spring, late night. A deserted, tree-lined south London street. Parked cars, street lights, shadows. A particular kind of stillness.

Me, just returned from a concert, sitting in my car, allowing a small silence to develop after the noise and bustle of the journey. Just as I reach for the door handle I see a movement on the pavement. Fifteen, maybe twenty yards away.

Fox.

It's wary at first, looking left and right like a good Green-Cross-Coder. It lowers its nose to the ground for a second, then emerges into the pool of light cast by the street lamp. Russet-silver coat, bushy tail, grizzled snout.

It trots out into the road and stops, slap bang in the middle, almost a statement of ownership. And now it's coming towards me. Ten yards, five. I still have my hand on the key in the ignition. And there it stops, looks up and stares me straight in the eye.

Maybe I'm imagining it. Did it actually make that contact, or do I just like the idea of this moment of cross-species intimacy? Maybe it's not even aware of my presence, sheltered as I am in my cocoon of metal and glass. In any case, it soon turns away, and continues down the road behind me. Brisk, relaxed, confident.

It remains the closest encounter I've had with a fox. My fox.

The cub assessing me from the long grass in West Norwood Cemetery twenty or more years later definitely knows I'm there. I can feel its gaze on me, can tell that it saw me first, was monitoring me, trying to work out what part I play in the strange world it's been thrust into.

Even with my rudimentary knowledge of mammalian behaviour, I know that foxes have a breeding season, and a little bit of maths enables me to work out that this cub is two months old, give or take. Small, fresh, cute as anything. But it's also wary, sitting motionless, unblinking, all its senses pointed towards me. It'll let me get this close. No further.

Two days earlier an old dog fox, perhaps its father, trotted past me on the path, paying me no more heed than any other Londoner would. This cub is already far advanced from the helpless creature that had its eyes closed for the first ten days of its life and depended entirely on its mother for the first month. It'll be catching its own food now, and will no doubt learn the ways of the urban fox before too long, but for now it shows an entirely appropriate wariness, giving me a wide berth and scampering away across the sunlit grass.

The holly is flowering. Small pink-tinged cream bubbles poking out in clumps from the tangle of spikes. They take me aback, simply because when I think about holly it's not the flowers that spring to mind. Leaves, yes – dark green and forbiddingly spiky – and berries, that deep red. But the flowers have somehow escaped my attention. I'm not sure how I imagined the berries came into existence, but that's just another example of what happens when you blunder through life not looking at anything beyond the surface.

Anyway, it's flowering, and I welcome the sight.

Even more welcome is a sound I hear in the woods on day three of this season. A sound to make you stop and give a little start. A sound I haven't heard for three years. A sound from high in the canopy and even higher in my listening spectrum.

Firecrest.

I stand stock still, uncertain. It's so easy to make these things up, to will them into existence. Maybe it's just a treecreeper, similarly high, right up there in the upper reaches of human hearing. Lacking any particular shape, these sounds are easily confused.

There it is again. *Zee-zee-zee-zee-zee.* Fast, agitated, slightly rising.

Yes. Firecrest.

Easy to see, when you look at the pictures, how the bird got its name. Flame orange stripe on the crown, flaring up to show the world just how huge and terrifying it is.

It's nothing of the kind, of course. In most respects the firecrest resembles its cousin the goldcrest. Tiny, olive-green, flitty. These factors combine to make both birds difficult to see, even when you know they're there. But while goldcrests are common and widespread, firecrests are not. Their population in this country is small, bolstered by passage migrants in spring and autumn. So this *zee-zee-zee-zee-zee* is quite the occasion. Here is a male firecrest with an interest in breeding.

If both birds were sitting in front of me, as in a field guide, I'd be able to distinguish them fairly easily. The eponymous crests follow similar patterns – black and orange or yellow stripes on the crown, drawing the eye – but the faces are different. The goldcrest's is open, plain except for a black button eye. The firecrest has a prominent eye stripe, giving it a sleeker, sharper look.

But such views exist only in dreams. This bird is high up, calling from the canopy, invisible. And that, in all probability, is how it will remain.

Maybe it will find a mate. And maybe, somewhere in this wood, they will construct a nest, a tiny ball-shaped cubbyhole of moss and spiders' webs and lichen, suspended between two twigs; and maybe they'll line it with hair and feathers picked up on forays around and about the place; and maybe in it they will raise a brood (or possibly even two) of half a dozen or so chicks; and maybe a proportion of them will evade predation and will reach adulthood, and a small population will be established.

Or maybe not. I'm enough of a realist to know that this encounter will be it, that the male won't find a partner, and he'll move on without my coming across him again.

So I hold the memory of that *zee-zee-zee-zee-zee* – a memory that, despite its comparative lack of intimacy, will last at least as long as that fox from long ago – and take it home with me.

Home, where, in defiance of the Japanese microseasons, peonies don't bloom; home, where purple-clustered allium flowers lurk inside their papery enclosing sheath, positively gagging to throw off the shackles; home, where an iris splays its purple and yellow florescence brazenly – obscenely, almost – across the flower bed.

Home, where spring springs its full blaze and points towards summer.

19

SWIFTS ARRIVE

5–9 May

Beginning of summer (*Rikka*, 立夏)

Frogs start singing
(*Kawazu hajimete naku*, 蛙始鳴)

You could believe the weather is looking at the ancient calendar and has noticed the name of the new season. It's warm enough to sit out in the sun, not so hot that you retreat into the shade muttering about how hot it is. It might just be because I've become more aware of the small rhythms of the year, but there is a discernible shift from spring–summer to summer–spring.

Goldfinch tinkles, robin chips in. Singing frogs, central to this microseason in Japan, are noticeable for their absence.

House sparrows fly up and cling to the wall next door, pecking away at the mortar. If at first this seems like eccentric behaviour, there is method to it. They might be mining the grit from the mortar to hold in their gizzards to help with breaking down seeds and suchlike; or they might be after the calcium from the limestone to toughen up their eggshells. Either way, it's not random. They would hardly expend such energy, flying up repeatedly from their perch in a nearby tree and back down again, without some benefit.

While I'm easily distracted by what a continuity announcer would no doubt call their 'zany antics', my eye is also drawn to a scene of more understated and slower drama closer at hand.

Next to me, a flowerpot. The last flowerings of geraniums, pale in the sun. Between two stalks a spider has spun a web of such intricate delicacy it quite takes the breath away. The spider itself is tiny, species unknown.*

It sits in the middle of the web, patience arachnified. There's the occasional tiny gust of wind, no more than a shiver, enough to send ripples through the web. Hoverflies and other tiddlers flit around, gathering nectar. One flies up and comes within a toucher of being ensnared. I wonder if it realises how close it came to being spider lunch.

This everyday spectacle is easily missed, for simple reasons of scale. Small things are harder to see. And if you're not interested, you can easily go through life without being aware of the micro-scopic universe around us. Even with that interest fully engaged, it takes an act of will to seek these things out. My noticing of the spider was almost coincidental, a function of my sitting next to it for a while and allowing my attention to wander, and it's not as if there aren't other things to distr— OHMYGOD SWIFTS SWIFTS SWIFTS!

What is it about them? Other birds – many birds – make the journey from Africa every year; other birds – mallards, to take a deliberately obvious example – are faster, although possibly deficient

---

* I tell myself I'll look it up later. I don't.

in the manoeuvrability department; other birds are in decline, plenty of them in a more parlous state, both nationally and globally, than *Apus apus*.*

But I hold a special place for swifts. I suspect I'm not alone.

They of all birds command the attention in flight. Even the sight of one swift squiggling around high above the house like an excitable parenthesis has me craning my neck to watch. And when they scream past my office window in tight formation I give myself over to them completely.

What it boils down to is their otherness, that feeling you get when you watch them that you're getting a glimpse of an alien world. All birds possess it to a certain extent; swifts embody it.

No doubt there's a sense of possession in there too, an unearned belief that these birds somehow belong to me. They happen to spend a portion of their year where I am. Ergo they are my swifts – not quite the same as other people's.

They return consistently on 6 or 7 May. Every year. Today is the 5th.

They're early.

And, I note with deep satisfaction, they're here in numbers. I see two at first, high over the house. And then, with a growing sense of pleasure, I see more, appearing in the blue sky as if from a portal. Four, eight, ten.

Twenty years ago, ten swifts would have been no more than a smattering; today it feels like a glut. Still, small mercies and all that.

---

* The scientific name, which translates to 'no foot no foot', derives from the old belief that because they were so proficient in the air and uncomfortable on the ground, swifts had no feet.

Behind them I see a different shape, one that sends me indoors for the binoculars. It takes a few seconds to find it in the boundless blue sky, but a recalibration does the job, and my instinct is confirmed. Broad wings, fan tail. A buzzard, soaring lazily anticlockwise, then drifting off and away and out of my sight behind the house.

There's something thrilling about this kind of sighting. I expect to see a buzzard perched on a fence post by a country lane, not circling over the suburban expanse of south London. But there's no shortage of food for an urban buzzard – rats and mice famously abound – and the woods a couple of miles east of our house offer the kind of woodland habitat where they might nest. I file the sighting under 'unusual, but not astonishing', make a mental note to visit Sydenham Hill Woods as soon as possible, and return to my communion with the swifts.

I'm immediately distracted from swiftwatch by a quick succession of staccato noises from above.

Tchhrrrrrrr – CHIP.

The *tchhrrrrrr* is the agitated alarm call of a great tit; the aggrieved CHIP the response of a great spotted woodpecker, rumbled in its attempted foray to the nesting box.

Proof, if it were needed, that there are chicks in there.

The great tit flies up, chases the woodpecker away. Given that the woodpecker is twice its size, and in possession of a fearsome stabber for a beak, this is an act of no mean bravery, and a good indication of the protective instincts of the parent.

Constant vigilance is required. Woodpeckers, magpies, jays – all on the lookout for an easy meal, and who can blame them? They're all in the same boat as the great tit, fellow combatants in the fight for survival.

It's the easiest thing in the world to take sides. Big bad magpie taking floofy great tit chicks. What a bastard. But floofy great tit chick will be fed on caterpillars and insects and maybe that spider. And my beloved swifts will end the lives of countless flying insects in their time on the planet. Play the 'every life is sacred' game and logic will soon get the better of you.

Spider and fly. Woodpecker and great tit. Buzzard and rabbit.

Life is not for the squeamish.

20

BEES ALL OVER THE PLACE

10–14 May

Beginning of summer (*Rikka*, 立夏)
Worms surface
(*Mimizu izuru*, 蚯蚓出)

For years I allowed the natural world to pass me by. It didn't leave me cold, but nor did it stoke the flames. I knew the countryside was a nice place to be, but I didn't seek it out. And while the residue of a childhood spent immersed in birds eventually rose again to claim me, of the world they lived in I knew next to nothing.

But some things, no matter how much I ignored them, were so etched in the backdrop of my childhood that even I would be hard-pushed to forget all about them. Daisy, cow parsley, horse chestnut, elder, bracken, dog-rose, red clover.

And this season, as I take my permitted daily walk, I feel as if they've come back to visit me all at once.

A single dog-rose, pretty in pale pink, greets me as I come to the edge of the grove. Cow parsley froths out over the path like champagne, its umbels* unstoppably resplendent. The green of the horse chestnut near the church – a fresh, bright green reminiscent of snooker-table baize or a Subbuteo pitch – is enhanced by the appearance of its pale, delicate candles. Elder comes into flower – pert sprays of cream lace. I will harvest them for cordial, but not just yet.

It all feels very 'summers of my childhood'.

It's probably not a coincidence that I'm drawn to these familiar touchstones. They are the ever-present, evoking feelings of nostalgia and comfort, memories of that fictional time when all was well in the best of all possible worlds. Reassurance when it's most needed.

Two days in, the weather turns. Wind from the north, a drop in temperature, a feeling of the rain that never quite comes. Two-thin-jumpers weather.

But I go out. Exercise is good for you, after all. Even slow, heel-dragging exercise, interrupted every twenty seconds because I need to look at the fractal geometry of that bracken, or the several different greens on that oak, or the blue pavement snow of a ceanothus that has decided to shed its flowers all in a heap, like it's mad as hell and not gonna take this any more.

And there, on the clover, bees.

The clover itself is coming into peak condition, and they are all over it like a rash. No wonder it used to be known as 'bee bread'. And the bees, now I look more closely, are of several different species.

Life used to be much simpler. Living in a fog of ignorance usually is.

---

* I didn't know the word 'umbel' as a child. I do now, so have to be forcibly restrained from throwing it into conversation willy-nilly.

For years I thought there were three kinds of bee: honey, bumble and other. And then I Discovered Nature and started to delve.

Big mistake.

There are, I learn when I get home and browse the *Field Guide to the Bees of Great Britain and Ireland*, hundreds of the beggars. To be precise: 270. Mining bees, furrow bees, mason bees, nomad bees, flower bees, carpenter bees, shaggy bees, yellow-face bees, plasterer bees, blood bees, leafcutter bees, sharp-tail bees, long-horned bees, bumblebees, and of course the one most people think of when you say the word 'bee': the good old Western honey bee, *Apis mellifera*.

It was quite a shock to learn, relatively late in life, that the word 'bumblebee' is a hopelessly vague way of describing the twenty-seven species of the genus *Bombus* that have been recorded in the UK. The good kind of shock – the kind that makes you recoil for a second before saying, 'Really? Tell me more.' Hence the field guide.

It's way above my pay grade, this book. As a beginner I should content myself with one of those laminated sheets that show only the commonest species and give you just the right amount of detail to absorb fairly easily.

But I like field guides. I like their heft, their detail, the weight of knowledge that's gone into their production. And I'm a sucker for a distribution map.

This one provides, as any good field guide should, far more detail than I'll ever need or be able to process. Of those 270 species, how many am I likely to see in the wilds of West Norwood? Fifteen or twenty, at most. And even then, most of them would fall squarely in the category 'unidentified buzzing thing'.

But I'm a completist by nature – I want all the information at my fingertips, even if most of it will only ever be theoretical. So I look with fascination at the anatomical drawings, taking in words such as 'tergite' and 'fovea' and 'supraclypeal plate', knowing that while some of the knowledge will stick, most of it won't. Knowledge, I've found as I get older, tends to do that.

But at the very least it helps pass the time.

And if nothing else it's quite the eye-opener to discover that there are insects going about the place with names like carrot mining bee, sheep's-bit dufourea and hairy-saddled colletes. I'm particularly exercised to discover the existence of something called a pantaloon bee.* I might never see one, but I can't help feeling that my world is ever so slightly enhanced by the knowledge that I share it with such a thing.

I'm looking the bees up because there's been a flurry of them. Bees don't get a mention in the Japanese version of the seasons, but if I were to start my own personal roster, this season might lean towards 'Bees all over the place'.

The individual I'm particularly interested in was doing two things. It was supping freely from a patch of clover in the cemetery, and it was refusing to sit still for long enough for me to get a good look at it. So, as with the pretty-sure-it-was-a-brindled-pug-moth of Season 11, I'm relying on my visual memory to help me.

If bee identification isn't quite the nightmare I experience with moths, it is nonetheless complicated enough to necessitate much brow-knitting and lip-pursing, but taking into consideration multiple factors, including tergite banding, malar gaps and its cute and fluffy white tail, I eventually come to the conclusion that I have no idea.

Bees, like life, are just a confusing mess.

---

* It's named after the baggy pollen brushes sported in a jaunty fashion by the female of the species. The male contents itself with a slimmer cut.

21

STARLING HULLABALOO

15–20 May

Beginning of summer (*Rikka*, 立夏)
Bamboo shoots sprout
(*Takenoko shōzu*, 竹笋生)

There's an art to a signature tune. Just a few notes, a memorable hook to announce yourself. Our robin has one. A two-note theme, full of jauntiness and élan. *Tsweee-WOOOO*.

And I look up, and more often than not it swoops across from the fence to the sweet-pea-training teepee, flicks its tail up to the left, shifts ninety degrees, flicks its tail up to the right, presents its orange breast to the world as if to say, 'Just you try it, go on, I dare you', and then hops onto the feeder. A few seconds, no more, then off.

There's a lot more to its repertoire, of course. The robin's song is notably sweet and silvery. Fluting phrases with a few seconds' gap in between, as if allowing each one to settle before trying a variation. The complexity of that song – used for mating or territorial purposes – isn't matched by this two-noter. It feels to me like an announcement: 'Coming to the feeder, like it or not – get off in the next five seconds or you're toast.' If that is its purpose, it's an effective ploy. This bird is rarely challenged.

It's not the only one with a signature tune. Our resident male blackbird regularly signs off its performance with the melody of the first line of 'Camptown Races'. In my head I finish it off with the answering 'doo dah, doo dah'.*

Much avian song defies transcription. Its complexity, often including 'non-musical' sounds, is immune to that kind of analysis. The blackbird's song is rich, mellifluous and full of variation, a striking mixture of clucks and gurgles and warbles intended to announce the bird's availability for mating, but having the serendipitous side-effect of striking joy deep into many a human heart. I would quail at the prospect of writing it out in musical notation, but 'Camptown Races' I can manage.

Both robin and blackbird signature tunes have an upbeat quality entirely in keeping with the tenor of the season. There is warmth in the air, and the swifts – absent for a couple of days thanks to the colder weather – have returned and are in full swoop. All the things that were in peak condition last season are now even peaker. Cow parsley, elder, alliums – all exuding the kind of energy you could use to power a small home. They're joined by the hawthorn blossom – the levels of tumbling prettiness it attains should carry a swoon warning.

This is a time of young things. A teenage robin catches my eye, perched on the edge of a scrubby bit in Streatham Common Woods. It's dissimilar enough to the adult bird – the eponymous red breast replaced by an all-over nondescript streaky brown – for people

---

* And yes, occasionally out loud. What of it?

to think they've seen something unusual when it turns up on the feeder. This one exudes a beaky defiance, but also that strange level of trust common in birds that haven't yet learned about the dangers of the world.

Those dangers come in all forms, as the mistle thrushes discover. My arrival in the vicinity of the nest is accompanied by the kind of hullabaloo that never bodes well for prospective parents. The mistle thrush's alarm call puts me in mind of the teleprinter from 1970s *Grandstand*, an agitated rattling on this occasion accompanied by the shouts of two carrion crows. Even though the action is hidden from my view by trees, it's not difficult to imagine what has happened. I fear the worst for the thrush chicks, and can't help wondering that if the crows were after a snack, they might have found it easier to rootle through one of the many overflowing bins nearby.

Back home, the clamour from the great tits in the nest box increases daily, as does the interest from those that would predate them – two carrion crows spend an agitated couple of minutes on the gutter above trying to work out how to get into the box for a tasty between-meals snack.

We're treated to a visit from a family of long-tailed tits, chasing each other in relay as they pass through. *Tseep-tseep-tseep* and gone. No sooner have they departed than a pair of parakeets circle overhead, land on the feeders with a clatter, throw some food on the floor and scarper.

Bloody hooligans.

But if all this activity – rude, energetic and utterly irrepressible – catches the attention as I sit on the terrace enjoying the warmest weather of the year so far, it's merely a sideshow. The main attraction plays out beyond the end of the garden, a near-continuous hubbub of excited chirrups and squeaks and squawks and whistles and youthful hijinks. Exuberance in bird form.

The juvenile starlings are having a party.

The stage they've reached in their development will be familiar to any parent of a toddler who has just learned to run. Anything and everything is possible.

The revels take place mostly out of sight, shielded from view by trees and sheds and general south-Londonery. But every couple of minutes an excitable bird pops up into the air as if shot out by a Nerf gun. Some of them go on longer excursions, agitatedly flapping and calling to each other as they do a lap of the surrounding neighbourhood. Others, either less developed or just not as adventurous, content themselves with a loop-the-loop before returning to base.

They're intoxicated by their new-found ability, and their enthusiasm is infectious, so I find myself smiling at each manifestation of their youthful vigour, and then it all settles down for a minute and a blue butterfly skitter-scatters across the lawn and lands on the holly, and I'm a blur as I run for the camera.

My eagerness is easily explained. I'm fairly sure that this is a holly blue butterfly. I do not have a photograph of a holly blue butterfly. I would like a photograph of a holly blue butterfly.

It seems like such a simple thing. The species isn't scarce. It isn't exactly retiring. Its disguise skills are, for a butterfly, in the mid-range. What it has in its favour, as far as not being photographed by enthusiastic but clumsy amateurs goes, is an ability to keep moving in a fast and apparently random manner. Further, it possesses an innate, unteachable skill. When at rest, it can anticipate the clicking of a camera shutter, and synchronise its take-off accordingly.

I would love to be able to tell a tale of triumph, to walk into the room brandishing a shiny photograph of a holly blue recumbent against a dark green holly leaf.

Would that life were so simple.

Looking back, I'm not even sure that's what it was. Probably a common blue. I've got loads of photos of those. Ah well.

But what with the swifts swifting and the young starlings young-starlinging and the robin–blackbird duet, and the whole darned peak-spring-almost-summerness of it all, such disappointments barely register.

22

WARMTH SETTLES IN

21–25 May

Lesser ripening (*Shōman,* 小満)
Silkworms start feasting on mulberry leaves
(*Kaiko okite kuwa o hamu,* 蚕起食桑)

The great tits have gone quiet.

For a couple of weeks the cheeping of the chicks from the nest box has been part of the garden soundtrack, but now there's an ominous silence. Like any parent, I fear the worst. I worry. I fret. I worry and fret, but it doesn't help. They've gone quiet. Not a peep.

They might have fledged while our backs were turned. It wouldn't be unusual. Out and gone to pastures new. Or they might all be dead, predated by the woodpecker or the crows or the magpies.

Naturally, my pessimistic brain keeps coming back to that thought.

Nature being nature, chicks die. If all the great tit chicks survived, and if they all went on to breed successfully, we'd be knee-deep in them within three years. This might seem overdramatic, but it's just maths. Great tits, and other small birds, allow for this by laying large clutches, knowing that a fair proportion won't make it to adult-hood. It's the way the world works, the way great tits have made it this far. Playing the odds. Survival maths. At a species level, they're very good at it.

But having followed this family's progress from the begin-ning, from the earliest site-scouting to incessant cheeping, it would be unnatural not to feel a pang. These are *our* great tits, *our* chicks, *our* floofy fluffbundles. No bastard magpie's having them for lunch.*

The hole in the soundscape nags at me, even if it's easily covered by other sounds. The swifts have settled in for their daily scream-by, treating me to a spectacular display every morning and defying me to tear my eyes away from them; the robin and blackbird rehearse their signature tunes with predictable regularity; there's the welcome sound of a blackcap singing from somewhere behind the shed on day two, and the whole is enhanced by a chorus of *tsweets*, *chiddleywips* and *graarghs* from a variety of species, all thoroughly pumped and hitting mid-season form.

Also well into its stride is the weather, which serves up reli-able warmth and sunshine, accompanied by temperatures that hit the British sweet spot and settle in for a good stint. Mid-twenties Celsius, the lightest and rufflingest of light ruffling breezes. 'Just

---

* At this point you might be wondering if there is a correlation between magpie population density and songbird decline. A study by the British Trust for Ornithology in 1998 showed none.

right' weather – to complain about it would mark you out as a curmudgeon of the first order. Or, just maybe, a gardener keen for a little moisture to penetrate the parched soil.

While there's still a great sense of burgeoning growth, some things are past their prime. Cow parsley is the most obvious plant to crest the rise and start the journey down the other side. Great swathes of it line the path down the side of Norwood Grove, gushing out from the railings like foamy water from a sprinkler. A few days ago, walking down that path was like being the victim of a botanical mugging; now it's more like a cheering crowd lining the streets of the London Marathon – vigorous and enthusiastic, but obeying the rules.

Here it was that the song thrush sang back in March, and here it was that the tamarisk sprayed its glorious pink froth all over the path for a couple of weeks in April. And here, to my pleasure and astonishment, I see a collared dove hanging out on the rooftop with a bevy of its wood-pigeon cousins.

I'm aware that to get excited about every instance of nature – hello, clouds! hello, sky! hello, small patch of frankly nondescript weed on the pavement! – is to invite accusations of Nature Hysteria Overload. A collared dove is nice enough, so pleasure is an appropriate reaction for those so inclined. But astonishment?

Well, up to a point.

Some context. The collared dove, barely known in Europe at the beginning of the twentieth century, swept all before it over the next fifty years, like an invading army playing the long game. By the mid-1950s it had nested in Britain for the first time. By the end of the century it was almost ubiquitous.

Almost.

Because while in plenty of areas of London it's abundant, in others it's completely absent. It's a bird of patches. And mine isn't one of them. I've never seen one within walking distance of my house.

But now I have.

It's a plain but elegant bird, its plumage touching on the range of cream, bone, buff, off-white, ivory, beige and so on you might see in a collection of linen jackets. Landlord white. The eponymous collar is a narrow black bar on the neck. Medium-sized, it looks positively dainty next to the wood pigeons. It's hard to imagine anyone choosing it as their absolute favourite. Certainly it lacks the charm of the even smaller turtle dove, whose population has been so appallingly denuded in recent years that a sighting is now an occasion of some significance. The turtle dove's call is a charming purr; the collared dove's a monotonous three-note coo.

Is it odd to get excited about this commonplace individual, slightly out of its usual range? Should I perhaps get worked up about the dragonfly I see later, up at the Rookery, its flat golden-brown abdomen suspended delicately in the air as it clings to the stem of a something-or-other plant, filigree wings immobile in the sunlight? It's not a species known to me – not that that's saying much – but that's what field guides are for, so I look it up later and learn that it's a four-spotted chaser, so named because of the two dark spots on the front edge of each wing. Hangs out at pond margins; defends its territory aggressively; likes a perch where it can look up at the sky and check out the silhouettes of potential predators and prey; eats sheep.*

---

* This bit isn't true.

Before I saw it, I knew the name. But going through the process of identification – seeing, studying, looking up – embeds it in the memory. I'll know it again.

Home. Sitting, thinking about things familiar, things unusual, the ever-evolving shape of life.

A flurry in the hazel, a sharp *chip*, an answering high-pitched *chrrrp*, and then another one, and suddenly the shrub is alive with *chrrrp*ing, and the adult great tit, the one with the pale nape, flies up to the feeder and grabs a buggy nibble and takes it down to a hungry mouth.

Not dead after all. Phew.

23

PEONIES BLOOM AT LAST

26–30 May

Lesser ripening (*Shōman,* 小満)
Safflowers bloom
(*Benibana sakau,* 紅花栄)

There is little to report. The weather continues warm and agreeable, this season merely a continuation of the last one. The changes, such as they are, are imperceptible. Grass grows, flowers bloom, tiny insects hover in spiralling columns above the lavender. A speckled wood butterfly flits its merry way through the shaded woods.

In the cemetery the blackcap, ever hopeful, sings its garbled song. Still no takers. Goldcrest flits, stock dove *hoo-hoos*, greenfinch *zuzzes*. I go for my walk and it is the quintessence of pleasantness and then I go home and out to the garden and the peonies have flowered with a BAM WHOOSH YES HERE WE ARE WE'RE HERE LOOK AT US JUST LOOK.

Maybe not imperceptible after all.

The unleashing of the peonies' energy is the most dramatic change of this season. One minute they were tight as a furled umbrella, the next they were out in all their flumpfed-up glory, somehow pulling off the twin trick of majesty and camp outrageousness. They won't be around for long, but they more than make their presence felt while they are.

This suddenness is a manifestation of a pattern I've begun to notice developing. While some microseasons are to all intents and purposes indistinguishable from their neighbours, others stand out. I will remember Season 23 for the peonies, as I will remember Seasons 4, 10, 16 and 19 for the drumming woodpecker, singing chiffchaff, blooming lily of the valley and screeching swifts respectively. Others, not so much. But the pleasure and interest comes just as much from watching those slow developments as from the memorable occasions, even if they're not so firmly attached to a specific time. And the whole process, allowing myself to be absorbed into the natural world as often as possible, is the most blessed respite imaginable.

How to stay sane in a time of pandemic.

The peonies are spectacular, but equally riotous is the cemetery's memorial rose garden, a corner that depresses the hell out of me in winter, with its raised stone beds arranged like pews before a central altarpiece. As these things go, it has been done well, the four-square geometry of the beds offset by an elegant crescent-shaped centrepiece, but I usually give it a wide berth, preferring to gravitate towards the wilder areas. Once a year, though, everything aligns, and the bounty of the flowering roses outweighs the municipal formality. This is its time, the majority of plants reaching peak condition, each one a life remembered. I wander round it, letting the colours, perfumes and vigour of the flowers do their business.

As I drift away I become aware of a brouhaha in the bushes to my right. Not the brouhaha of a fight or fracas, but the result of frenetic activity, and with it, a buzzing. I am immediately imbued with the spirit of Winnie-the-Pooh.

Bees!

The sound they're producing is not the low hum normally associated with bees. It's higher, tauter, reminiscent of a dentist's drill, but more concentrated and with energy levels turned to eleven. I track it down to a voluminous rose bush, the flower with its petals spread to allow access to the treasure in the middle. It's a bumblebee – probably white-tailed but don't quote me – clinging to the anthers as if its life depends on it. It delivers a good ten seconds of high-pitched buzzing before releasing its grip, lowering the pitch of its buzz and moving to the next flower.

What it's doing is this.

Some plants play fast and loose with their pollen, welcoming all comers. Others are more miserly, figuring that they've worked hard to produce it so they want it to go to only the best homes. They pack the pollen tight into the anthers, leaving only a tiny slit from which it can be retrieved. The technique required to do this involves grabbing the anther and giving it a good shake. Pollen bursts, bee grabs pollen, caches it in the 'baskets' on its legs, makes off with it. It has plenty of pollen for its own purposes, but inevitably takes along a bit extra, which it unwittingly transfers to the next flower it visits. The bee gets its just reward for its cleverness and hard work; the flower is granted its wish for the pollen to be spread in an effective and economical way.

Everyday transactions going on in their millions, right under our noses, keeping the world going.

The sign is printed in bold on A4 paper and taped to the wall at head height with eye-catching red tape: 'THEY ARE BEES NOT WASPS. THEY ARE VERY NICE AND DON'T STING! (It is illegal to try and get rid of them.)'

And now I look up and see them. Ten, twenty, probably many more, swirling around at first-floor-window height. Not a swarm by any means, but a good gathering nonetheless. No doubt the nest is not far away.

I wonder how many people it took knocking on the door to complain before the owners of the house felt compelled to post the note. And I wonder, too, at the human instinct, when faced with something we perceive as a threat or a pest or just something that's in our way, to destroy it, even when all it's doing is buzzing around minding its own business.

I take this thought for a walk, imagining a conversation between two recently deceased individuals of unspecified species.

'Humans?'

'Yeah. How about you?'

'Humans.'

'What did you do?'

'Built a nest. You?'

'Dunno really. I think I was just there.'

'What *is* their problem?'

'No idea.'

These glum thoughts dog me as I continue on my long walk around the neighbourhood. They're slightly dissipated by the sight of a cinnabar moth, its striking vermilion-and-black colouring catching the eye; and by the sounds of a family of nuthatches careering around in the canopy calling to each other in the woods; and by a really VERY LOUD great tit calling when I get home, as if welcoming me and telling me to snap out of it. And by the time it gets to dusk my mood has almost recovered its former optimism.

There are now officially sixteen hours of daylight. Good times for lovers of really early mornings, or for those, like me, who lack the get-up-and-go to get up and go when the sun rises before five, but who relish the lengthening evenings. What could be better than watching the daylight fade, to an accompaniment of crepuscular blackbird song and swooping swifts?

Nothing. That's what.

24

WOODPECKERS FEED
THEIR OFFSPRING

31 May–5 June

Lesser ripening (*Shōman,* 小満)
Wheat ripens and is harvested
(*Mugi no toki itaru,* 麦秋至)

I'm on a trudge.

I wish I could call it a saunter, but you need to be carefree to saunter. Even 'walk' isn't right. Not today. Today it's a trudge.

It's mostly the weather. For three days it was perfectly reasonable. Warm enough without hitting full swelter; a smattering of clouds of the requisite kind; gentle breezes. Early summer done right.

And then it decided to be autumn for a bit. Just to keep us on our toes. Low grey clouds, sullen as a teenager; quasi single-figure temperatures reduced further by the mysterious 'wind chill'.* The kind

---

* I understand the concept of 'wind chill'. It's something we're all familiar with. But explain it to me ten times and I still won't quite understand how you put a figure on it.

of weather you tolerate in November because it's what you expect. You might even enjoy it in a 'going for a blustery walk is fun' kind of way, if that's your thing. But in June it's just dismal, mood-dampening nonsense. It doesn't even rain. Pointless weather, as much use as a Kleenex umbrella.

In these conditions the daily walk becomes a trial. A heavy-legged one at that. My default is to march up and down the local hills with an air of purpose, but today I'm content merely to keep going in a dogged kind of way, wanting it all to be over so the 'feet up with a well-earned cup of tea' stage comes sooner.

What I need is something to cheer me up.

Enter a pied wagtail, as reliable a cheerer-upper as you'll ever find.

These little black and white birds are known by London birders as 'Chiswick flyover' – after the elevated section of the M4 in the west of the city – because of their habit of flying over your head with a brisk *chi-zick* call. On the ground, foraging for scraps, tail flicking busily – they are well named – their whirring gait recalls a clockwork toy. They like motorway service stations, supermarket car parks, station platforms. This one seems to favour a patch of pavement by the parade at the top of the hill. Bike rack, bin, pied wagtail.

It's happy enough to be on the pavement – there's good pick-ings around – and happy enough to let me stand near it – no more than a couple of yards. Urban birds face different challenges, com-pared with their rural counterparts. Higher levels of heat, light and air pollution take their toll, but on the other hand there is usually a source of free food nearby for the canny and adaptable feeder. And living in close proximity to humans often makes them more trusting.

This little whirrer almost seems to relish the attention I'm giving it. Inevitably, this being the era in which no thought or experience can go unrecorded, I take out my phone and start filming it. I follow it as it skitters in front of the vape shop; I follow it as it whizzes past the dry cleaners; I follow it as it careers perilously close to the open door of the cafe.

I become aware of agitation from within. The owner, presumably wondering what the hell I'm doing, is communicating her objection through the plate glass. And now she's at the door, challenging me. The pied wagtail, feckless accomplice, flies away.

Quite what she imagines I'm going to gain by randomly filming the bottom two feet of her shop front, I'm not sure. But in a world where threat can materialise from nowhere I can see that this perceived invasion of privacy might stir feelings of paranoia.

It's a delicate moment. I worry that my innocent explanation – 'I was just filming this little bird' – might be met with disbelief or even hostility, and that a deeper exploration of my motives might be required.

But she's seen the bird fly away, and when understanding dawns she lets me off the hook with a laugh and a flap of the hand. She might not be of the pied-wagtail-filming persuasion, but at least she's open-minded enough to admit the possibility of the existence of pied-wagtail-filming as a viable leisure activity, and not to restrict the rights of pied-wagtail-filmers.

I continue my walk. It even turns, at times, into a saunter.

Rewind three days, to the beginning of the season. A time of sauntering, for sure. This is very much more like it. The soft dappling of sunlight on a dirt path. Insects swirling against clear blue skies. The background chuntering of a variety of songbirds. That sort of thing.

The garden is being taken over by tall, slender grasses. Halfway down, where the flowerbeds bulge out into the middle of the garden, leaving a narrow curved pathway of grass, I have to usher them to one side, their tips nodding gently as I weave my way past them.

The swifts are very much in evidence, eight of them wheeling around in free formation at medium height. So too are the great spotted woodpeckers, the adult male accompanying one of its offspring, prising insects from the bark of the cordyline halfway down the garden and giving them to the juvenile, which sits in the crook of the tree, its crown bright red in the sun, waiting patiently for its meal. It'll be fending for itself soon enough.

The day of the allium is past, their spiky purple globes gone over to green bobbles. Honesty throws out slender, pale green seed pods. Their moon shape and silvery translucence give them their scientific name, *Lunaria annua*, and make them a staple of dried-flower arrangements once they've gone over. I count the seeds. Six in that one. A poppy, two-tone pink, flops open in that sprawling way they have, revealing a pair of dark green insects scrabbling around among the pistils. These, I learn, are thick-legged flower beetles, and they are quite the thing. Looking closely, I see the differences between the two insects. The female is slender, with a copper sheen to the metallic-green body; the male is darker, its thighs like a drug-fuelled bodybuilder. Popeye the thick-legged flower beetle.

At the bottom of the garden a bramble, no respecter of boundaries, tumbles over the low wall separating us from our back neighbours. I'm fond of its familiar shambling shape, particularly here, where it's out of the way and its lacerating thorns can do no harm. The pink-tinged white flowers are pretty too. And there, poking shyly out of the rough tangle, are the first faint stirrings of a pale green fruit.

Hello, autumn.

25

LEAF MINERS RUN AMOK

6–10 June

Grain beards and seeds (*Bōshu*, 芒種)
Praying mantises hatch
(*Kamakiri shōzu*, 蟷螂生)

Wait. Autumn? In June?

Of course not.

Except ... perhaps.

Take the green sandpiper, a small brown-and-white wading bird to be found, if you're lucky, on a muddy lakeshore near you.* For some birders, autumn starts with the first migratory movements of these birds from their breeding grounds in Scandinavia. Just about now, as it happens.

Counter-intuitive though it may seem to think of autumn before summer's got going, this is just a manifestation of the ever-shifting world of bird migration.

---

* Depending on where you live – Terms and Conditions apply.

Why a bird might decide to risk its life by flying thousands of miles over land and sea depends on the species, but is generally driven by availability of resources. A swallow, for example, living most of its life in central or southern Africa, will travel to Europe for the breeding season because food is more readily available there at that time, making it much easier to raise a family. Similarly birds summering in the far north will benefit from long hours of daylight to maximise foraging opportunities, and the comparative lack of predators will make breeding a less hazardous undertaking than in Britain, where mammals would make breakfast of their young quicker than you can say 'gosling smoothie'.

But if the reasons for migration are clear enough, how they negotiate the journey is more mysterious. We know many birds use the length of daylight as a cue to set off. We know they build up fat deposits before embarking on these long journeys to give them a better chance of survival. We know that once under way they use magnetoreception – the ability to detect the earth's magnetic field – to find their way. We know they might use any of a range of techniques to hone further their instinct to end up in the right place. Some seabirds use their astonishing olfactory abilities to navigate the featureless sea. Others might build up a mental map of key areas and useful landmarks to alert them to imminent arrival at their ultimate destination. Others might use the sun as a compass to keep them on track.

But despite all this knowledge, and an ever more advanced understanding of migration's myriad complexities, the reality of it is still enough to induce astonishment. Millions of birds, some of them impossibly tiny, undertake these monumental journeys every year. And it's going on all the time. Barely have the last spotted flycatchers arrived from Africa in May than those green sandpipers set off. Whatever the season, something, somewhere, is on the move.

If my thoughts turn prematurely to the season of decay, they're backed up by the weather, which doubles down on the previous season's low temperatures, as if daring us to turn the heating back on. Ever defiant, I don a second jumper instead. But no matter how often I repeat, 'It's June, it's June, it's June', the world seems determined to prove me wrong.

The horse chestnut in the church grounds is in on it too. Its leaves, resplendent a few days ago, are wilting. It's not autumn, it just looks like it. And for that we can lay the blame squarely at the door of the horse chestnut leaf miner moth (*Cameraria ohridella*). Or, to be strictly accurate, its caterpillars.

The moths themselves – no bigger than a grain of rice – look attractive enough in a mothy kind of way. Sleek chestnut brown with little tufty behinds and tiny black-and-white bars evenly spaced on the wings. But it's the caterpillars that do the damage. The moths lay eggs on the leaves, and the larvae, once hatched, wriggle between the leaf's two thin layers and start chomping, protected from predators by the leaf itself – after all, a blue tit would prefer to nab a caterpillar from a leaf's surface than go to the faff of digging around inside it.

The caterpillars go their merry way, maybe a million of them in a single tree.* The damage to the leaves means their ability to convert sunlight into sugar is compromised, the tree is weakened and more susceptible to other diseases, and we think autumn has come early as the tiny white blotches turn to elongated brown ones,

---

* This is an estimate. I haven't counted them.

and then spread to colour and shrivel the whole leaf. As summer progresses, the tree turns copper, and come September it drops its leaves early.

The attack of the horse chestnut leaf miner is a recent phenomenon. First recorded in Macedonia in 1985, it reached this country in 2002. As with the collared dove, when conditions are favourable, things can move fast.

I stand under the churchyard horse chestnut. It's a striking tree, noble of shape. One of the trees of my childhood, and despite its Balkan origins an emblem of the English countryside.

My thoughts are interrupted by a *chi-zick* from behind me, and I turn just in time to see the familiar bouncing shape of a pied wagtail flying up into the church porch. Always welcome, never snubbed. It comes out again a minute later, flying over my head and down the high street. I wait. Sure enough, two minutes later it's back, swooping up into the same recess with what can only be described as verve and élan. Another minute and it's out again.

Chicks are clearly being fed.

This everyday tale of tireless parenting occupies me as I enter the cemetery, where I'm immediately presented with another example in the form of a soft, regular cheeping. I look round, expecting the usual game of hide-and-seek, but the wren chick – half fluff, half feather – is standing brazenly on a bench.

I realise, now I have eyes on it, that it's providing just half of the soundtrack. The answering cheep is the work of its parent, hidden in the undergrowth a couple of yards to the right. The parent bird knows to stay hidden. The chick doesn't. It just wants to explore.

It emits a plaintive *tseep*, cocks its head, assesses the answering *tsip*. Another *tseep*. Another *tsip*.

I can see the yellow around its beak – exaggeratedly large, like a clown with smeared make-up. This is a feature of many recently fledged birds. Their gape – the inside of the mouth – is coloured to catch the parent's attention. 'Feed me! Here!' As the bird develops and begins to fend for itself, the gape's importance diminishes. But vestiges remain, particularly where the mandibles join together.* This might be this wren's first foray beyond the nest. The urge to protect it is strong.

It finally accedes to its parent's wishes, and hops down out of danger.

Phew.

---

* This, I learn to my delight, is known as the 'gape flange'.

26

EARLY SUMMER STORMS

11–15 June

Grain beards and seeds (*Bōshu,* 芒種)
Rotten grass becomes fireflies
(*Kusaretaru kusa hotaru to naru,* 腐草為螢)

I was never a tree climber. Too scared. While friends clambered up, agile and fearless, I'd make it onto a lower branch and cling on for all I was worth, not daring to look down in case the ground had disappeared.

But age brings a sense of proportion, and now, if there's a branch low enough for me to haul my creaking body onto, and a convenient perch for my backside, I can be persuaded to grapple my way up to at least, ooh, five feet above the ground.

There is just such a tree in the copse at the top of the common. It's the kind of tree that dispenses with the old-fashioned single straight-up trunk, and instead seems to have several of them, each as solid as the other, splayed out from a central node. One of them is perfect for my purposes – low, broad and almost horizontal – and if I find myself in the area I'll stop for a rest.

From there I can see great tits and blue tits and the occasional blackcap furtling around in the higher branches of surrounding trees; from there I get distracted by a sudden flurry and a weird grunting cackle – a squirrel, bounding to the end of a branch and giving one of its occasional confusing vocalisations; and from there I listen to a blackbird singing in a way that leads me to conclude that it's the Marvin Gaye of the blackbird world – a brilliant display of richness, range and variety, the kind of singing to make you stop and listen.

It's the height of luxury. Sitting on a bench watching the world go by is pleasurable enough; sitting in a tree and being treated to a virtuoso recital, free of charge, takes it to a different level.

I'm not the only tree-grappler in town. Two children, very much the age for such activities, eye the lowest-hanging branches of the magnificent cedar of Lebanon in the Rookery with ill-concealed desire. The branches are particularly tempting – long, broad and elegant, sweeping so low to the ground they almost brush against the grass. The children's parents stop them just in time. Just as well. This is a venerable tree, three hundred or more years old. You wouldn't want to be the one responsible for damaging it. The children retreat reluctantly and scamper off to find their entertainment elsewhere.

All this takes place on the one calm day of the season. The rest of the time, blustery winds are the norm. Crows make flying look even harder work than usual; trees fling themselves back and forth like 1980s headbangers; a lesser black-backed gull is blown over the garden, banking sharply on a sudden gust, then resuming its progress with game persistence. Following close behind it, the kind of rainstorm that gives rainstorms a good name. Its USP is that it dumps a reservoir-load of water on the house to a backdrop of blazing sunshine. The more ferociously it rains, the more intense the light illuminating it. Weeks have passed without a change in the weather; now we have two ends of the spectrum at once. It's a spectacular, almost psychedelic experience. And then it fades away almost as quickly as it started, as these summer rains often do, leaving the way clear for that special thing, a warm post-rain walk. The word 'petrichor' – the now-famous smell of rain on warm ground – trembles on my lips. You can almost see it rising from the pavements.

The cemetery is full of activity. It manifests itself mostly in rustles and flickers from the tops of trees and deep in the undergrowth, but it's good to know it's there. A green woodpecker gives me the benefit of its laughing call from somewhere in the dense thicket to the right. Then it breaks ranks, a flash of movement flickering in and out of vision amid the foliage before bouncing out of sight.

But if the birds are in a secretive mood, the butterflies are upfront and central, and I'm soon treated to the sight of a red admiral posing on a gravestone. A pert little pyramid of orange, black and white.

It's come from France, maybe. Somewhere over the sea, at any rate, flying to a high altitude where the wind will make the journey easier. If my mind boggles at the thought of bird migration, it throws up its hands and concedes defeat when contemplating the same phenomenon in butterflies. No matter how often I read that 'the red admiral is a strongly migratory species', part of me will still protest, 'But . . . I mean, *how*?'

This one, unaware of my admiration for it, sits quietly, soaking up the sun. Our communion is interrupted by alarums nearby. A constant, percussive chattering, pinging first in one ear and then the other.

Wrens. Two of them, calling to each other from each side of the scrubby patch below me. I can't see them in the shady tangle of fallen tree trunks, ivy, collapsed gravestones and general mass of scrubby vegetation. But wherever they are, they're agitated about something.

Wrens are adaptable. They'll nest anywhere they can find a crevice, and this area is full of prime locations. Somewhere in the snarl-up before me is a nest, probably with chicks. And something is threatening them. I can't discount the possibility that what they're chattering at is me.

I like to think of myself as a friend to the birds, fancying that my benevolence will shine from me like a beacon. But to them I'm just like any other threat. Big, noisy, unpredictable. Liable to wreak havoc on them, their property or their children at any time. My good intentions count for nothing. So I keep my distance and observe, trying to locate the target of their persistent scolding. The general thrust of their communication is clear enough, even if we lack the insight to comprehend the exact vocabulary.

The chattering intensifies, my eye is caught by a small movement off to the left, and all becomes clear.

Cat.

The cemetery is part-time home to a handful of them, seekers of adventure away from the banality of their domestic surroundings. This one's lurking in predatory fashion behind a gravestone. I shoo it away, and it scuttles off.

The wrens emerge behind me, raising the intensity of their chattering yet further, as if to say, 'Yeah, and don't come back!' One hops up onto the corner of a flat tombstone and treats me to a final tirade before disappearing into the shadows.

I like to think it's thanking me.

27

BUTTERFLIES ALL OVER THE PLACE

16–20 June

Grain beards and seeds (*Bōshu,* 芒種)
Plums turn yellow
(*Ume no mi kibamu,* 梅子黄)

It's not a restful sound.

Chichichi ch i ch i ch i chichichichich i ch i ch i ch ichichichichi.

And so on, for an hour now, unrelenting, changing speed – fast, slow, fast – as if controlled by someone winding a wheel.

A blackbird, out of sight, apparently moving around low in the trees behind the fence next door. The acoustic signature of the *chichi* changes timbre, but the sound remains the same. I'm a big fan of bird noises of all descriptions, but just this once I'd like it to shut up.

Maybe it's scolding a persistent predator; perhaps it's an expression of distress at the loss of a fledgling; or maybe it's just letting the world know there's unspecified trouble about – in which case it has my full agreement. Whatever the cause, it's an unsettling sound. I take myself away from it and go for a long, slow, meandering walk, taking in back streets hitherto unexplored, little corners of the neighbourhood that aren't particularly on my way to anywhere but are perfectly suited for an aimless June afternoon when there's nothing much to do.

People are moving slowly, enjoying the warmth without the heaviness of the previous day that made leaden-limbed sluggards of us all. My eye is caught by a small black blotch on the pavement in front of me. I move closer and examine it. It's a stag beetle, my first of the year, its smooth armoured black shell glinting gently against the matt grey of the pavement. It's a female, lacking the huge antler-like mandibles protruding from its head that denote the male of the species. I stifle my internal celebration when I see its complete still-ness and the little smear of yellow near its rear end. This beetle is completely, incontrovertibly dead.

It's distressing to think of it meeting its end under the careless tread of a human foot. All it wanted was a warm spot – pavements and tarmac are perfect for this, but inevitably put beetles unwittingly in the way of increased risk of accidental death. Even more upsetting is the possibility that it was crushed deliberately, human distrust and fear of anything considered scary leading us to wanton acts of barbarism against completely harmless species.

Boo to us.

If there's a flagship species in the fight against tidying up, the stag beetle might just be it. What they need is rotting wood. We don't like rotting wood that much. We think it's messy and redolent of decay and not in keeping with our aspirations. If a tree falls down our instinct is to remove it; if a gatepost rots we rush to install a new one.

But for the stag beetle larva, that urge to keep everything looking fresh and new is a disaster. They spend up to seven years developing, feeding on the rotting wood we abhor. So the simple act of leaving a fallen tree where it lies is an act of basic kindness for them. And for plenty of other organisms, for that matter.

The adults have short lives, devoted completely to reproduction. Emerge in May, find a mate,* die in August. And in between times, try not to be crushed by a human.

Onwards, dropping in at the cemetery on the way home.

There are a lot of yellow flowers, few of which I recognise. I take photographs, telling myself I'll look them up later.

No prizes for guessing what I don't do later.

This season feels to me like a marker. Spring is fading, summer moving in. There's a sense that the phase of unbridled growth has nearly shot its bolt, and the brow of the year's hill is coming into view. Growth, decay, repeat.

Some things have reached the decay stage already. The cow parsley is now completely desiccated, its parched brown stems contrasting with the vigorous green of the wealth of grasses that have been allowed to grow in one specific area. No doubt a grass expert could lead me through the various species represented in this small and carefully ignored patch of land. But I – like many people, I suspect – make do with 'grasses'.

There are those who, weaned on neat and tidy bowling-green type lawns, might think it looks a mess. To butterflies, it affords the same kind of luxury as rotting wood does stag beetles.

* The males do this by flying around on warm evenings, trying to impress the females with the size of their mandibles, which they also use to fight off rivals.

Take the large skipper, a gingery species whose preference is for anywhere with long grass. I see two of them almost instantly, basking with their wings splayed in a 'V'.

Or the ringlet, an exceptionally dapper butterfly. I catch sight of a dark shadow bobbing lazily across my eyeline and landing on a small patch to my left. Sure enough, there it is, basking on a rough bit, dark brown verging on black, with neat and thin white piping bordering its wings.

But the prize for 'Butterfly of the Day' goes to the marbled white I see clinging to one of those tall grasses. You know the kind – light brown, wheaty, blowing in the breeze.

The marbled white – large, in butterfly terms – is a flying advertisement for the joys of monochrome, its striking black-and-white pattern visible even in flight. It's also, I gather, a fairly recent arrival to this area. I admire and celebrate it for a few minutes, and when it finally flutters off, I wish it nothing but good things for the rest of its short life.

I stop for a rest. A familiar bench, by a familiar path. I listen.

In order of volume:

> Soft wind soughing* in trees
> Robins calling presumably in same trees
> Man, laughing, possibly at me, although he is quite a
>   way away
> Magpie, cackling, definitely at me
> Faraway dog, yappy type

---

* This word, along with 'cerulean', 'liminal' and 'susurration', is almost obligatory in a book of nature writing. I feel I have done my duty.

Goldfinch, tinkling

Power tool, distant

Police siren

Blackbird, singing – welcome change from its
   chattering compadre

Parakeet – less welcome

Wind in trees, gusting now

Wren singing, close, piercing

Helicopter, drowning everything briefly

The helicopter breaks the spell. I move on. Back to the warm streets and home. I open the back door, ready for a rest.

   Chichichi ch i ch i ch i chichichichich i ch i ch i ch ichichichichi.

28

INSECTS GATHER IN THE HEAT

21–26 June

Summer solstice (*Geshi*, 夏至)
Self-heal withers
(*Natsukarekusa karuru*, 乃東枯)

You get used to the sound of London. Not just the obvious noise – the cars, the building site down the road, the man five doors down who just *loves* power tools, the bus changing gear as it goes up the hill, the over-the-road neighbour who plays his music nice and loud every Friday night – but the background. The sound of millions of people going about their daily lives. It's silence, in a way – not that there's really any such thing – but the quality of that silence differs fundamentally from the silence of a Hampshire village, say, or a small market town in Nottinghamshire, or a remote Scottish island.

It went, briefly, during late March and April, as people were forced to suspend activities. Then it crept back – not to its previous levels, but just enough that if you stopped and listened you'd think, 'Oh yes, there it is again.'

Today, though, it's subdued. Not by lack of activity, but by heat. For the first time this year, the temperature tops 30 degrees Celsius, and Brits everywhere dust off the words 'sweltering', 'phew!' and 'don't get me wrong, I like it warm, but this is too hot, isn't it?' And it has a dampening effect on the atmosphere, a duvet of somnolence draped over London.

But nobody's told the treecreeper.

My first sighting of it in several weeks is frustratingly brief. I hold any encounter with this bird dear. It's not just that they're hard to see, their brown, mousey plumage helping them blend in with the bark. I like their habits too. A treecreeper will work its way up a tree from the bottom in a loose spiral, stopping every few seconds to probe the bark for insects with its curved needle bill, and bracing itself with its stiff, stubby tail. When it feels as if it's exhausted the tree's possibilities, or perhaps just on a whim, it flies to the bottom of another one. Repeat. It's a joy to watch, if you can keep up.

I can't.

This one appears almost the moment I set foot in the woods, clinging to the bottom of the oak about ten yards away, then skittering up it in manic bursts. Stop, probe, flit, stop, probe, flit, until it's nearly swallowed up by the tangle of branches above. I manage to keep track of it as it flies to the next tree. And then it just disappears, as if auditioning for a part in *Alice in Wonderland*. One second it was there, the white of its belly showing up against the uniform brownness around it; then it was gone, almost certainly through a portal to another world.

Curious. But no matter. There are other things to divert me, not least the sheer glory of the day. The prospect of a few days of uninterrupted blue skies allows a sort of peace to descend, the impression of all being well with the world easier to maintain than when the wind and rain swirl around your head under a carapace of grey.

In the garden, tall slender things of startling prettiness abound – *Thalictrum, Knautia macedonica,* Angel's Fishing Rods – their leggy delicacy lending lightness to the heavy air. The blackbird has changed its tune from constant alarming to constant *pock-pock*ing as it darts up to take advantage of the free supply of jostaberries that have plumped to perfection in the heat. The swifts are almost constant companions – sometimes whizzing over the terrace so low I can hear the whoosh of displaced air, sometimes tracing elegant squiggles high in the sky. On the third morning they take time out of their swooping activities to mob a peregrine. It jinks and dodges, but there are fifteen of them, they're persistent, and eventually it admits defeat, flapping resignedly off to seek its meal elsewhere.

There are other reasons to feel cheerful. Butterflies, lured out by the sunshine, are legion. I can't tell the difference between a small white (*Pieris rapae*) and a large white (*Pieris brassicae*) when they're on the wing – and, to be honest, I struggle to do so when they're sitting still. Despite the names, size isn't necessarily the most reliable indicator, identification often hanging on the extent of the black markings on the wing tips. So I hedge my bets and assume that of the two dozen or so I see at various times during the long afternoon at least one of them is the less abundant large white. In any case, I welcome their simple prettiness. Perhaps if I were a gardener, driven to distraction by their cabbage-munching habit, my reaction would be less positive.

There is a general bonanza of insects, bringing with them memories of times when we could see such abundance without worrying about The State of Things. In the little pond area in the Rookery, this abundance manifests itself in the form of flies. Many, many flies, either sitting on the covering of algae on the water or jinking around just above it. If a gathering of this kind were to appear in your sitting room, you'd call the fumigators and consider moving to the North Pole. Here, their activity is a sideshow to the damselflies performing aerobatic miracles just above their heads.

A chiffchaff sings its two-note song from the other side of the grove, but it's a lacklustre effort, feeble in comparison to its energetic offerings a couple of months ago, redolent of a bird that's given up and is just phoning it in. It's a lone voice in the heat of the afternoon. The next morning, when in a fit of energy I get up and out of the house at a time you might just about describe as 'early', the voices of birds compete with each other in a way that recalls the peak of the dawn chorus a month earlier. I hear the voices of twenty-two species,* a texture of song complex enough to gull me into thinking we're still in mid-season.

But it's an illusion. This is more akin to a last hurrah. Birdsong is fading, a lot of the voices are contact or alarm calls, and the sound is boosted by the chatterings of fledglings. The solstice has passed. The Earth's axial tilt reaches its peak, 23.44 degrees. From now until the winter solstice on 21 December, the hours of daylight reduce, and we enter the out-breath phase of the year's cycle.

Onwards.

---

* If you insist: wren, chiffchaff, blackbird, blackcap, song thrush, ring-necked parakeet, carrion crow, great spotted woodpecker, green woodpecker, blue tit, nuthatch, wood pigeon, dunnock, greenfinch, goldcrest, coal tit, long-tailed tit, magpie, chaffinch, robin, great tit, starling.

29

COOL WINDS
SOMETIMES BLOW

27 June–1 July

Summer solstice (*Geshi*, 夏至)
Irises bloom (*Ayame hana saku*, 菖蒲華)

The ebb and flow of the year's weather has so far paid scant attention to the rigours of the microseasons system. But just this once it aligns itself with the change of season, turning on a sixpence overnight and bequeathing to this little package of days the unbeloved title 'Meh times in the squall zone'. The sun and warmth were fun while they lasted, but England is England. A drop of ten degrees in a day is par for the course.

Everything's relative. Temperatures hovering just below the 20-degree mark would have been greeted with cries of hoop-la in March. Less so when you have to replace the unquestioned T-shirt and shorts with a just-in-case thin jumper.

There are grounds for optimism. Thank heaven, for once, for the parakeets, welcome splashes of colour on a grey day. Thank heaven, too, for hollyhocks. They're popular in the front gardens on the way to the common, and beginning to enter their full florescence, lanky stalks leaning at alarming angles under the weight of gaudy blooms. Irises too, as per the Japanese precedent, show in various stages of blowsiness, adding zest to an otherwise flat atmosphere.

Up the hill, through the estate, the wind blowing an empty Lucozade bottle into my shins. Pigeons on the grass, unconcerned by my passage.

In the woods, the wind sea-like in the canopy. There's a fragrance in the air, strangely familiar. I inhale deeply, trying to place it. It's full, rich and sweet. I pause, curious. This really is a smell I know. It makes me think, for some reason, of London streets. I wonder for a few seconds what kind of flower might exude that kind of aroma on a coldish late-June afternoon, looking around the woods to try to find its source. A small group of teenagers is sitting on the ground near the fenced-off area, chatting, laughing, smoking . . .

Ah yes. Of course.

That smell. It's not a plant. Well, not any more. The leaves have been dried, crumbled, rolled up and lit, and now I have it clear in my head I wonder how I could have thought it was a smell of nature.

I leave them to it and move on.

In the Rookery, a more innocent scene. A quiet drama of childhood rebellion playing out by the pond. Two children – young enough to show unfettered curiosity, old enough to cause damage if left to their own devices – squat together, prodding at the water with short sticks. Their mother hovers behind them, nervous. One of the children puts down the stick and dips her hand into the water.

'Don't do that! Dirty! Disgusting!'

Alarm in the voice.

I can't particularly blame her. The water's surface is covered in bright green algae – the kind that can go from nothing to ubiquitous in what seems like ten minutes. It would be easy to think that the water underneath is not only muddy, but also stagnant, harbouring hordes of microscopic squigglers ready to jump into the bloodstream of an unsuspecting child and cause untold harm and misery.

But try telling that to a child armed with a stick and an admirable curiosity for the splashy. They ignore her, as children do, and continue with their dabbling. I am, despite the disturbance they're causing to the water, on their side. Curiosity is the parent of discovery, and splashing things with sticks is fun. I'm almost tempted to join them.

Sticks are fine things. You can dabble in ponds with them. You can throw them for dogs to fetch. And if they're of the right build – stout, with a hand-snug end – you can stride through the woods using one as an aid, not just for the walking but for the general quality of the experience. And that is exactly what another fine young person is doing as I trudge my way back through the woods half an hour later.

I've spent some quality time with a common carder bee – ginger fuzz illuminated by a weakly emerging sun – as it busies itself on a slender stalk of *Verbena bonariensis*.* There were hoverflies too – fast and zippy. I said a passing hello to a ladybird – the kind familiar from my childhood, two spots adorning its domed red shell. And, as I

---

* I'm getting good at identifying the ones I know. It's the ones I don't know that cause me grief.

watch, the child strides into the thicket at the edge of the clearing, where there is a simply splendid thing.

A den, scrappily built with a mixture of stout and slender branches and twigs. A fine den, made with pride, for sitting in and hiding from people and pretending you're on an adventure. Which, indeed, you are.

There is hope for humanity yet.

Home, where the drab of the afternoon is enlivened by swifts. For once, these masters of the air have competition, the gusty wind making them bank and wheel and glide and come again like skateboarders, too cool to fall.

I watch them for a while, then go inside to make a cup of tea. Automatic actions. Kettle, sink, tap. Look out of the window as the water gushes into oh hello there's a jay on the feeder.

This is not an expected development.

The magic of jays lies not just in their status as the most colourful British corvid. That peachy front, cinnamon on the back, pure white rump, and the flash of electric blue on the wing are all in stark contrast to their cousins' funereal garb. But it's not the whole story, not even when you throw in the distinctive pot-bellied and splay-winged flight shape, greasepaint moustache, and a streaked crown that sometimes flares into a mildly comical crest.

Perhaps it's their ability with acorns. When the time is right, they gather them, stashing up to nine in their pouch-like crop and carrying one in their beak for good measure. Then they bury them in holes near and far, for later consumption. That they remember later on where they've hidden them is astonishing.

I don't think of summer as a time for jays. Autumn is their moment, when acorns are everywhere. They overcome their natural shyness and become, for a few weeks, very visible. Audible, too, as reflected in their Welsh name, *sgrech y coed*, or 'screecher of the woods'.

But this one is bold as brass, jumping down from the feeder and strutting about in front of me. There's a distance, even through glass, at which an encounter with a wild thing passes from 'ooh look' to 'aah yeeesss'. This jay, no more than five yards away, is firmly in the latter zone, giving the added frisson of a close encounter. I stay absolutely still, knowing that any movement might mean the end of our one-sided communion.

It hops around, cocks its head, hops again, and then something spooks it – not me, honest, I was like a statue – and it's gone in a flurry, leaving me with a vivid memory and a half-full kettle.

30

LAVENDER ASSUMES MASSIVE PROPORTIONS

2–6 July

Summer solstice (*Geshi*, 夏至)
Crow-dipper sprouts
(*Hange shōzu*, 半夏生)

'Ladybird, ladybird, fly away home. Your house is on fire and your children are gone.'

Cheery stuff, passed on as part of an occasionally grisly oral tradition dating back centuries. I learned it as a child – along with other classics, including 'Hello, Mr Magpie, how's your lady wife?' – as did many others of my generation.

Back then, I knew little about ladybirds except that I liked them. I liked their neatness, the sheen on their wings, the way they just pootled around aimlessly then off with a whirr for no apparent reason.

I liked that they would happily crawl on my hand.

To my unknowing eyes, ladybirds came in one kind. Red with black polka dots. The number of spots varied from individual to individual, and I enjoyed counting them, but I assumed they were all basically the same species: 'ladybird'. Maybe I thought the number of spots was a lifestyle choice, little suspecting that there are nearly fifty species of this attractive and widely loved beetle in the UK.

Gratifyingly for the novice, identification of ladybirds often comes down to the simplest of skills: an ability to count. All praise to the pragmatic soul who decided their names should include their most prominent feature. Red ladybird with two spots? That's a 2-spot ladybird. How about that one, with one-two-three-four-five spots? A 5-spot ladybird. It's even reflected in their scientific names: *Coccinella 5-punctata*, *Thea 22-punctata* and so on.

The one sitting on the mint leaf on the third day of this season is, if my counting is to be relied on, a 7-spot ladybird (*Coccinella 7-punctata*), and it brings on a small Proustian moment, whizzing me in a temporal wormhole back to 1976 with such clarity that I can almost hear the theme tune to *Tomorrow's World*. While these little beetles are redolent to me of high summer, I'll take them whenever I find them, and even though they've been around for weeks by now, this season they seem to be everywhere, so it counts as another notch on the 'sumer is icumen in'* stick.

The unwelcome squalls of the previous season haven't yet been banished, but it's settled down a bit, and the temperature is inviting enough for me to sit in the kitchen with one flap of the sliding doors open, a slight breeze tickling the curtain as a surprise shower briefly pummels the lavender, which has by stealth taken over the view from

---

* If you've ever seen the film *The Wicker Man*, this thirteenth-century round ('Sumer is icumen in; Lhude sing cuccu!') will immediately conjure disturbing images.

the kitchen. Starting as a small shop-bought shrub when we moved in ten years ago, it's found conditions to its liking, somehow growing to the size of a small village. Each year we think it's topped out, and each year it seems to find an extra level of luxuriance in peak season.

No matter. It is deliciously fragrant, and in a few weeks will play host to hordes of pollinators, a few of which are already exploring its nooks and crannies. One of them breaks rank and flies across, hovering between me and my laptop screen for a few seconds before zinging back to its business in the lavender.

Back in the day I might have thought it a bee or even a wasp, but while I have found my bee studies terminally confusing, a few things have managed to stick, one of them being a rudimentary ability to differentiate bees from hoverflies.

The tendency of some hoverfly species to mimic stinging insects such as bees, wasps and hornets is one of those things that must have seemed like a good idea at the time. It's known as Batesian mimicry, after H. W. Bates, the nineteenth-century natu-ralist who developed the theory after a decade in the Amazon rainforest studying butterflies. The idea is that a harmless thing mimics a poisonous thing. Potential predators, aware of the dangers of the poisonous thing, avoid it, so allowing the harmless thing to go about its daily business without fear of molestation.

The tactic has its downside. While a bird's instinct is to steer clear of something that might sting it, a human's, all too often, is to kill it. This undoubtedly leads to the death of countless innocent buzzers each year at the hands of people whose identification skills could do with some brushing up.

It's an easy mistake to make. In fact it's really quite hard not to make it. Distinguishing some bees from their mimic hoverflies is tough, and while cool-headed common sense might dictate an 'usher it along and stay out of its way' policy, innate fear of pain can lead people to more intemperate measures.

If these summery seasons are predominantly a time of insects, the avian world isn't entirely invisible. There is grim manifestation of this in the dead great tit chick I find directly under the nesting box one morning. The fledging of the first brood over a month ago was followed by a brief lull, but recently the cheeping from up above has started again, and it's been clear that a second brood has hatched.

It's difficult to tell exactly what happened, but maybe it just wasn't strong enough. While I know that a proportion of chicks don't reach adulthood, to have the evidence so starkly presented brings on a sense of melancholy.

More cheering is the young blue tit that appears on the feeder later that day. Its yellow feathers don't yet have the glow of an adult's; the thin black head markings, so clearly defined in older birds, are vague and patchy, and its general appearance is on the scruffy side of acceptable. It's still getting used to the demands of life, and hasn't yet got the hang of the concept of danger, so it sticks around for a while, even dropping down to the floor a few times to scrabble around for fallen seeds, before fluttering away, gawky and uncoordinated, to safety.

Dusk falls. The wind relents. A blackbird sings. Life goes on.

31

BIRDS IN MOULT

7–11 July

Lesser heat (*Shōsho*, 小暑)
Warm winds blow
(*Atsukaze itaru*, 温風至)

It's an unexpected duet, stopping me in my tracks. A blackcap and a blackbird, their contrasting songs – scrabble and flute – somehow complementing each other perfectly, dovetailing for just a few seconds before first the blackcap stops, then the blackbird, and while I can wish for them to start up again as hard as I like, I can't will that perfect moment back into existence. Perhaps it's for the best.

This kind of birdsong in early July has an end-of-season air to it, almost like a last hurrah. The blackcap's, in particular, lacks the usual zest. The complexity of the song – almost precisely in inverse proportion to the bird's plain, soft, grey plumage – has delighted and intrigued me every time I've heard it this spring, and I'm fairly certain this will be the last one I hear until next year.

We're on the cusp of the quiet time, the full bloom of the dawn chorus now a distant memory. Its intensity has waned over the last two months, and now it's dribbling away into silence as birds, each according to their own cycle, tackle the next part of the year, the recovery phase. No territories to defend, no partners to attract. The kids are growing up, and recuperation is the order of the day.

An adult blue tit appears at the feeder. It looks, not to put too fine a point on it, knackered, its feathers worn and frayed. While for some birds moulting is more or less continuous, for others it's packed into a short period around this time, refreshing their feathers in preparation for autumn and winter. It's an energy-sapping process, taking a month or more. As they wait for their flight feathers to regrow they're more vulnerable than usual to predators, so their default position at this time of year is buried deep in the undergrowth, from where you might hear the occasional chipping alarm call, but little else in the way of noise.

But as one phenomenon fades, another burgeons. It's not something that immediately draws attention to itself, but look a bit closer and in among the general greenery you can discern the slow plumping of fruits and berries.

Most obvious, in the garden, are the apples. Our little columnar tree next to the fence has a bit of a list to it, exaggerated by the weight of the fruit now emerging from the foliage. They're not yet ripe for picking, but it won't be long. We'll have a few for ourselves, leave some for the birds, and inevitably some will fall to the ground, slowly rotting and adding to the richness of the soil, part of the eternal cycle.

If I'm temporarily uplifted by the blackcap–blackbird duet, the cheer is short-lived. For this is a grey season, stubbornly refusing to conform to our idea of what summers should be like. The warm winds of the Japanese equivalent are in evidence, but they're not benevolent. I know that summer is rarely a straightforward tale of

clear blue skies and continued warmth, but natural human entitle-
ment leads me to believe I deserve at least an hour of sunshine in a
single five-day period.

On the third morning, I get it. Clear skies and not a breath of
wind. Blessed relief after the general bluster of the last ten days. Add
to this luxury the sight of fifteen swifts rollicking around the treetops
and my cup overfloweth.

It can't last. The clouds roll back in mid-morning – one of those
occasions when you can see the weather coming towards you like
an advancing army. A wisp of breeze turns to a gust, which turns to
a squall, bringing with it the kind of rain that seems to come from
knee height, and before long we're engulfed in it. Wall to wall, unremitting, grim.

I can love rain. It's not a straightforward case of 'sun is good and
rain is bad and ne'er the twain shall meet'. In the right circumstances
– wearing the appropriate clothing, knowing dryness is an attainable
prospect – rain can fill the heart with mysterious pleasure, a feeling
that however uncomfortable you might be in the moment, you are
at least experiencing life to the full.

My attitude to wind is more straightforward.

I don't like it.

Light breezes are fine. You can hit me with light breezes till
the cows come home. I'll even enjoy, to an extent, walking into a
strong but steady wind. And there have been times when I've been
overtaken by a temporary surge of euphoria in the teeth of a gale.
But my default reaction, as the wind picks up my cap and sends it
cartwheeling across the road and under the wheels of the 468 bus,
is to be filled with a desire to be back home with the doors closed
and curtains drawn.

I can appreciate, from a distance, the magic of wind. Its invisibility, its freedom, the way it seems to come from nowhere and disappear again. And there is something mesmerising about clouds scudding across the sky, or trees whipping back and forth, or a black-headed gull grappling with a sudden gust, making the necessary adjustments to wings and flap speed and gamely carrying on rather than throwing in the towel and flopping exhausted onto our back lawn.

I just don't particularly like being in it.

Perhaps it's something to do with the way it unsettles the soul, or reminds us of our own powerlessness in the face of an invisible, unknowable force.

The ancients knew all about that. Innumerable weather gods – of storms, wind, thunder, lightning, tornados, typhoons, hurricanes and myriad other meteorological phenomena, though strangely not of pleasantly warm sunshine – received innumerable prayers and offerings. And their personifications are often fierce. The green-skinned Japanese deity Fūjin was most often portrayed with a large bag on his* shoulder, full of winds ready to unleash on humanity. His counterpart Raijin, the thunder god, hair streaming behind him, beats thunder drums with large hammers. Fearsome figures, ready to punish us for our misdeeds.

We know better now. We know that rain is condensed water vapour plus gravity; we know that wind is moving air caused by differences in atmospheric pressure; we know the causes of thunder and lightning and tornados and typhoons and hurricanes.

---

* Irascible weather gods are overwhelmingly male.

It doesn't make them any less terrifying when they hit. And while the wind that shakes my office windows is comparatively light in the grand scheme of things, at the back of the mind lurks that primitive fear of the forces of nature that make mock of human strength.

So I sit in the office, faintly morose, watching it do its thing. And then, half an hour before dusk, the wind calms, the skies clear and the blue sky is punctuated by just a few unthreatening pink-tinged grey fluffies, and four goldfinches clatter onto the feeders and off again before you can blink, and then it's just me and the swifts and the rising, waning moon.

32

FLYING ANTS
FILL THE SKY

12–16 July

Lesser heat (*Shōsho*, 小暑)

First lotus blossoms
(*Hasu hajimete hiraku*, 蓮始開)

On 15 July 971, the body of St Swithun was moved from its resting place just outside the Saxon minster in Winchester, where he had been bishop for just over a decade a hundred years earlier, to a precious shrine inside the building. Legend has it that on his deathbed he had asked to be buried outdoors, there to be adorned with raindrops and the steps of passers-by. Legend also has it that the day of his removal coincided with a terrible forty-day storm, possibly brought on by his wrath at being removed from his preferred resting place.

And so a superstition was born.

There's nothing in it, of course. Rain on St Swithun's Day has never resulted in forty days of anything except the relentless flow of time.

But this year, 15 July – in our part of West Norwood, at least – coincides with what has come to be known as Flying Ant Day, so I greet the dawn of the 16th with a touch of nervousness. Forty days of sun would be fantastic. Forty days of rain less good but bearable. Forty days of flying ants and we'd be entering plague territory, which, given the way 2020 has gone so far, would be about par for the course.

The prospect of forty days of flying ants is enough to make even this insectophile quail, but I'm able to bear one day of them, knowing that this too shall pass. They're only fulfilling their purpose, and as usual it's to do with sex. Because Flying Ant Day is when the drone males and mature queens of the species black garden ant take to the air and share their love. It's a handy way to expand a colony that has reached the limits of its potential on the ground. Striking out by air is a way to meet new ants and thereby broaden the gene pool.

Despite the name, it's a season rather than a single day. The ants are responding to local conditions, emerging for their annual swarming on warm, still days, often after rain. Open your eyes for long enough while in the middle of a swarm (while keeping your mouth closed, naturally), and you might see a male and a virgin queen conjoined in what's known as 'nuptial flight'. For the virgin queen, this is just one of many couplings she will engage in during this short season – for the male, it'll be the last thing he does. After the nuptial flight, the virgin queen lands, finds herself a nice quiet corner where she can lay her eggs, rubs her own wings off and settles in for the long haul. The males, their duty to the continuation of the species fulfilled, die.

It's nature in action, an opportunity to learn a bit more about the world around us, to expand our horizons and embrace the myriad non-human ways of being that have been successful on this planet since way before we were around. And yet, because of our aversion to creepies and crawlies and buzzy things getting in our hair, it's a day viewed by many as something to be endured, something to exclaim disgustedly about, an opportunity to take to the message board of your local Facebook group and ask, 'How do I kill those effing ants they're driving me crazy.'

My attention is drawn to it by a group of six black-headed gulls. They're performing a sort of interpretive dance over the cemetery, jinking and diving as they try to make the most of the unexpected feast. As I walk back up the hill the odd ant whizzes past my face, and by the time I'm home they're making their presence felt in no uncertain terms. But it's a relatively light infestation, enough to make you incline your head and say, 'Ah yes, flying ant day', but not so intense that they cause inconvenience. Accordingly, my reaction is one of curiosity rather than flapping panic.

As I watch them do their thing, I briefly wonder what it must be like to be a male ant, programmed to do your bit for the species and then fall on your sword. Then I pick the ripe cherry tomato from the plant in the pot on the terrace, and eat it, feeling the explosion of flavour in my mouth.

Two days earlier. Not an ant in sight, nor any prospect of one, because it's clear and light and – when the sun hides behind one of the floofy clouds dotting the sky – ever so slightly chilly. It's weather that makes you put on a T-shirt, which then proves inadequate so you put on a thin jumper, and then the sun comes out so you're too hot and you take the jumper off again, at which point the sun does its floofy-cloud-hiding thing and the cycle begins again.

And so the long day wears on.

In the cemetery, a fox hangs around the low water fountain by the memorial rose garden, bolder than brass. It takes a few sips, looks at me incuriously, then trots towards me. It has a black smudge on its muzzle. There is a poise to it, an assuredness born of security. It doesn't fear the shotgun or the foxhound – indeed it has little to worry about as long as it stays within the confines of the traffic-free cemetery. There's plenty of food around to scavenge, and its diet is supplemented by people who come to the cemetery with scraps of bread, their desire to help the animals in perfect balance with their desire to be close to something wild.

A wood pigeon appears to my right, rises to crest an invisible brow, claps its wings behind its back twice – *kla'klack!* – then glides down, plump breast to the fore, wings held at a shallow angle. It's a display flight, but I will never be persuaded that it's not also enormous fun. It's followed almost immediately by a family of long-tailed tits moving through the trees behind me, *tseep*ing lightly to each other, bringing a little flurry of energy to an otherwise quiet day.

Despite these moments of activity, there's a feeling of stasis, of waiting. An in-between period. The weather toys with the idea of launching into high summer, decides against it just for the moment, and settles in for a couple of days of 'not too bad'.

Nothing much happens, but it does it well.

The fox realises it won't get anything from me and trots off, its tail quivering, to my paranoid mind, with slight indignation.

33

ACORNS FALL TO THE GROUND

17–22 July

Lesser heat (*Shōsho*, 小暑)
Hawks learn to fly
(*Taka sunawachi waza o narau*, 鷹乃学習)

Summer – at least what we think we mean by summer – returns. Not with a vengeance, but with a warm benevolence that puts a smile back on the face.

We lost it for a few days, and everyone, myself included, behaved as if it would never come back, like a child thinking that because their father has hunkered down behind the sofa he's gone for ever, when in fact he's just gearing up for a hilarious jack-in-the-box-style stunt that will scare the little imp senseless and no doubt leave painful mental scars. But it's back, so I celebrate with a leisurely saunter round the patch.

Two peregrines on the church tower, stock still, facing different directions. It's not a good sign, at least from the point of view of breeding. The ideal number of peregrines at this stage of the year would be at least three, and preferably five or six. And instead of glum perching we should be witnessing the parents accompanying the young on their first gawky, angular attempts at flying, trying to shepherd them into some sort of self-sufficiency before allowing them to take on the world by themselves. Busy parents don't have time to sit around looking broodingly into the middle distance. It all points to breeding failure, and takes a bit of the gloss off my afternoon.

The cemetery, basking in warm sunshine, makes up for it, somehow taking on an almost Mediterranean feel. It's not just the warmth. Something to do with the angle of the sun, maybe, the light it casts. Somnolence in the air, insects on the wing.

Nevertheless, I think of autumn. Looking ahead that far feels counter-intuitive just as summer is reaching its peak, but there's no escaping it. Perhaps it's because I'm already on the lookout for the signs, but I see them everywhere. Conker husks, bright green and spiky, stand out against the backdrop of the trees' diseased leaves. Brambles run the gamut of colours from pale pink to deep purple-black. An ash, by all appearances fighting a losing battle with the dreaded 'ash dieback' fungus that has swept across Europe in recent years, still manages to throw out heavy swags of keys. Their weight and fecundity distract for just a bit from the tree's general decay.

And then there are the acorns.

Easily confused as I am, it took me a while to differentiate between sessile oak (*Quercus petraea*, stalked leaves, clustered acorns) and pedunculate oak (*Quercus robur*, unstalked leaves, stalked acorns like clay pipes) – but now I have them clear in my head I can approach them with a bit more confidence. One pedunculate in particular catches the eye, its evocative shape silhouetted against the blue sky, leaves dark green and prolific. I could, as I have done many times, walk past it with little more than a tacit acknowledgement of its reassuring oakiness. But my own mantra floats into my head – 'look, look again, look better' – so I stop, and inevitably reap the reward.

The acorns I first noticed a couple of seasons ago – as flat-domed bumps poking out of their little cups – have filled out, and are beginning to show their familiar shape. But next to the smooth matt dome of the new fruit sits a misshapen ridged lump, nobbly and glistening. This, I'm pleased to recognise, is the oak knopper gall – the work of the oak knopper gall wasp – and it's one of the very few I know. Yellowy-green and sticky to the touch, these galls look disturbing and wrong at first, an unattractive contrast with the smooth perfection of the neighbouring acorns. But these misshapes, while not entirely benevolent, don't inflict the same kind of damage on the tree as the horse chestnut leaf miner inflicts on its host. It would be easy to think that the burden of multiple parasites taking over the tree's fruit might weaken it, but this doesn't seem to be the case. Some years will see more galls than acorns, but the balance is redressed over time, and the tree coexists perfectly happily with its guest.

The wasp's life cycle is somewhat complex. The female lays eggs in the acorn. The tree responds by producing the galls, which provide both shelter and food for the developing larva. After a while, in early autumn, the gall will turn brown and drop off. The following spring the fully developed wasp (always female) wriggles out of the gall and flies off to find a different kind of oak, the turkey oak (*Quercus cerris*) – on the catkins of which it lays further eggs, which in turn produce the next generation (of both sexes), which return to the pedunculate oak to lay their eggs again. A two-generation process requiring two separate tree species – which leads this impartial observer to wonder how such a convoluted process evolved.

As if that weren't enough, the knopper gall in turn plays host not only to a variety of tiny but harmless insect tenants – inquilines, to use the scientific term – but also to its own parasites. These take the form of even smaller wasps, which lay their eggs, sight unseen, through the gall walls. The remarkable thing about this – all of it is remarkable to my easily astounded eyes – is that they never pick the wrong host, nor do they inoculate an already occupied gall. As so often when confronted by the mysteries of nature, my first and enduring question is 'But . . . how?'

This layer of relationships – host, parasite, hyperparasite – is testament to the richness and diversity of life that exists, unsuspected by many, in the most apparently mundane of environments. But it's also a reminder that a tree isn't just a tree. It plays host to a bewildering variety of life, from the squirrels that scamper along its branches* to the fungi that live in symbiosis with it beneath the soil – and with myriad wrigglers and creepers and borers and squeakers in between.

Not so much a tree as a teeming city.

---

* Endearingly, the Bavarian word for 'squirrel' is *Eichkätzchen*, or 'oak kitten'.

34

BUTTERFLIES BASK IN HEAT

23–28 July

Greater heat (*Taisho*, 大暑)

Paulownia trees produce seeds
(*Kiri hajimete hana o musubu*, 桐始結花)

The cuckoos have been spitting again. Every year it's the same. They descend en masse and gob all over our chrysanthemums, coating the stems with their bubbly spittle.

It's not the cuckoos, of course. Apart from anything else, a cuckoo in south London would be welcomed with open arms and invited to cast its sputum wherever it pleased. Their two-note song was part of the soundtrack to my rural childhood, but now I can easily go a whole summer – like this one, in all probability – without hearing or seeing one, unless I choose to make a special journey to somewhere they frequent. They occasionally touch down in Streatham Common Woods or Crystal Palace Park on their way to friendlier habitats, but I'm never there when they do.

The bubbling froth whose folk name is 'cuckoo spit'* appears on many plants in the garden, and it seems to have reached a peak this season. Or maybe it's just that it's appearing on the plants I can see from my seat on the terrace, from where it manifests itself as tiny white specks in a sea of greens. Move closer, carefully brush away the foam, and you'll reveal a tiny insect. This is the nymph of the spittlebug (also known as 'froghopper'), which drills into the host plant shortly after its birth and siphons out the sap, boosting its volume with air from a special opening in its nethers. And there it lives, cosily insulated against temperature change, and protected from predators by the foam's acrid taste.

I don't move closer, preferring to let the little mites get on with their lives. I'm reliably assured by those who know that even a significant population does little damage to the host plant, so my 'live and let live' policy goes unchallenged.

Elsewhere in the garden, the eye is drawn to poppy seed heads, their desiccated and pert plumpness making them look like the kind of thing you could sell as 'distressed newel posts' to millionaire doll's house collectors for £500 a pop. Also in the dry-goods department, the honesty seed pods are at the yellowing stage, the outline of each seed clearly visible through the drying, translucent skin. On the other side of the garden, the plumping of the apples progresses in almost direct opposition, as if draining the moisture from everything else.

Once again I'm deceived by the weather. The weather app's no help, offering a range of incorrect temperatures and an overall assessment of the day ahead that bears no relation to reality. I look outside,

* Or 'frog spit', depending on who you talk to.

see grey clouds and swaying trees and, taking a punt, I opt for a thin sweater.

I remove it in a muck sweat two minutes later. Of course it's not cold. It's late July. What kind of idiot am I? As I could and should have foreseen, despite the appearance of chill and bluster from inside, the overwhelming feeling when out and about is of mugginess. And within quarter of an hour, the clouds have thinned out enough for the first thing to greet me when I reach the common to be a comma butterfly basking on a post, its orange shape distinctly outlined against the grain of the wood.

You have to look hard for clues to the origins of this butterfly's name in its appearance, and you won't find them when it's basking with its wings open. Only when they're closed will you see the little white loop on the dark brown of the hindwing. More distinctive is that outline, with its ragged, scalloped edges – unlike any other British butterfly. With wings closed it's been compared to a dead leaf; with wings open it reminds me of that strange jigsaw piece that you think isn't going to fit so you leave it on the side and eventually oh yes of course there it goes.

It turns out to be an afternoon of lepidoptera.

In the Rookery, clinging to a thistle stalk, a blackish-blue mothy shape with handlebar antennae and crimson spots. Stalking it carefully, I get close enough to count the spots. Six. Almost as easy as identifying a ladybird.

This is a six-spot burnet, a day-flying moth of striking appearance. There are seven species of burnet moth in Britain (four of them are very localised and scarce), and they're all similar in appearance. They fly in broad daylight, safe in the knowledge that their bright colouring will act as a warning to predators: 'Poisonous! Do Not

Touch!' The word for this widespread tactic, whether the warning is colours, sounds or smells, is 'aposematic', and it's one of those words I read and pledge to remember before immediately forgetting. Perhaps rendering it in print will help.

The poison in question, in the case of the six-spot burnet moth, is hydrogen cyanide. Their caterpillars' ability to metabolise this deadly substance from its favoured food plant, bird's-foot-trefoil, is impressive enough, but they can also produce more of it if they run short, which is a handy trick to have up your sleeve. And, conveniently, the females also combine the toxic chemical with a variety of pheromones to attract males.

As I read about such things, it strikes me – not for the first time – how extraordinary life is. I still struggle, when contemplating these simple everyday miracles, to find the appropriate balance, to stop myself from enthusing to the world in general, 'Oh my God, will you just look at that, do you know what it can do?'

Perhaps it's simple-minded of me to walk about in open-mouthed wonder at all these natural phenomena. Gall wasps, burnet moths, flying ants, spittlebug nymphs and all the rest of them. Such things are, after all, merely the business of the world. It would be even more extraordinary if we were surrounded by nothing of note, nothing complex and fascinating, nothing at all.

Looking at a six-spot burnet moth and appreciating it as a thing of beauty is, for many people, plenty to be going on with. But learning about the way it lives, breeds, feeds and interacts with the world around it gives us insight into what it's like to be something other than human. And that feels both worthwhile and important.

35

SWIFTS FLY HOME

29 July–2 August

Greater heat (*Taisho*, 大暑)
Earth is damp, air is humid
(*Tsuchi uruōte mushi atsushi*, 土潤溽暑)

They've gone.

No more screaming fly-bys. No more high-flying wing-waggles. No more spectacular tree-height dusk displays of daring acrobatics.

No more swifts.

The sky, that midsummer blue with the highest of fractured clouds slipping gently across it – crazy paving for the heavens – is empty.

They slip away overnight through the same portal they came in on, an apparently unanimous decision, leaving behind them the usual memories and a faint taste of regret. However many times I see them, however long I spend gawping at their display, I always want just one more moment with them, to be able to say goodbye on my terms.

But when it's time, it's time, and now the only sound in the garden is the occasional tinkle of a goldfinch.

There are consolations. A dunnock, not seen for weeks, appears on the terrace, hops around for a few seconds then disappears into the murky depths of the lavender city. The grasses in the garden nod their heads in the gentlest breeze, glowing in the sultry sun. A nameless weed on the pavement outside the house throws up tiny, pretty yellow flowers with delicate white edges, defying me to redefine the meaning of the word 'weed'.

Earth is dry, air likewise. The season warms up, peaking on day three with the kind of heat that makes English people want to put their heads in the fridge.

The smooth curve of the drainpipe above the kitchen door has a blemish. It might blend in perfectly were it not for the angled pattern of creamy yellow stripes giving its presence away. It sits entirely still for minutes on end, then in a flutter relocates itself just inches away.

Jersey tiger moth. It's not a swift, but I'm glad to see it anyway. This large day-flying moth has been a reliable marker of high summer in our garden for a few years now. Relative newcomers to Britain, their range is expanding, presumably in keeping with climate change, and no patch of high summer is complete without one of them appearing as if from nowhere in the garden, accompanied by a cry of 'Jersey tiger!'

Unlike many of their cousins, they're easy to identify. Other tiger moth species are more leopard-print-like, the stripes morphing into blotches or spots, but the Jersey tiger is a real tiger, and once you've got the pattern in your head there's no need to leaf through guides trying to match picture to reality.

It sits, immobile, striped triangle on black plastic. Attractive enough in repose, when it takes wing it elicits a gasp of delight from the unwary, the startling orange of its undercrackers – or, to be more scientific, hindwings – irresistibly festive.

You could think it a butterfly. It's day-flying and colourful, after all, and I suspect that, if pressed on the distinction between the two, most people would offer that moths are nocturnal while butterflies are not.

If only it were that simple. There are, inevitably, exceptions.

Moths are nocturnal, except the ones that aren't; butterflies have brightly coloured wings, except the ones that don't; moths rest with their wings spread, while butterflies hold them above their backs – except for all the ones that behave differently. It's like learning Russian irregular verbs.

The most reliable distinction seems to be in the antennae – if you can get a good look at them, you'll see that the antennae of butterflies have small balls or clubs on the end. The antennae of moths vary in appearance – my favourites are the extravagantly feathery ones, some of which have the unruliness of an old man's eyebrows – but they are uniformly club-free.

The other way of doing it, at least in Britain, would be to learn the exact appearance of all the sixty-odd butterflies that occur here. If it doesn't look like one of those, it's a moth.

The scrap of fabric I see a few minutes after the Jersey tiger might be a moth, or it might not. It sticks around for such a short time I can't be certain. But as I see it flit into the maple at the bottom of the garden, something in my novice butterflying brain says a hopeful 'Oh, hello.'

It's the concept known to birders as 'jizz',* that feeling you get from the merest glimpse of something that tells you what it is. I have enough experience now as a birder for it to be fairly reliable with a limited number of familiar species. With butterflies it's scattergun at best.

But that doesn't stop me.

I see the movement, follow it as well as I can, then zero in on the suspected branch. But no sooner have I located it and clocked the little white zigzag on its brown wing than it's off.

Little white zigzag. At least I think it was.

I want it to be a white-letter hairstreak; but my lack of knowledge works against me. And I have no photographic evidence to back me up.

Consultation with the field guide leaves me none the wiser. What I want is confirmation that these butterflies do indeed hang out in suburban gardens. What I get is inconclusive. They spend most of their time in treetops, can be found wherever there are elms, and sometimes come down to lower levels to feed on things like brambles. I mark it in my head as 'not known' and get on with my day.

Ah well. Whatever it was, it brightened an already bright afternoon. And that's the main thing. Sometimes it's important to embrace the concept of not knowing.

---

* Supposedly derived from the acronym of 'General Impression of Size and Shape'.

The fifth day mirrors the first. Warm without being hot, clear skies adorned with thinly spread, unthreatening clouds, light breezes to ruffle the sleeve.

A white-tailed bumblebee stumbles blearily into the kitchen, does two laps, then tries to escape through the closed window. I watch it banging its head against the glass for a couple of minutes, and just for a moment lose patience.

'It's over there,' I half yell, pointing towards the wide-open sliding doors. 'You literally came in through it two minutes ago.'

It must be the heat.

I relent, and open the window. It zigzags its way out without so much as a murmur of thanks.

The Jersey tiger (I presume the same one) puts in a brief appearance late in the afternoon before disappearing to a secret moth hiding place, a reminder that what we encounter is the tiniest fraction of what's there.

Flies – the magnetised kind with poles aligned to your food – cause a mild nuisance, a minor blot on the evening's general pleasantness.

A faint *squee* from on high. I look up.

Five swifts, almost a mirage, filling up on high-flying insects before their journey. Are they ours? Maybe. I watch them for a bit, and then they're gone, as if I'd conjured them up with the power of wishful thinking.

36

HEAT STIFLES,
EVENINGS STAY LIGHT

3–7 August

Greater heat (*Taisho,* 大暑)
Great rains sometimes fall
(*Taiu tokidoki furu,* 大雨時行)

The transition from season to season is seamless. Same warmth, same winds, same everything. No rains falling, great or otherwise.

The garden is at least 10 per cent butterfly. They're everywhere. Whites, small and large, flitting scraps of festivity – I still can't tell the difference, but still count them both; the gatekeeper, chocolate brown enlivened by orange patches and little black spots with pin-prick white double-eyes on the wing; meadow brown, larger, plainer, the colours looking as if they've been through the wash at the wrong temperature. The gatekeeper is the smaller and nimbler of the two, the perky younger cousin. It sits on the lavender, wings open, bathing in the sun. Its flying season is short – no more than six weeks, peaking right now. This is its time.

I become aware, somewhere in the ether, of something else.

What is the instinct that makes you look? I felt it with the cormorant, way back at the beginning of the year. And with the wisteria, shortly afterwards. And countless times since. From nowhere, an indefinable impulse to turn your attention towards a certain place, knowing you'll see something of interest. Or maybe the thing that's appeared registers itself on your subconscious before the conscious brain kicks in: 'If you look directly up right now you will find something to your advantage.'

In this case, it's not a cormorant. It's something much tinier, more elegant, less likely to eat fish. It scatters to and fro, eventually landing on the straggly mint that grows higgledy-piggledy out of the bottom of the garden steps.

It's an appropriate choice of landing spot, because this is a mint moth, a winsome little tidger, no bigger than a Cadbury's milk chocolate button, and just as delicious to behold. Seen in the right light (and this is the right light) it's velvety purple, with little gold dots on its splayed wings. When distracted by larger things, it's easy to miss. I'm glad I didn't.

Day five. The light breezes disappear, and the clouds go with them. Hot hot hot.

The afternoon lull. I refill the feeders. Strange as it may seem, the practice of feeding birds in summer is quite controversial. Some say it's mollycoddling, should be reserved for the harsh winter months, when food is scarce and birds need a helping hand. Others counter this argument by pointing out the needs of young birds, and the necessity of a safe, regular food source. The naysayers counter that young birds might choke on large food parts. Those who have read the research might counter with a study that showed that great tits either avoided feeding their fledglings with the larger bits of food or took those bits to a safe place away from the feeder and broke them down into easily manageable scraps before ferrying them to the little ones.

I opt to feed.

The food bag is large, the feeder small, and I am hurried and clumsy. Mixed seed cascades onto the garden table, through the cracks and onto the ground.

I leave it, figuring that something will come and tidy it up soon enough. If it's a squirrel I'll probably chase it away, because we have a hierarchy, and squirrels, seen as undeserving pests dashing the food from the beaks of the deserving birds, rank low.

It's not a squirrel. It's a wood pigeon, strutting plumptiously up the steps and laying into the banquet with admirable gusto.

I'm fond of our wood pigeons. Like their cousins, the streetwise feral pigeons, there's more to them than meets the eye. Feral pigeons have a lean, athletic look to them, and the air of being about to sidle up behind you and relieve you of your wallet; wood pigeons, plump and arrogant, would expect you to hand it over on demand as if it was their right.

They're a familiar sight in our garden, either fossicking around under the feeders, hoovering up the mess left behind by the smaller birds (great tits and goldfinches are shockingly profligate eaters), perched precariously at the top of one of the small cypresses behind the shed, or barging their way busily through the airspace over the garden. They're brazen and obvious and I wouldn't be without them. The wood pigeon is the bird I see the most often. I can't remember a day when I didn't see one. But I rarely get to examine them from a distance of five yards.

It continues with its pecking, watching me as carefully as I'm watching it. I'm aware of the fragility of the encounter, and keen to maintain the thread of contact.

It has slate-grey plumage, morphing to a soft purple on the breast. Round the neck, a white ring, laid over its collar like a gym-user's towel. The eye, beady black set in the lightest sage green. A little bit scary when you look at it for too long. Claws, scaly and gnarled, a reminder of prehistoric origins. The beak, a bit stubby – not elegant but doing the job.

It is a thing of beauty. Only its ubiquity tells us otherwise. Plus, I grant you, its pest-like status for farmers driven to distraction by its distressing habit of munching their crops. Easy for me, the town-dweller, to be blind to the genuine difficulties caused by things that have caused much misery to those whose livelihood depends on such things.

Nevertheless, I stand by my fundamental point. There's beauty to be found in the everyday. Confucius had something to say about that too:* 'Everything has beauty, but not everyone can see it.'

It's gratifying when my own observations are corroborated by ancient philosophers.

Late evening. Sunset is at 8.41 p.m. Silence, warmth. I sit outside, quarter-watching snooker. The rest of my attention is on the sky.

---

* This sounds as though I spend my time immersed in improving literature. I don't. I'm pretty sure I saw it on Twitter.

It's easy to think that urban starwatching is a mug's game because of the pernicious effect of light pollution. And so, to an extent, it is. But moments of clarity are possible, and tonight is just such a night.

The snooker is drifting to a predictable conclusion, so I ditch it, take myself to the small patch of lawn at the bottom of the steps, lie on my back, and allow my eyes to adjust.

If I really wanted to get the best celestial experience I'd take myself to a hill, maybe further out of town, or at least away from the worst of the light. But this is better than nothing.

As my eyes accustom themselves to the darkness, pinpricks of light emerge in the sky. I don't know their names, but on this occasion it doesn't matter. Sometimes all you need is a general contemplation of the large and the small, the immensity and extent of the universe.

Perspective, so elusive, can be good.

37

FLIES ALL OVER THE PLACE

8–12 August

Beginning of autumn (*Risshū,* 立秋)
Cool winds blow (*Suzukaze itaru,* 涼風至)

The fifteen days of 'Greater Heat' only briefly delivered on the promise of the name; it falls to 'Beginning of Autumn' to usher in a heatwave. And not for the first time, the name of the microseason is completely out of kilter with reality – what winds do blow are of the 'fan heater with both elements turned to 11' variety.

Default temperatures of 30 degrees or more bring back memories of 1976, the benchmark of heatwaves for anyone alive at the time. And because August is inextricably linked with 'the summer holidays', to associate it with the word 'autumn' feels counter-intuitive. But, as already advertised, autumn has been quietly doing its thing for a while now, and while temperatures might indicate one thing, the progress of the natural world tells a different story. The two are connected, for sure, but not always precisely aligned.

The lavender has developed from village to small city. From a distance of five yards it emits a low hum. Only when you get right up close to it do you see just how many insects are thrumming and crawling over its pale lilac flowers, each following its own path and rhythm. Bees, butterflies, hoverflies, a selection of other, nameless pollinators.

Also like a small city is the melon rind I accidentally leave out on the kitchen counter. But in that case the visitors are less welcome. I'd love to be able to say I view all nature with the equanimity of a truly disinterested and fascinated observer. But these flies can just fuck off.

They are everywhere, appearing from nowhere and descending on the merest crumb at a moment's notice. A buzzing, whirring nightmare of unpredictable movement, botherment and ickiness.

And relax.

No doubt these flies would be greeted with cries of enthusiasm by a passing dipterist, who would point out the many amazing qualities exhibited by the 120,000 or so members of the genus *Diptera* (they're known as 'true flies', as if all the other kinds are pretending – which I suppose some of them are). But to most people they're just flies, there are too many of them, and they're unwelcome. Something to do with their role as vectors of disease, no doubt. Something to do with the way they gravitate towards our food. Something to do with perceptions of dirtiness.

But it's also their ability to bother us, to keep bothering us, to not stop bothering us when we flap at them – a finely honed instinct to buzz around our heads in the most annoying way, as if they've all graduated from a training course called 'How to Piss Off Humans'. They remind me of the culminating scene in *King Kong*, the great ape harangued by aeroplanes while halfway up the Empire State Building and trying to protect its delicate human charge (Fay Wray, Jessica Lange or Naomi Watts, depending on your vintage). Strange how tiny things can strike consternation and revulsion into the human heart.

They disperse in a flurry as I flap them away. They'll be back. They always are.

Late afternoon. In the humid heat, a phenomenon to take the breath away. Clear blue sky, except for a large cloud, low down. The cloud billows upwards, full to bursting, backlit by the late-afternoon sun. Its fringes appear lined by a thin string of luminescence. A shaft of sunlight breaks clear of the cloud's guard like a striker on goal, lights up the bottom-right corner of the sky and shows up our neighbour's ash tree as a dark silhouette. Numinous, memorable, gone in an instant as the light breeze changes the angles and restores normality to proceedings.

The next day. Thunderiness weighs down the city, hanging over it like a massive blanket of doom.

It has to break soon.

Rumours abound. This afternoon, they say. There will be thunder and lightning and significant rain and most of all there will be blessed release from the limb-sagging languor that restricts all activity.

There are none of these things. Just a continued feeling of impending, non-specific portent getting in the way of productive activity.

The lightning radar map proves every bit as addictive as the multicoloured swirls of the wind map all those weeks ago. Blobs appear on it out of nowhere, radiating outwards like raindrops on a still pond. *Ping ping ping.* A flurry over Roehampton. Kingston gets it in the neck. Hammersmith, Fulham, Putney. But not West Norwood.

It's the sneeze that never comes. The chance of a storm gradually subsides; the feeling of torpor doesn't.

Pit-chew! Pit-chew! Pit-chew!

I've got so used to the sultry silence that any avian sound has my head jerking up, and nothing more so than the unseasonal call that pierces the heat haze.

Pit-chew! Pit-chew! Pit-chew!

Coal tit. Little fella. Black and white head, buff underparts, blue-grey back. Fast, active, flitty.

It's a sound so out of kilter with the time of year I find myself wondering briefly if it's some sort of weird hallucination. But on it carries, for five minutes, monotonously repeating the same sound from somewhere in the cedar of Lebanon two doors down.

Pit-chew! Pit-chew! Pit-chew! Small gap. *Pit-chew! Pit-chew! Pit-chew! Pit-chew! Pit-chew! Pit-chew!*

It might be a young bird, so intoxicated with the joys of life that it feels it has to announce itself to the world. That seems the most likely explanation, more plausible than a knackered parent suddenly summoning the energy to go again at a time when all it really wants is to sleep for a month.

Pit-chew! Pit-chew! Pit-chew! Pit-chew!

Then it falls silent as abruptly as it started, never to be heard again.

Another afternoon. The humidity has lessened; the heat remains.

I lie on the grass. Partly to cool down, partly because seeing things from another angle gives you a different perspective. I have a book too, but it's tiring to hold it at a convenient reading angle, so I put it down, allowing my gaze to drift across the sky, looking for nothing in particular and, as luck would have it, finding it.

Eyelids droop, eyes close. Just resting them, you understand.

A distant *squee*, an aural rip in the sky. Eyes jerk open, start scanning.

High up, fast, gone in a few seconds.

Two swifts, not hanging around.

The thrill of seeing them is counteracted by that feeling you get when, after protracted goodbyes, your visitors return ten minutes later because someone forgot their gloves.

And that, surely, is that for the year.

38

BIRD SOUNDS START AGAIN

13–17 August

Beginning of autumn (*Risshū*, 立秋)
Evening cicadas sing
(*Higurashi naku*, 寒蝉鳴)

Out with the moth book again. It's that time of year.

The specimen in question has infiltrated the bedroom and is flapping around in that way they have. It's not one of those large blundering ones that seem to make a disproportionate amount of noise for their size, but it's eye-catching nonetheless, simply because it's the only moving thing in the room.

It has several lights to choose from, eventually landing on the one by my bedside. It sits there for a few seconds before deciding it prefers the reassuring solidity of the bedside book pile. *Bleak House*, as it happens – added to the pile at the beginning of lockdown, and resolutely unread ever since.

This moth belongs to the distressingly large category I call 'shades of beige'. It's no less attractive for that – closer examination of its slight and delicate form shows up the yellowish tints in its colouring, and highlights the rippling effect of the changing hues. A reminder that beauty doesn't always come in gaudy packages.

I try to find it in the book, but it's late, I'm tired, and moths are too confusing, so I allow myself to be satisfied by the simple fact of its existence, not fussing so much about pinning a label to it. Sometimes it's better that way.

These days are resolutely undramatic in the weather department, eliciting no more than a 'meh' and a shrug. Some cloud, some sun, a faint mizzle from time to time. Neither pleasant nor foul – just there. The Ed Sheeran of weather.

The garden gets on with its slow business. The only notable additions are the tendrils of wisteria that appear overnight, snaking through the gaps in next door's fence and curling their way onto the terrace. On the other side, our vine and jasmine pull a similar stunt of encroachment on next door.

Out and about, the hollyhocks are so top-heavy now that they lean out over the pavement as if trying to hail a cab. Not to be out-done, a thistle – so solid it nearly achieves tree status – towers over them, looking down on their weakness with spiky disdain. Leaves on the pavements, brown and crinkled. Not just the horse chest-nuts, with their premature decay, but oak too, with the odd acorn among them.

As I enter the woods I experience one of those slow, dawning realisations that creeps up on you from behind.

The birds have started making noises again.

The background hasn't been completely silent these last few weeks – where there are parakeets, there is noise, after all – but the small birds have mostly been hunkering down out of sight, keeping their opinions to themselves. My walks have occasionally been punctuated by little sounds – contact calls, complaints, general comments – but they've been the exception rather than the norm.

But now, as close to imperceptibly as makes no difference, the air is beginning to wake up. The soft *chrrr* of a blue tit, followed closely by the more piercing *tsee* of a great tit. The agitated *tik tik tik* of a robin. Maybe, unless I'm mistaken, the light *pock* of a nuthatch.

The beginning of a new phase.

A boy walks past, serious, carrying a stick. This simple act gains my instant approval. Boys carrying sticks are the very stuff on which a better world can be built, after all. It gives him a sense of purpose that would otherwise be lacking. It soon transpires that this purpose is to chase a wood pigeon with a view to bashing it as hard as possible about the head and shoulders. It's a game as old as the hills, and one the pigeon will always win, but it doesn't stop the boy giving it his best shot. The bird lures him in by staying put as he scampers towards it, stick raised above his head in wobbling menace. Then, at the last minute, off it flies with a clatter of wings. The boy registers the mildest disappointment, then immediately repurposes the stick, swishing it on the ground in fast, violent arcs.

This is exactly as it should be, and I leave him to it, feeling obscurely reassured for the future.

On the way home, I take a detour from my usual route. Cross the road, through the estate, down the grass bank – back streets all the way. I'm drawn to a sound in the clump of small trees on the corner. The trees are of indeterminate species (to my eyes, at least)

– scrubby, clumpy, offering dense cover for the kind of things that like dense cover.

The sound is enough to bring relief on the drabbest of days, an arrhythmic agglomeration of chirp, the work of a dozen or more birds hidden in the depths, giving a decent impression of a busy cafe kitchen in full swing.

House sparrows.

It's been so long since the sparrows I regard as 'ours' have come to the garden that I'd almost given up on seeing them again. This little gathering of about a dozen birds might not be the exact same ones I got used to seeing earlier in the year, but they'll do as proof of continuing existence.

How extraordinary, though, that such an encounter should be a cause for celebration. Their former ubiquity – such that they were widely regarded as pests, especially on farmland – is now a dim memory, and even in my lifetime their number has declined to a startling extent: 69 per cent between 1977 and 2010, although there have been signs of stabilisation and even recovery in recent years. So now, when I come across a pocket of them – and there are a few dotted around the area – I give a little cheer and stay a while.

There is something about sparrows that almost requires anthropomorphism. Cheeky chappies, 'cock sparrer', spadge, spug, sparky – the kind of names and descriptions you might apply to people.

Their appearance – dumpy and upright, the plumage a mixture of brown, grey and black – makes them the original 'little brown job'. And their behaviour, at once both confiding and shy, endears them to us while allowing them to retain a slight air of mystery. My experiences with them have often gone this way – come for the chirps, stay for the peering into a bush vainly trying to catch sight of one.

I pass within a few yards of the trees, and they fall suddenly silent, like a rowdy classroom feigning studiousness at the appearance of a teacher at the end of the corridor. I cock an ear. Silence. I get the feeling that if they could, they would ask the trees to say, 'There are definitely no sparrows in us, nothing to see here, move on.'

So on I move. I haven't walked ten yards before I hear the first tentative chirp from behind me, and within a few seconds they're back up to full volume.

Good old spugs.

39

ROBINS SING AUTUMN SONG

18–22 August

Beginning of autumn (*Risshū*, 立秋)
Thick fog descends
(*Fukaki kiri matō*, 蒙霧升降)

Clear. Warm. Dry. A summer's day.

A sharp staccato *chip* has me jerking my head up, scanning the treeline. Nothing at first, but then an unmistakable silhouette jumps up to the top of the cedar, *chipping* all the while – sharp beak pointed up at a 45-degree angle.

Hail the return of the great spotted woodpecker.

They come and go in phases – sometimes a daily sight, sometimes absent for weeks. It would be good to know where they nest, but even I baulk at knocking on every door in the neighbourhood and asking, 'Excuse me, can I check your garden for a woodpecker's nest?', so I'll have to remain in blissful ignorance.

It chips for a few minutes, the rhythm not quite regular. I'm never quite sure what purpose this call serves. Is it an announcement to the world, a portent of impending danger, or just a nervous tic? Whatever, I appreciate it, and take it as a direct message from the bird, alerting me to its presence.

How we massage everything so it has human significance.

Take the robin. Specifically, the robin that starts singing just five minutes after the woodpecker's chipping stops. It's the first robin's song I've heard for weeks – a soft, sibilant, almost hesitant sound, as if testing the waters before going all in. A warm-up after weeks of silence.

Those in the know will tell you the robin has two songs. There's the spring song – upbeat, uplifting, a sound you could almost believe is designed purely to bring joy to the human heart; and then there's the autumn song, a more downbeat, melancholy affair.

Anthropomorphism ahoy.

I listen to recordings of the song of robins. They vary from phrase to phrase. Some have a jumbly energy near the beginning before tailing off; others are more measured; still others are the aural equivalent of a puppy chasing an unravelling ball of wool across a wooden floor. It is true that if you listen carefully you will discern differences: the song of the mating season has more variation, is fuller in tone. But perhaps that's because it has to be – there is more general background sound to contend with, for one thing, and the purpose of the song is to attract a mate. The more vibrant and ear-catching it is, the greater the likelihood of success. For the rest of the year – save the short period in midsummer when moulting, not singing, is the focus of the bird's energies – the song is used to defend a feeding territory. In times of hardship, the female joins in as well. The requirement now is not to attract, but to repel. Get off my land. There's no need for them to shout or elaborate – it's enough to be both audible and visible.

What we humans do is conflate these sounds with our own feelings. Spring song is energetic and hopeful; autumn song melancholy and sad.* But there's no place for such sentimentality in the robin's make-up. It's all about survival.

I know all this. But still I hear this robin, harbinger of the next phase of the year, and against the received wisdom, which would have a mild autumnal gloom enter my heart, smile a quiet and happy smile.

Grey. Cold. Wet. An autumn day.

No robin today. No anything except the drip-drip-drip of water on the water-butt cover outside the kitchen. From it I can tell exactly how heavily it's raining. It reaches its peak around lunchtime – an impressive 168 beats per minute. But as the afternoon wears on the gloom lightens and the rain eases, and by five or so it has stopped altogether, a landmark celebrated by a sharp staccato *chip* from the top of the cedar.

Right on time, almost to the minute.

I look up, and there is the woodpecker again. Same place, same pose, same procedure.

It's almost as if it knows what I like.

Rain. Wind. Clouds. Rain. Clouds. More wind. Sun. Make your mind up.

---

* I'm well aware that these seasonal emotions don't apply to everyone, but they're common enough to make the generalisation.

I see the shape of the wind in the silver birches at the front of the house, and only when they've calmed down do I go out.

By the parade, overhead, a darting triangle. Then another. And one more. A little flurry of them, appearing from behind the petrol station and chasing their friends into the tree by the traffic lights.

Starlings.

The traffic rumbles past, heedless. People go about their business, hunched and downfacing. The starlings can't settle, the landing of one prompting another to fly up and relocate on another branch, almost like a chain reaction. I can just about hear the outline of their whistles above the growl of a passing bus.

Through the woods, onto the path, into the Rookery, find a bench, sit. It's the kind of afternoon that almost compels you to sit and do nothing. High clouds, a mixture of wisp and fluff, sail gently by, the turbulence of the morning a distant memory. People wander past, dawdling, eating ice cream, chatting, keeping a vague eye on the kids, passing the time. They come here because it is a pleasant and peaceful place. There is no urgency to anything. Time passes slowly, which is all to the good.

I'm filled, not coincidentally, with a feeling of well-being. The key to this peace of mind is simple and obvious: as well as allowing myself time to sit in a place of calm, I've left my phone behind.

I love my phone. I love the possibilities it affords, the things I can use it for – a world of information in a small device that sits snugly in my pocket. I can take a photograph with it that would have required professional equipment just twenty years ago. I can find out what birds are nearby, identify bumblebees, learn Japanese, make a feature film, record Grammy-winning albums.

And when all else fails I can even use it to speak to a fellow human being.

But to sit here on this quiet bench, watching the quiet world pass by on a quiet afternoon, allowing it all to drape itself around my shoulders and fill me with calm, without feeling the need to reach into my pocket and check that, yes, the world is still falling apart at the seams ... well, it's a good and important thing to do, now and again.

So I sit and watch, and it is an hour well spent. A series of moments, a time of timelessness, stretching into eternity.

40

FRUIT FALLS TO THE GROUND

23–27 August

Limit of heat (*Shosho*, 処暑)

Cotton flowers bloom
(*Wata no hana shibe hiraku,* 綿柎開)

They call it 'Limit of Heat', but we're well past that. That's what it feels like, anyway. We're firmly in 'English weather' territory, the progression from summer to autumn showing not just in the mixed conditions and moderate temperatures, but in a general feeling that things have gone over the top.

I stand on the terrace, looking up at half-and-half skies and debating whether I can be bothered to go for a good long trek or just flummock around the house all day.

Five seconds. That's all it takes. There and then gone. All angles and movement and that 'not-a-pigeon' shape that makes you snap your head up and run for the door. But by the time I've got out onto the terrace to get a proper look it's disappeared behind the trees and no amount of wishing will persuade it to reappear. I scan the skies, trying to turn the outline of a wispy cloud into a peregrine. No dice.

A wood pigeon, perched on the cedar two doors down, heckles me with a disdainful coo.

I've got used to seeing the peregrines on the church tower. I've seen them flying high over the back streets of West Dulwich. And there was that memorable feathery gull encounter in the cemetery. But for a long time they were completely absent from the quadrant to the south of the church, where we live. I put this down to the birds' natural distaste for the less salubrious areas of south London.

But perhaps I wasn't looking hard enough.

The two sightings I've had of a peregrine over the garden this year have lasted a combined total of about fifteen seconds. They are, I'm fairly certain, the direct result of a simple act: looking more. Who knows what I'd see if I devoted my entire life to scanning the skies?

It brings home two simple truths: there's a lot more out there than anyone sees, and you can't see without looking.

While I'm excited to see this bird overcome its natural aversion to the seamier part of town, and always happy to see a peregrine anywhere, I have secret hopes of an even more noteworthy sighting. Because while peregrines are of course magnificent in every way, there's been a more elusive bird of prey hanging about not far away recently, and I would pay good money for it to wander over my way.

The glamorous allure of the hobby (*Falco subbuteo*) is easily enough explained. Like swifts, they come from Africa for the summer; like swifts, they're fast, agile and thrilling; like swifts, once seen they command the attention. In fact, with a short tail and their wings swept back in flight, they don't look unlike giant swifts, and their agility is such that if a swift has anything to fear from a bird of prey, it's most likely from a hobby.

A hobby (the name comes from an old French word, *hober*, meaning 'to jump about') is the one bird capable of taking out a swift in the air, although they more commonly content themselves with dragonflies. With powerful, angular flight, deep wingbeats, and an ability to change direction in mid-air that seems to defy the laws of aerodynamics, a hobby on the hunt is a mesmerising sight. And if local reports are to be believed, there's been one hanging around from time to time just a couple of miles away.

This, for me, would be birding gold.

But if I think I can find it just by turning up, I'm sadly mistaken. My occasional forays in that direction have been fruitless. But it's better to live in hope than to be a miserable git, so I live in hope, and try to conjure a sighting with a combination of magical willpower and constant scanning of the skies.

Look up. Always look up.

There's wind overnight. It's strong enough to blow over the umbrella on the terrace and uproot a fence panel two doors down. Summer's fading fast.

The forecast has it all dying down mid-afternoon, so I again take the soft option and leave my walk till everything is calm.

Dried seed pods hang stiff from green branches; apples lie scattered on the ground, either rotting to squelch or nibbled by various insects; the dying ash tree to the right of the path sprouts a bracket fungus large enough to eat a meal off. But these incontrovertible signs of autumn have a vivid counterpoint. Peeping up through the parched ground, a tentative carpet of tiny fractal fronds. Cow parsley, its fresh green contrasting with the backdrop of varying shades of brown. As other things fade, in comes the new growth. Yet another reminder of the circularity of things. It will creep upwards until temperatures drop to 4 degrees Celsius, when the chemistry of cold will kick in and keep growth at bay.

More oak galls, this time in the form of dozens of little pale-brown circular appendages stuck to the backs of leaves, as if someone has glued a bowl of miniature Cheerios to them. These are the pleasingly named spangle galls.* An expert would be able to say which of the four UK species they are; I'm just content to have narrowed them down that far.

The brambles have gone over, and what shrivelled berries remain are beset by flies. It's a forlorn sight, redolent of the in-between phase we're in, the mirror of the 'anticipation' stage just before spring flaunts its wares. The good bits of summer seem a distant memory, but the full glory of autumn lies too far ahead.

My hobby sense is on overdrive, turning every fleeting glimpse of anything avian into the angle-winged raptor. Even a pigeon coming in to land from a distance is enough to get me going. A bird-of-prey-shaped object flashes into the periphery of my vision and out again, ducking down behind the treeline. I sprint round the corner to catch up with it, and see it climbing up towards its habitual perch on the church tower.

Peregrine. It's not a hobby, but it'll do nicely.

---

* I say 'pleasingly' partly because 'spangle' is a pleasing word, but also because it calls to mind the sweets of the same name, which were a childhood favourite.

41

CONKERS BEGIN
TO FALL

28 August–1 September

Limit of heat (*Shosho*, 処暑)

Heat starts to die down
(*Tenchi hajimete samushi*, 天地始粛)

It's lying on the path in front of me, its just-shelled freshness imploring me to pick it up. The husk lies to one side, papery pith cup left to wither, the protective spikes nothing like as frightening as they'd like to think. Up on the tree, the leaves that are left are a forlorn sight, brown and crumpled by the depredations of the leaf miners. Their time is past. It is the time of the conker.

I bend down and pick it up. The soft sheen of it, that mahogany glow, the satisfying nearly round shape, its complete and utter conkerness. How am I supposed to resist?

I'm not. Into the pocket it goes, to accompany the three acorns from earlier. Some people have worry beads. Others might have a key ring or a pocketknife or a perfectly contoured pebble. But at this time of year all I need is a conker in my pocket to hold and rotate and smooth my fingers over as I walk down the street. A strange, warm comfort.

A few decades ago I might have rejected it and looked for something chunkier, with a bit more heft. Then I would have drilled a hole in it, threaded a shoelace through the hole, knotted it tightly and given it a few practice swings before launching it into what I hoped would be one of the great conker careers. If I were minded to game the system I might have soaked it in vinegar or baked it in a low oven. But while I wasn't averse to a bit of sharp practice in other areas of my life, that always seemed both too much of a faff and rather dubious in its results.

Perhaps that explains why I never achieved anything more than a 'six-er'.

Like the bearded tit (neither bearded nor a tit), the horse chestnut is misnamed. It is neither a horse nor a chestnut. The former observation is obvious from the merest glance, yet the true origin of that part of the tree's name is in the misguided belief that the seeds, when ground up, were beneficial to sick horses. They're not. They're poisonous.

As for the 'chestnut' bit, it turns out that it's only distantly related to the 'true' chestnut family, so it's all a bit of a mess.

The horse chestnut might feel like a British tree, but it's a relatively recent import, native to the Balkan peninsula and arriving here only in the late sixteenth century. We made up for lost time though, planting it widely in parks and other public places, and its majestic stature and long life have guaranteed it a strong place in the nation's affections.

It took a couple of centuries for the game of conkers to emerge. The first recorded game took place on the Isle of Wight in 1848. A version of the game had already been around for a couple of decades, played with hazelnuts or seashells. But it's easy to see why conkers replaced them. Quite apart from their weight and heft and general excellence, if you get the impact right they also shatter into small pieces in a most satisfying way – for the winner, at least.

Even the sight of a conker is enough to induce waves of soggy nostalgia. I admit it's a bittersweet feeling, given my relentless losing record at the game in my youth, but there's pleasure to be had in it nevertheless, and in these unprecedented times we take pleasure where we can find it.

When the sun is at a particular angle, and I stand in a particular spot, I can see it perfectly; move a yard and it's invisible. I experiment with angles, trying to place myself in a position to admire this tiny thing and its miraculous construction.

It's an orb web spider, one of the commoner species you find knocking about the place, and while I'm keen enough on the sight of it – small and golden in the early-morning sun – I reserve most of my enthusiasm for the web.

It's easy to overdo open-mouthed wonder at the glories of nature – I realise that. It's exhausting to be in a constant state of excitement, and even though we look for magic in everything, we don't always find it. Some things are mundane, even ugly. But sometimes it's worth setting aside world-weariness for a few seconds so we can allow ourselves to be swept away by the glory of everyday things.

And so it is with spiders' webs.

It's not just their beauty when viewed from the perfect angle on a sunny autumnal morning, although that would be enough for me.

Beauty is all very well, and abundant in nature, but it's also subjective, and there will be millions – some of them no doubt reading these words while quelling a vague sense of trepidation – for whom the intrinsic glory of a spider's web is overshadowed by feelings of fear and revulsion at the prospect of the creature that made it. But there's more to it than that. Because a spider's web is a miracle of engineering. Everything about it inspires admiration, even awe – the first radial threads, the intricate and precise spacing of the tendrils that make up the bulk of the web, the use of sticky and non-sticky threads for different parts, the extraordinary tensile strength and elasticity of the materials produced by the spider to make it. That the finished product happens to look delicately beautiful to human eyes when caught by sunlight or laden with early-morning dew, and simply spectacular when adorned with the sharp crystals of hoar frost, is one of those happy coincidences on which our appreciation of the natural world is built.

So I spend some time not just looking at the web, but thinking about the process that made it, and I do allow myself a little moment of open-mouthed wonder.

And then I move on down the garden and come across a dead pigeon on the grass, and the magic is somehow forgotten.

42

DRAGONFLIES LAY
EGGS ON WATER

2–7 September

Limit of heat (*Shosho*, 処暑)

Rice ripens
(*Kokumono sunawachi minoru*, 禾乃登)

The streets.

Rumble of traffic. Gentle wind in trees. Soft *chrrr* of blue tit.

Furious cawing, stage left.

I'm familiar with the vocabulary of carrion crows. Sometimes one of our locals will sit on the cedar and give out a series of bellowed, drawn-out caws – low and raw, neck extended, as if summoning the other crows to prayer. At other times there will be a back-and-forth between several of them, each at their own pitch, like an argument with everyone repeating their own point of view and resolutely ignoring anyone else's.

This is different. Hearing the pure rage in the voices I assume this sound is the corvid equivalent of 'fuck the fuck off, you fucking fucker'.

I look up, scan for a bit, find them. Three agitated black shapes, flapping, shouting, tumbling, occasionally backing off then lunging upwards – a dramatic sight against the clear blue sky.

In the middle, pale and slender next to the dark forms of the crows, and apparently unperturbed by their attentions, a kestrel. It doesn't try to evade them, nor does it change its course. It merely carries on towards wherever it's going. The crows continue their tumbling attack, never actually coming within striking distance, just making themselves irritating. Whether the threat it poses to the crows is real or imagined is debatable. Maybe it encroached on their territory, or had its eye on a meal they'd earmarked for themselves.

It's an everyday battle, briefly glimpsed. These animals live their lives, unaware they have an audience. To see a small slice of them always feels like a privilege.

The Rookery.

The formal bit, well-planted beds separated by flagstoned paths laid out in a geometric pattern. Driven by the theory that everything is 10 per cent better next to water, I'm drawn to the corner with the fountain.

Make that 50 per cent. Because zipping around just above the water, like crazed remote-control mini-drones, are half a dozen dragonflies.

Whichever angle you view them from, dragonflies* are ace. There's the prehistoric vibe, for starters – there are dragonfly fossils from 325 million years ago, and whenever I see one an image pops

* And damselflies – let's not leave them out.

into my head of one of its ancestors, its wingspan up to 75 centi-metres, challenging everything we think we understand about both aerodynamics and the proper size of things.

And then there's the flight, a mesmerising sight – zoom STOP whizz STOP dash STOP – all speed and control and mastery of the air.

Then, when you find one sitting quietly on a moss-covered stone and it lets you close enough to take a photograph or look at it through close-focus binoculars, you get a chance to examine the intricate delicacy of its wings and the looming strangeness of its com-pound eyes, and you go on your way with that extra spring in your step you get whenever you encounter anything of beauty or interest.

Do I know what species they are? Of course not. In-depth study of Odonata, like fixing the dripping bathroom tap, is one of those things I've never quite got round to. But I've absorbed enough from my occasional delvings into the subject to hazard a guess, and I reckon these are common darters – red male, golden-brown female, darting behaviour. I look them up later and discover that separating the various darter species is 'problematic', so I leave it at that and content myself with the memory of the sight of them. And what a sight it is.

They're attractive enough seen from above against the dark backdrop of fountain water. But I have the feeling that to appreciate them fully I need to get down to their level. From there I get more perspective on their speed and mobility, the outlines of their slender bodies seen more clearly against the light stone of the fountain wall. One pair in particular catches the eye. They're attached to each other, female's head to male's tail. The male swings the female down with a rhythmic whipping action, her tail just brushing the water.

A woman nearby has stopped, possibly more intrigued by the sight of me lying on the flagstones than by the dragonflies.

'What are they doing?'

A half-remembered snippet floats into my head.

'I think – but don't quote me – they're laying eggs on the water. I think.'

'Ah.' I'm not sure she believes me. 'Fascinating.' And she wanders off, leaving me in my quest for the perfect dragonfly photograph.

I look it up later. I was right. Score one for the casual habit of random reading.

The cemetery.

My arrival is heralded by a distant chipping sound. Great spotted woodpecker. A welcome portent for a productive visit.

There's a properly autumnal feeling in the air – I've already been lured by the blue skies into opening the sliding doors, only to close them again on feeling the strength and nip of the breeze – and it's enhanced by the sight of an enormous shelf-like growth surging from the trunk of one of the oaks near the crematorium at the top of the hill. It's the orange-yellow bracket fungus known as 'chicken-of-the-woods'. There are eight individual growths in total – five huge, like steaks, interleaved with three smaller.

They look so fresh you could believe they've been summoned by the morning's rain shower, emerging like a time-lapse sequence, then waiting for an unsuspecting passer-by like me to harvest them, take them home and fry them with garlic. But despite my confident identification, I draw the line at foraging. I know enough about mushrooms to know how very little I know, so I leave that kind of thing to the experts. I leave the fungus behind and carry on down the hill, hanging right along the Doulton Path. I gravitate towards this path as a firm-earthed alternative to the more obvious paved route that runs parallel to it. And now I get a bonus.

From deep in the bushes to my left I hear a soft burbling, so quiet it's almost inaudible above the soft tread of my feet.

There are bird sounds I recognise instantly – blackbird's song, swift's *squee*, jay's shriek – and there are others that leave me perplexed. This is somewhere in between. Familiar, but not, the shapes and contours resembling something I know well, but refusing to coalesce into something concretely recognisable.

A scrabble here, a jangle there. Silence. A jumble of scratches, followed by a softer fluting sound. All on the edge of audibility, as if coming from another room. I put on my best listening face and stand stiller than still, my head cocked towards the bush.

Two women walk past, chatting. I'm tempted to shush them, but a small internal voice reminds me, just in time, that not everyone shares my priorities. And somehow, once they've passed, my brain clears and I recognise the bird for what it is.

It's a blackcap. Specifically, the subsong – typically made by young birds or adults outside the breeding season. It continues for another couple of minutes – chatty, fizzy, full of suppressed energy.

It's another intimate glimpse into alien lives – the fighting crows and the kestrel, the egg-laying dragonflies, and now this bird, singing to and for itself, unaware and uncaring that it might give another living thing the purest and most personal of pleasures.

43

IVY FLOWERS

8–12 September

White dew (*Hakuro*, 白露)
Dew glistens white on grass
(*Kusa no tsuyu shiroshi*, 草露白)

It doesn't seem like a fair fight. The flies are recently snared, struggling helplessly and with dwindling energy. The spider tiptoes out from the middle, using the non-sticky threads that form the main structure of the web. Then it wraps the flies up, one by one, rotating them nimbly while spinning out a continuous thread from its abdomen until they're completely encased. The process combines the theatricality of a magician pulling handkerchiefs from their sleeve with the brisk efficiency of a secretary doing the filing. The flies are now securely trapped for later consumption and the spider retreats to the centre of the web for a breather. Take the rest of the day off. You've earned it.

I have, for once, come out early, and am rewarded with the promised dew, even if the glistening effect is muted under the high but uniform early-morning cloud. What I notice most of all, apart from the warmth in the air, is the dampness on my walking shoes. And dampness, especially at this time of year and prompted by the attention-grabbing appearance of the chicken-of-the-woods, brings thoughts of fungi.

The fascination of fungi isn't limited to their appearance. The pert perfection of a fresh growth of inkcaps; the bright red, white-flecked allure of fly agaric, the classic toadstool; the bloated promise of a puffball; and, yes, even the phallic impudence of the stinkhorn – all these are enticing enough, but when you consider the hidden world they represent, interest turns to fascination turns to awe. These alien forms that grace us with their presence – sometimes obvious and out in the open, but more often tucked away in damp nooks or teasing us with their ability to blend in with any background – are ambassadors from a subterranean world of beguiling strangeness. It's a world full of words like 'hyphae' and 'mycelium' and 'mycorrhizal' – words trying to make sense of a world of inextricably tangled, complex connections linking fungi with trees and other green plants, and drawing into their milieu a host of other life forms along the way. When I read about the 'Wood Wide Web' I undergo the usual thought processes, starting with 'wow this is amazing', progressing through 'I don't understand', on to 'let me just read that again', and most often culminating with a combination of 'wow' again and 'yes, but how do they *know*?' This last stage, incidentally, is born more of a layperson's bewilderment in the face of science than of a fundamental distrust of scientists.

Knowing that mushrooms are merely the fruiting bodies of a larger organism – one that exists on a level whose intricacies we're only just beginning to understand and unravel – adds a layer to my appreciation of them. It also helps me feel less guilty when my clumsy feet accidentally boot one towards an unsuspecting carrion crow. I haven't killed a mushroom, merely harvested it.

The crow, unimpressed, flies away from me with a judgemental *graarrk*.

It's around this time of year that my eye is drawn to ivy.

Ivy gets a bad press. Things that grow a lot often do. Its reputation for sucking the lifeblood from buildings and for weighing down fences to the point of collapse prompts many people to adopt a zero-tolerance approach. Rip it out, kill it, burn the remains. Anything to keep nature from overrunning us. It's an approach that at this time of year has conservationists wringing their hands with frustration. Because just as the gardener thinks of 'tidying up', ivy's getting into mid-season form.

Not only is it a cosy habitat for nesting birds – and the denser the better, as far as they're concerned – autumn-flowering plants such as ivy provide a handy source of food for pollinators, among which we in the UK can now count the ivy bee.

The ivy bee is a relatively recent arrival here, but since its first record in 2001 it has made fast progress northwards, and now takes its place as one of those things that people so inclined look forward to every autumn.

Some species seem to have gained their names randomly – the ivy bee isn't one of them. Its preference for ivy flowers is just one of many reasons for the overenthusiastic gardener to stay their hand and spare that rampant ivy for just a few more weeks.

Having grappled with bee identification earlier in the year, I am at least one step further on than I might have been, and as I scan the cascades of dark green ivy looking for its bobbly flowers and associated buzzers, I'm particularly on the lookout for anything with a warm ginger fuzz around the head and shoulders. This feature, according to the field guides, renders the ivy bee 'unmistakable' – the novice will squint vaguely at the yellow-and-black thing buzzing around the ivy flowers, get frustrated that it won't sit still, and then say, 'Yes, well I *think* I see . . .'

I take the latter approach, and with judicious use of my close-up binoculars am able to declare after ten minutes that none of the insects busying themselves around the cascading ivy are ivy bees. Honey bees, yes; other nameless buzzers, absolutely; but the one thing they have in common is the complete lack of ginger fuzz in the requisite areas.

I quell my inner child ('everyone else has ivy bees, *I* want ivy bees, it's not *fair*') and allow myself to be soothed by the industry of those insects that are there – and there are plenty of them. They might not be as glamorous as my target species, but they are doing equally good work vis-à-vis the ecosystem in general. Species snobbery isn't a good look.

After a few minutes, I've had my fill, and continue with the walk. The light is fading, the clouds are low and a dullness has fallen on proceedings.

Then, round the corner, a cascade of leaves, running the gamut of colours from bright red through all the oranges and somehow morphing to green in a way that positively screams: 'Photograph me. Put me on Instagram. Do it now.'

Nature is so desperate for attention these days.

44

BATS
SOMETIMES SWARM

13–17 September

White dew (*Hakuro*, 白露)
Wagtails sing (*Sekirei naku*, 鶺鴒鳴)

Chi-zick!

I like to think it's calling to catch my attention. 'Look at this!'

Flutter bounce flutter bounce land trot.

It's a good start. I've found myself looking at the season names, hoping they'll somehow reflect their Japanese equivalents. Sometimes geography doesn't allow for it – blooming cotton flowers and ripening rice are in short supply in the wilds of West Norwood – but coming out for a walk on the first day of 'Wagtails sing' and almost immediately hearing and seeing a wagtail feels like a decent portent.

The pedant will point out that the wagtail of Japanese folklore – the Japanese wagtail (*Motacilla grandis*) – isn't the same species as the pied wagtail (*Motacilla alba*) that's just executed its signature move in front of me. The ruthless pedant will further note that the song of the Japanese wagtail is at least worthy of the name – a winsome agglomeration of warbles and swoops and clicks – while our pied wagtail contents itself with unimaginative variations on the *chi-zick* theme.

But I'll take these confluences wherever I can get them.

The wagtail has some significance in Japanese folklore. Indeed, if their version of the universe's creation is taken at face value, we'd be nowhere without them.

When Izanami and Izanagi, the young gods left in charge of the fledgling universe, found themselves at a loss as to how to proceed with its development, the elder gods sent down a pair of wagtails to show them the righteous path. Modern sensibilities might wish to gloss over the details – Izanagi, the female, had dared to speak before Izanami, the male, which was seen to be against the natural order of things. But the idea of wagtails as messengers from the gods, imparting wisdom from on high, is enticing.

Wagtails sing. Or call. Whichever you prefer. And when they do, they send a grain of joy our way.

It's no more than two inches from stem to stern, weighs almost nothing, and is among my most precious possessions.

I should really say 'from quill to tip', because this treasured object, sitting on my desk with delicate perfection, is a feather. Specifically, one of the secondary flight feathers of the great spotted woodpecker.

Identifying a bird from a single feather can be tricky, the colours and patterning often not tallying with the overall image of the bird.

It's like being asked to name a painting from a small fragment. Only when you see it in context does its place in the whole become clear.

With the woodpecker's, though, it's relatively simple. It's predominantly black, the thicker part to the right of the shaft adorned with four and a bit roundish white blobs, each one slightly truncated by the edge of the feather.

Hold it up to the light and it has a hint of translucence.

If you came across an object like this without knowing its purpose, you might be struck by its beauty. Link it in your mind with the miracle of flight, and it takes on special meaning.

I know it's a flight feather because of its shape. It curves gently with an elegance that defies analysis (no doubt there's a mathematical equation to describe it, but to apply it would somehow denude it of its poetry). And I'm guessing it's a secondary feather because of its size. The primaries are long and narrow, can be individually rotated, and are a bird's primary source of thrust. They're attached to the part of the wing known as the 'hand' – in other words, the bit furthest from the body. The secondaries – shorter and broader – work more as a unit, helping give the bird lift. They're attached to the forearm, or ulna. There are also tertials, the innermost wing feathers, attached to the humerus, whose function isn't for flight but to protect the folded wing.

Each of these feathers has a specific individual shape and structure, according to its function, and they all work together to help the bird execute its own particular brand of flight as efficiently as possible.

The woodpecker won't miss this feather too much. This is moulting season, and the bird is gradually divesting itself of its worn plumage. It's a slow process, starting after the breeding season's finished, in June or July, and lasting about four months. But the next time I see it – maybe tomorrow, maybe next week – I'll imagine the little gap under its ulna and send it a silent message of thanks.

I've neglected bats.

It's not their fault. It's my own carelessness. They could help matters by flying around in broad daylight like birds, but that would strip away some of the mystique.

No, what's really happened is that I've been lazy – disinclined to go for dusky walks, not willing to seek out their company in the places they're known to hang out. For all I know we might have bats flitting through the night sky over our garden most evenings, but my tendency is to hunker down, eschewing nocturnal activity. Sheer laziness.

In a bid to rectify this failing, I take myself up to Streatham Common on evening three, armed with special night vision and a bat detector. There's bound to be a bat or two flitting around in the crepuscular shadows, and while I'm barely conversant with the workings of the detector, the only way to find out about it is to try.

For many people, the prospect of an encounter with a bat is not anticipated eagerly. Bats are creatures of the night – creepy, malevolent and sinister. They suck your blood, get in your hair, and when they're done with all that they act as vectors of deadly diseases. And should you get a chance to see one up close, its appearance would only confirm these prejudices – only the most committed chiroptophile would describe them as cuddly.

But once you dispense with the prejudice and misinformation, the truth is that bats are benevolent creatures, happy to go about their business without meddling in ours. Throw in the whole echo-location thing, their status as the only flying mammals, and the extraordinary arms race they have going on with moths, among much else, and they reveal themselves as creatures of dark fascination. Whether that fascination manifests itself as fear or wonder (or perhaps a mixture of the two) is entirely up to the individual.

I wander around, not quite knowing where I might find them, but just sort of hoping they'll appear as if by magic. I have the detector set to the frequency most likely to detect our commonest bat, the pipistrelle, but I have little to go on except what I've gleaned from various guides and a childish hopeful innocence.

My reward is exactly what you'd expect from an endeavour of such naive speculation.

But it's a pleasant evening, imbued with that special mid-September warmth, like a bonus summer night. The presence of a bat or two would enhance it, for sure, but at least the hope of encountering one has lured me out of the house for a walk.

I retrace my steps. It's now almost completely dark, but for the soft circle of light thrown out by a street lamp and the constant background glow of London. From the woods to my left comes a short, querulous *hooo*. A tawny owl, buried deep. No detector required.

I wait, hoping for a repeat. But there's nothing. The owl has said its piece.

45

HOUSE MARTINS LEAVE

18–22 September

White dew (*Hakuro,* 白露)
Swallows leave (*Tsubame saru,* 玄鳥去)

These are the September days I like to remember – on the cusp between summer and autumn, combining the best elements of both. There's a dewy chill early on, burning off by mid-morning and yielding to comfortable warmth. There's a clarity to the light, summer's high sun beginning to give way to the slanting angles of autumn. And there are leaves on the ground. Not quite enough yet for a proper shruffle, but tempting enough anyway. They accumulate in clusters – here thinly spread on the pavement on the railway bridge, there drifting into a small pile in the unfrequented corner by the pub. And mingling among them, about one for every thousand leaves,* a sign of the times: the white-trimmed pale-blue rectangle of a discarded face mask.

---

* Give or take – I haven't counted them.

No matter how used I get to the thoughtlessness of littering, my distaste for it doesn't wane. I sometimes arm myself with a bin bag and pick it up as I go on my walk, hopeless though it might be as an act of defiance. But the casual discarding of masks feels like a particularly pernicious development, an extra layer of grim.

I try to distract myself by looking up at the church tower. Are the peregrines there?

No. Bah.

But there is compensation, in the form of two smaller birds flying high over the church. Fast, nimble, flitty. Their flight is slightly jerky, and even in the short time I observe them they change places three times, like breakaway cyclists sharing the work on a tough stage in the Tour de France. The sun illuminates their undercarriage for a moment, then they execute a small banked turn, enough to show the dark metallic flash of their backs – enough for the words 'house martin' to appear in my head.

My ability to identify birds from the merest glimpse of their disappearing backsides is intermittent and unreliable. Sometimes the identification is instantaneous (starling!) and quite wrong (oh no, wait, blackbird); sometimes the identification comes with caveats and question marks (coal tit? I think?) and a second glimpse or a different angle is required for certainty; and sometimes I get it right first time. Those are the good times, and this is one of them.

These house martins, part of my life for twenty seconds at most, are a particular treat. Like their cousins, swallows, they're not really urban birds, and the only time I see them is when they pass through on migration. Their appearance today, flying with purpose – and, I'm pleased to note, in the right direction for Africa – is a reminder that the season is in full swing, with the peak just a couple of weeks away. I won't see much of it on my patch, but these two tiny birds, low enough to be visible with the naked eye, trigger the imagination, and remind me just how little migration we witness first hand. For each bird seen or heard, imagine hundreds more passing out of sight high overhead. What we know about this mysterious process is swamped by what we don't, and while technological advances increase our understanding all the time, there is much that is, and will remain, unknowable. These birds give me the briefest glimpse into an alien world of extraordinary resilience and endeavour. They will continue their journey, for the most part unobserved, until they reach their destination somewhere south of the Sahara, where they will spend the winter, returning next spring to the same place for another breeding cycle.

Repeat until dead.

In the cemetery, on the Doulton Path, near where I encountered the burbling blackcap, there's an old crypt, its arched entrance long ago bricked in. Ivy sits on top of the miniature building, a sheaf of leaves hanging over the edge like a lockdown haircut. Even better, though, is the way the tendrils have inveigled their way out from behind the brickwork, creeping between bricks and arch. One strand loops around, hugging the contours of the wall and extending a narrow finger across the bricks.

I would watch the film that had this as its opening shot.

There's something enticing about the clash of architectural symmetry and natural haphazardness, but also about the sense that, given enough time, the ivy would swallow the crypt entirely.

Ivy's encroaching qualities are particularly suited to a place where they try as much as possible to let wilderness be wilderness, and that is one of the attractions of this cemetery. Order has its place, but disorder is important too. Newly painted railings offer one form of satisfaction – the freshness of renewal, a sign that things are being maintained. But leave them a few years, let paint flake, tendrils twine, and you have a different picture. Decay, melancholy perhaps, the contrast of 'natural' versus 'man-made'.

As I reach the end of the path and emerge into the sunshine, a little orange scrap flutters over my shoulder and lands on the kerb. It's a small copper butterfly – notably pert and delicate – and while it would be easy to focus just on the butterfly itself, I can't help but notice the contrast between its extreme beauty and the drab functionality of its chosen perch.

There's a satisfying crunching underfoot. Acorns, and loads of them.

Every few years – between seven and ten – the vast majority of trees in the beech family (which includes oaks) decides to produce a bumper crop of nuts. These years – 'mast years' – seem to be linked to weather in the preceding spring, when the trees are flowering. Warm and windy conditions ensure prolific pollination on a mass scale, and therefore bountiful nut production. This abundance is hard work for the tree, but worth the effort. Its growth might be restricted in the short term, but it's ensuring the survival of the next generation, because they produce so many seeds that it would be impossible for their predators – in our case mostly squirrels and jays, with the odd mouse and suchlike chipping in – to eat them all.

It's not coincidental that I've seen more jays around the place this year than ever before, and the crunching of my feet on this acorn-carpeted path is given a topical counterpoint by the appear-ance of one above my head. But instead of announcing itself with its habitual loud shriek, it gives forth a mewing sound that would be familiar to any owner of a hungry and demanding cat.

The mimicking abilities of certain species of bird are well docu-mented – starlings are notorious for it – and jays are among the finest exponents of the art, able to incorporate a variety of other species, including felines and humans, in their repertoire. This rendition is so convincing that if I didn't have the bird in my sight line, I would be scanning the undergrowth for a skulking tabby.

It doesn't last long. My jay encounters rarely do. Its habitual shy-ness kicks in, and it's off with a flurry and a flash of its white backside, into the trees and out of my life until the next time.

46

SOME LEAVES
TURN YELLOW

23–27 September

Autumn equinox (*Shūbun*, 秋分)

Thunder ceases

(*Kaminari sunawachi koe o osamu*, 雷乃収声)

For several months I didn't even go on a train. Now, when I turn up raring to go, a familiar disappointment from The Before Times awaits.

Cancelled.

It's a mild inconvenience, at worst. There is no urgency to my journey. The next train's in half an hour. I can easily kill time by wandering the streets.

Aimless meandering is a lost art. A slow, contemplative walk, going nowhere in particular, the only goal the lack of a goal. This half-hour hiatus is the perfect opportunity for such a meander.

My reward is instant. A cheery *chi-zick* from above, then the familiar bouncing flight, ending in a flurry and a twirl and a soft landing on the station roof.

I don't know whether this pied wagtail is the same as the one I see regularly over the high street or around the church. Maybe, maybe not. But however many there are in the area, and whichever one this is, a pied-wagtail day is better than a no-pied-wagtail day.

The meander takes me to a small, hitherto unexplored corner – up the hill, past the leisure centre, squiggle along the footpath and then back round down the hill. It's uneventful enough, I get to see a new bit of my area, and it helps pass the time.

And then the noise starts, a sort of malcontented chuntering interspersed with snuffly grunts and the occasional hoarse squawk.

It fools me every time. I hear a noise from the trees, think, 'What bird is that?', and experience a sort of bewildered disappointment when the matching of name to sound doesn't leap into my head. Then I see a twanging branch, perhaps a glimpse of grey furry tail with a hint of russet, and all becomes clear. Darn those pesky squirrels.

While our experience of squirrels might lead us to associate them with silent, bird-food-snaffling acrobatics, they have an impressive repertoire of vocalisations: grunting, snuffling, rasping, and the aforementioned hoarse squawk, which might be described as their 'signature' sound. This one, sitting on a branch about five metres up, is working through the whole range, chattering to itself almost constantly as if carrying on a conversation with the voices in its head. An extended monologue on subjects unknown. It's enough to keep me there, wondering what's going to come next.

After a good five minutes of free-form riffing, it finishes off with a triumphant bark, scampers down the branch and up the trunk and away and out of my sight.

Needless to say, I miss the next train by two minutes.

‰

A race has started in the garden. Robinia versus gleditsia.* Two trees, somewhat alike in appearance, dominating the left-hand side of the garden from over the fence – and very welcome they are too. Anything that draws attention from the geometric partitions that delineate where one person's property ends and the next begins is fine by me. The utopian ideal would be to dispense with fences, soften the boundaries, trust people to do the right thing and not to encroach.

A man can dream, can't he?

The race in question concerns leaves, and their seasonal colour change.

The robinia has made the first move, the yellowing of the tips visible from my office window while the gleditsia remains, for the most part, resolutely green. I say 'for the most part' because even within the palette of verdure there is wide variation. The old growth in the main body of the tree maintains a healthy dark green that wouldn't look out of place on a vintage British sports car; the new leaves nearer the top are a lighter shade, lending them a kind of jaunty freshness.

These variations are a subtle reminder of the slow progress of the seasons, how the changes might slip past you unnoticed until one day you look up and the green tree has turned into a yellow one. But while the trees are playing the long game, the weather has taken a turn overnight, and not in a good way. Any impression that summer still has a trick up its sleeve is dispelled by a drop in temperature, backed up by light rain, and confirmed by swirling winds.

A fine way to celebrate the equinox.

---

* I'm aware that scientific names can put people off – these trees are also known as 'false acacia' and 'honey locust' respectively.

The stickler, consulting Wikipedia's handy chart, will point out that the equinox – that instant when the middle of the visible sun is exactly above the equator – happened at 13.31 on 22 September, while the season bearing its name didn't start until the 23rd. They might further stickle with the observation that the day of equilux – exactly twelve hours of daylight from sunrise to sunset – might vary according to how you measure the exact moments of sunrise and sunset, and especially depends on where on the planet you are. According to my calendar, the equilux occurs in Britain on the 25th, smack in the middle of this first portion of the equinox season.

But these quibbles aside, the broader point remains: it's autumn. The great descent from summer to winter solstice, the gradual shortening of our daylight hours, has reached its halfway point. Summer-haters will breathe that bit more easily; winter-haters will hunch a bit more deeply into their coats.

We might tick off the year's progress according to our own personal dates of interest – Christmas, Easter, birthdays, anniversaries, bank holidays, school terms and so on – but The Big Four – the solstices and equinoxes – are the true markers of its passage. While the equinoxes don't carry quite the same weight as the solstices – they're a point on a straight line rather than the turning of a corner – I mark this one in the same way I mark the halfway point on a long car journey. We're getting there. Look, Peterborough already.

These moments are a way of tracking the larger rhythms, the big in- and out-breaths of the planet's annual cycle, and – to get slightly fanciful for just a minute – at least to make the effort to retain some contact with the kind of cycles our ancestors knew.

Whether that's a useful endeavour is, naturally, for the individual to decide.

47

STARLINGS START
TO GATHER

28 September–2 October

Autumn equinox (*Shūbun*, 秋分)
Insects hole up underground
(*Mushi kakurete to o fusagu*, 蟄虫坏戸)

I wake to the sight of trees flinging themselves around wantonly, the sound of car tyres on wet tarmac, water dripping down the window.

Turned out nice again.

The plan was to go out the night before, find a high spot, set up the telescope and have a good look at the Harvest moon.

I monitored the forecast, and found myself scrutinising the sky nervously as the day went on. When the cloud rolled in around six o'clock, as I knew in my heart of hearts it would, I turned my attention unwillingly to other things.

It seizes me occasionally, this desire to spend time observing the night sky. By no means a dedicated sky-watcher, I can let whole months go by without thinking too hard about it, but from time to time – often around a full moon, when it's at its most obvious – it feels the right thing to do, as if contemplating the wonder of life on earth isn't quite enough to make me feel tiny and insignificant.

My telescope is most often deployed for its primary purpose, birdwatching. But it comes in handy for the moon too. Through the telescope I can see the moon's craters, its dips and crevices, can make out its curvature. It becomes something three-dimensional rather than the flat disc it can sometimes seem. And when it's full I can almost feel its weight, its connection with Earth, that invisible pull exerting such a strong and strange hold on us, often without our realising it. Through the telescope the moon becomes more real, almost touchable.

I know enough to be able to find the Sea of Tranquillity, and if the mood takes me I'll focus on it and ponder briefly the ridiculous notion that men once stood on that very spot, 250,000 miles away. But mostly I just look at it and lose myself for a while in its silvery light.

The Harvest moon is simply the full moon that occurs nearest the autumn equinox. It rises early and shines bright enough for you to work late bringing the harvest in. Great for farmers back in the day – of less significance to the average urbanite nowadays.

Were I in Japan, the occasion would have more significance. The moon is one of the pillars of autumn in Japanese seasonal poetry, and the festival of *tsukimi* (moon-viewing) contains a ritual element lacking in Western culture. It might involve decorations of seasonal pampas grass, special rice dumplings and offerings of sweet potato to the moon. Take it back a few hundred years and the ritual would take place on a boat, as we sat back and admired the moon's reflection on the water.

But this is England in 2020, so the ritual element consists of no more than noticing it, and perhaps taking an atrocious shot with my phone and posting it to Twitter with a self-deprecating comment about the quality of the photograph.

When it comes to it, though, the thick cloud cover puts paid to all of that, and while the particular nature of the Harvest moon means it sticks around, apparently full, for several evenings, each night is cloudier than the last and, after three evenings, and with a gloomy eye on the forecast, I give it up as a forlorn hope.

I haven't seen the peregrines for weeks.

It's become a habit, as I walk down the hill, to check the possible perches on the church. Sometimes there's just one of them, easy to spot, sitting out on a ledge, watching the world go by. Sometimes they're both there. Sometimes, after a few minutes of scanning, what I thought was a shadow turns, like a Magic Eye puzzle, into feathers and wings and beak.

Recently there has been nothing.

Today, instead, my eye is caught by flutterings at the very top of the tower. Starlings. Little mobile scraps, no more than twenty or thirty of them, but restless and agitated, as unable to settle down as a class of schoolchildren near the end of term, and constantly displacing each other – a fluid stream of bird.

Their presence is sign enough that the peregrines are away. Such confidence would be unthinkable if there were a threat around. Whether they'll adopt that spot as their favoured winter roost will depend a great deal on whether the predators return.

Laughably paltry by the standards of fifty years ago, this kind of nano-murmuration is nonetheless welcome, and another little sign that the year is turning. Winter is the season of the huge and spectacular gatherings of starlings that used to be commonplace, and now, in an age when videos are easily made and disseminated, attract audiences both in real life and on social media. But if my little group,* along with the others I see about the place as I roam my patch, is so small as to appear somewhat quaint, it doesn't diminish the little moment of pleasure when I hear the whirring of their wings. It's their energy that does it, I think. Little black dynamos, fizzing the air around them.

They're adaptable birds, so the plummeting of the population (down by 66 per cent or so since the early 1970s) is something of a mystery. Whether they'll find a nice patch of grass, full of worms and other invertebrates, to see them through the winter, or whether they'll supplement their diet with berries and whatever pickings the gulls leave behind from their litter scavenging, I'll look forward to seeing them whizzing about the place over the next few months.

There is avian activity everywhere, as if the entire order has been energised by the example of the starlings. Gulls wheel around above the high street in a way that strongly suggests the presence of a bin truck. They're joined by a quartet of carrion crows, the paths of the competing birds tracing a complex and mesmerising ballet. In the cemetery, families of tits – blue, great, long-tailed, you name it – call to each other constantly, warning each other of dangers real or imagined. Robins sing, parakeets frenzy, pigeons pigeon. It almost – *almost* – feels like spring. But then I notice the russet tinges of the trees, the droop of the leaves, the frosted sloes on the blackthorn

---

* Yes, they're mine – just try to take them away from me.

bush, the spillikins mess of needles on the ground. The watershed of full autumn colour-change is still just round the corner. Soon, though. Soon.

The memorial rose garden is emphatically set to 'melancholy', the majority of plants done for the season. One bush catches the eye, a few drooping blooms still hanging on. As I look at it, almost as if triggered by the attention, a single petal detaches itself, and floats gently down to join the little pool of pink on the grass below.

48

EVENING
SKIES BLAZE

3–7 October

Autumn equinox (*Shūbun*, 秋分)
Farmers drain fields
(*Mizu hajimete karuru*, 水始涸)

I don't particularly want to be awake, but sometimes you just need to accept that the level of alertness your brain springs on you at five in the morning isn't going to yield to serial dozing, no matter how much you'd like it to. So the only option is to leap out of bed like a gazelle that's just received good news, and set about the day with vim and gusto.

There are those who greet every morning this way, and while I would never count myself among their number, it's good to join as a guest from time to time. And today in particular this approach has its reward, in the guise of the perfect morning sky.

They come along once in a while, all the more welcome for their comparative scarcity. Today's form of perfection lies in the combination of the autumn light – direct, sharp, bright – and the position and shape of the moon. It hangs in the sky in the exact position an artist with an eye for proportion would choose – not centred in an obvious way, but just off to the left, possibly aligned with the Golden Section, the spot that feels instinctively right and turns out to conform to a fundamental mathematical truth. The artist would be careful to grade the blue of this just-post-dawn sky with this kind of precision, the gradations running from the palest at the horizon to a darker shade overhead. And then they'd take particular care over the portrayal of the moon itself – a sliver of potato print on light blue paper. And finally, at the fringes, there would be some indications that this isn't an idealised scene, but rooted in solid everydayness. Rooftops, the loose straggle of some trees, perhaps a crane or some scaffolding poking up above the roofline; maybe even, if you look really hard, an early-morning aeroplane banking ready for landing, leaving a faint comet tail of vapour behind.

Morning, everyone. Lovely morning.

It feels churlish to complain, because there was that nice spell, and it's generally been dry for the time of year, but I complain anyway.

I blame the wind. And of course the rain. But mostly the squirrel.

The squirrel didn't do it on purpose. It was just running along a branch, the way they do. But when there's been a deluge, and when the branch in question is heavily laden with leaves, and when an unthinking human walks underneath the branch, and when there's a sudden gust of wind to complement the scampering of the squirrel, extreme dampness inevitably ensues. It's the shock of it more than anything else. Dampness is fine, under the right circumstances; surprising dampness less so.

The midday deluge that caused my momentary drenching was short-lived but intense, an aftershock from Storm Alex, which lashed us for the first two days of the season. We were never in the full firing line of this storm – we just got the tail end, a general turbulence of the air with occasional bouts of violence, as if it was reminding us what it could do if it really put its mind to it. We got a day of rain, the odd branch spreadeagled across the pavement, and an upturned bench; southern France and northern Italy got widespread, heavy flooding, mudslides, cars and houses washed away, death.

So in the grand scheme of things, a small drenching barely registers.

If my mood is briefly subdued by this moment of wetness, it's almost instantly buoyed by the effect of the post-rain sunshine that quickly moves in. It's bright and low, glaring off the wet tarmac with a particular intensity, the kind of light that would cause a pile-up on a motorway. Here in the pedestrian zone it merely enhances the feelings of well-being.

As so often, post-rain sun acts as a stimulant on the birds of the cemetery, and for ten minutes or so the air is alive with chattering and fluttering. The species are irrelevant – it's the profusion of the sounds that is striking.

The lifting of mood brought on by this is strange and perceptible. Partly it's the visual and aural stimulus, an awakening of the senses. But perhaps it works at a deeper level too – the contact with other living things gives us some kind of reassurance that we're not alone in the world.

✕

The other end of the day.

The turbulence of the weather brings changeable skies, and it's in those minutes before dusk that they come into their own. The clouds seem to be in just the right place to catch the setting sun, and the result is briefly spectacular. Heavy grey cloud, tinged underneath with jaundiced yellow. Half a minute later, the universe has shifted and the yellow tinge has morphed to a warm orange glow. Then the cloud thins a touch, disperses enough to allow a pale mottled pink to develop.

We have a sunset on our hands.

With the instinct of a seasoned social media addict, I reach for my phone. Never mind that everyone in London will be doing exactly the same thing. My photos will be the ones to stand out from the crowd.

I duly take them, duly post a couple of the most striking, and they duly get a flurry of likes. Approval! For possessing a rudimentary eye for beauty and an ability to use the internet!

What a time to be alive.

The act of taking the photos and posting them online has its own pleasure. Other people, as I expected, are doing the same, and there's the brief warmth engendered by shared experience. But I can't escape the thought that perhaps it would have been better just to look at the sky, to drink it in, to allow it to be a personal, private experience. If a spectacular dusk sky appears, with shades of orange, yellow and pink, and nobody photographs it to post on social media, does it happen at all?

As quickly as it started, it's finished, replaced by darkening hues of grey and blue. I could have missed it entirely in the time it takes to make a cup of coffee.

And then, as if expressly ordered in by the return of the drab, four goldfinches, absent for several weeks, are back, their irrepressible chattiness doing good things to the soul. Bounce bounce, flit flit, tinkle tinkle. Sit on the top of the tree for ten seconds, gossip a bit, then off again.

49

MAPLE REACHES PEAK OF GLORY

8–12 October

Cold dew (*Kanro*, 寒露)

Wild geese return
(*Kōgan kitaru*, 鴻雁来)

It's not just dew. It's autumn dew. The sun has less heat, clear nights chill rapidly, the dew point is reached more readily. And its appearance as a pillar of the Japanese calendar is another example of the formalisation of the natural phenomena on which the system of the seasons is built.

If we have an equivalent in England, it's the annual game of dare that is Heating On Or Not Yet?

I nearly crack on day three. Nearly, but not quite. Instead, I get another jumper, an extra pair of socks.

It's not so much the air temperature as the mood. There's something afoot. The gradual encroachment of dusk into daylight hours doesn't help, but there's also a dampening greyness that lowers the temperature of the soul.

The garden is a saving grace, its warming colour palette tempering the chill. The spread of yellow through robinia and gleditsia is gathering momentum – robinia keeping up its early strong pace, gleditsia biding its time, poised to attack. The lightening of their colours down the left of the garden is offset by the glory of the small maple on the other side. For months at a time it's elegant but relatively anonymous. But come the moment, and it takes centre stage.

It's been showing promise for a couple of weeks now, the autumn colours spreading from leaf tips inwards. And now it's a riot, a glowing pool of oranges and browns and reds that positively invites immersion.

You can take simple pleasure from observing this process without understanding the science behind it – these warm colours lie well within the spectrum marked 'brain-pleasing', and that's enough for most people. I did this for years, the lessons of O-level biology either forgotten completely or lurking undisturbed under layers of Other Stuff. And then someone pointed out that the colour change isn't a change so much as an unveiling. The chemicals responsible for those autumn colours – carotenoids and flavonoids – don't appear from nowhere. They're always there in the leaves, waiting for the chlorophyll to disappear so they can strut their stuff. It's like a heat-sensitive mug, revealing its true nature only under certain circumstances.

This knowledge – fairly common knowledge, I now discover with some sheepishness – is like the explanation of a simple conjuring trick to a child. The demystification doesn't strip away the wonder – it deepens it.

※

It's rarity season.

It's been building over the last few weeks, the alerts on my BirdGuides app gradually increasing in variety and unusualness, and now there's a flurry of excitement as activity hits its peak.

The hotspots for these sightings are the extremities. The Scilly Isles, Shetland, Portland, Spurn. First ports of call for exhausted birds blown off course, these names are enough to set a birder's pulse racing. My relationship with these sightings is mixed. I understand the excitement. Any endeavour or enthusiasm holds the possibility of a once-in-a-lifetime experience, and it's only human to be stirred by such opportunities. But while I keep an eye on these occurrences, and am happy for those whose enthusiasm outstrips mine, I don't feel the need to drive 150 miles to stare at a damp bush in the hope that a hungry lanceolated warbler will come out to play for a second. That blue tit hanging upside-down from the feeder will do me fine.

That's what I say, at least.

Because if a hoopoe landed on a lawn two miles down the road – or ten, or possibly even twenty – you wouldn't see me for dust. And when I hear whispers of a common nighthawk – a solidly American bird that has been seen fewer than two dozen times in Britain – over a field in Sussex, I do go at least as far as looking up how long the journey would take. Because a nighthawk, a slender, crepuscular bird not dissimilar to our nightjar, is an intrinsically exciting thing, regardless of geography. But in the end common sense prevails. Travelling large distances to see an individual bird isn't really for me. The nighthawk sticks around for a day, and then, as birds tend to, disappears.

As if to confirm the wisdom of my decision, a blue tit pops up to the feeder and hangs upside-down for a few seconds, for no apparent reason other than to entertain me.

My head is turned by the nighthawk and other tales of adventure pinging into my phone. Perhaps it's a sign that my devotion to my local patch is wearing a little thin. But the thing that really sets my heart a-yearning is a one-word tweet from a northern birder.

'Geese!'

That simple exclamation conjures an image. Not of the local park geese – Canada, Egyptian, greylag – which are available for scrutiny all year, but of long, straggly echelons high in the sky, raucous and unruly, announcing their arrival with great shouting honks.

Pink-footed geese, fresh in from their Arctic breeding grounds to spend the winter here, where the weather is milder and food more plentiful. They speak to me of open spaces, fresh air and salt tang, of wildness and freedom – commodities in short supply in SE27.

But if the glories of goose migration are denied me, there are other manifestations of bird movement closer to home.

Look up 'bird migration' and you'll find tales of adventure and endurance, almost unimaginable journeys undertaken by little specks of things that fit in the palm of your hand. Record-breaking journeys such as the one undertaken by a bar-tailed godwit, which flew 12,000 kilometres non-stop from Alaska to New Zealand. Or the extraordinary endeavour of the Arctic tern, travelling almost from pole to pole and then back again in search of eternal summer.

But while those glamorous journeys earn our awe, spare a thought for the unsung, the overlooked, the humdrum. Because migration isn't restricted to the long-distance.

Every winter, the populations of many of our everyday garden birds – robins and blackbirds, to name just two – are boosted by visitors from northern Europe. It's easy to think of these birds as locals, never straying from their patch – 'Ah look, there's "our" robin' – but it's salutary to remember that 'your' robin might not be yours. It might be Denmark's.

Wood pigeons are at it too, going from we don't quite know exactly where to . . . well, we don't quite know exactly where. What we do know, and can witness if we're so minded and prepared to stand on a hill early in the morning during October, is that these movements happen all over the place, and sometimes involve thousands of birds.

The hundred or so wood pigeons I see barging their way over the back of the house on day two of this season, their undersides burnished by the glow of the morning sun, are a sight to behold, a flurry of activity in an otherwise still morning. It's impossible to tell whether they're flying from West Norwood Cemetery to Streatham Common, and have decided to swing by my place just to say hello, or whether they're engaged in a more ambitious journey. But when you're used to seeing them about the place in threes and fours, a gathering of twenty-five times that number registers. And they divert me for long enough to forget about the geese just for a moment.

50

REDWINGS ARRIVE

13–17 October

Cold dew (*Kanro*, 寒露)
Chrysanthemums bloom
(*Kiku no hana hiraku,* 菊花開)

The weather waxes average. Cool but not cold, damp but not wet, cloudy but not threatening. I take the glass-half-full approach, and enjoy the clear spells for what they are.

Out and about, my ears are on high alert – not just for the usual avian sounds, the ones that perk me up as I walk the streets – but for something specific. A high-pitched noise variously described by the field guides as *seeip, seep seep, tseerp, steep,* and the rather alarming *stüüüf.**

For this is the time of the redwing.

If swifts are my bird of summer – and they very much are – redwings run them close when autumn comes. But even though I'm

---

* The variety of transliterations for a relatively simple bird sound gives you some insight into the difficulty of the art form.

prepared for them, every year I have to get my ear in again. The first one always takes me by surprise, no matter how diligently I think I'm listening, no matter how attuned I think I am to the potential for that *tseep*.

Despite my close attention, the sound doesn't appear. But one day soon it will, and then we'll know we're properly on to the next stage.

In the cemetery, a young couple, of contrasting demeanours. He, amiable, almost cheerful, certainly contented. She, with the air of one there only under duress. They walk slowly, arms linked. Even from the other side of the path their conversation is clearly audible.

'I like this place because it's different.'

There's a small pause before her reply, just long enough for her distaste to register.

'Different? Depressing, more like.'

And that, by beautiful coincidence, is all I hear.

This idea – that a cemetery is inherently depressing – might on the face of it seem self-evident. You are, after all, surrounded by death.

And yet for me the cemetery has become so indispensable as a source of solace, a place to visit when in need of soothing thoughts, a little oasis of calm and contentment and Good Things, that I'm taken aback by the thought. Where I see a place teeming with life – trees and bushes and flowers and birds and fascinating unexplored corners – someone else might see only the gravestones, the munici-pal feel of the memorial rose garden, the looming presence of the crematorium – and their thoughts might turn to endings rather than continuation.

Each, as the saying goes, to their own.

A nondescript patch of grass, between road and path. Square, scrappy, damp. The kind of place I walk past every day with barely a second glance. But today I notice a little blemish, something that makes me stop and look.

A small semicircle of tiny silver-white mushrooms – freshly risen, almost impossibly pert and delicate, quivering with newness.

Such things are an invitation for a photograph, and the best way to get a worthwhile image is to get right down to their level. There are three possible disincentives for such a move: wet trousers, dodgy knees and the judgement of strangers. None of these things has stopped me from such actions in the past, and they're not going to stop me now.

I squat down, realise I'm not low enough, and go all the way, measuring my length on the path. As I do so, I become aware of scrutiny. A dog, trotting round in front of me, a concerned expression on its face. Behind, its owner, who now appears in front of me, his expression not so much concerned as perplexed.

I decide to break the ice.

'Morning.'

A hesitation.

'Morning.'

'Just photographing these mushrooms ... in case you were wondering.'

It's not immediately clear whether this helps. But after a short pause, he offers a quarter-smile, and a two-word appraisal.

'Oh. Good.'

There are many simple joys in life.

Standing on your local station platform, on your way to work for the first time in over six months, hearing the familiar *chi-zick!* overhead, then looking up and seeing that bouncing pied wagtail silhouette – oval body, straight tail – against the clear October sky as it bounces off towards the church, and flattering yourself that it saw you, recognised you as that benevolent occasional stranger, and this was its way of wishing you luck. That's a good one.

Spending the day in a room of like-minded people, working towards a common goal, knowing that each of them is doing the very best they can, not least because you have all spent the last six months wondering when, if ever, this kind of activity would be possible again. That's high on the list too. And if they happen to be some of the finest musicians in the country, then that's a happy coincidence, adding lustre to the occasion, but really it's just the fact of it happening at all that makes it memorable.

Coming back from the day's work with time in hand for a quick walk round your favourite local place, and suddenly finding that, without your really being aware of it, you are now entirely surrounded by long-tailed tits, their high-pitched conversational chattering coming at you from all angles as you try, and fail, to get a proper sight of them; and then spotting a carrion crow pecking viciously at something on the path ahead of you and realising it's a cuddly toy of favourite cartoon plumber Mario and, carried away with the giddiness of it all – the pied wagtail, the long-tailed tits, the carrion crow and its hapless victim, but mostly the strangeness of everything that's happened in the year, and particularly the not-normal normal day you've just had – doing a sort of laugh that turns into a little cry and then back into a laugh again.

That might be the best of them all.

*Tseep.**

It takes a moment to register.

Tseep.

Wait. Hang on.

My brain gradually processes the sound, and leads me to the word I've had on my mind for the last few days.

Redwing.

The bird remains invisible, but I don't need to see it. Just hearing the sound is enough.

Stand down, everyone. The redwings are here.

---

* Or, if you prefer, *seeip, seep seep, tseerp, steep,* or *stüüüf.*

51

PLANE TREES SHED THEIR LEAVES

18–22 October

Cold dew (*Kanro*, 寒露)
Crickets chirp around the door
(*Kirigirisu to ni ari*, 蟋蟀在戶)

This is a damp, blustery season. Another one. The upside to such weather, if you're looking for one, is that if you don't like it there'll be something else along in a minute. And so it proves. Rain and wind morph to partly blue skies and then back again. There is brightness available to the canny consumer, but the trick is to go out in the gaps. One appears in that quiet period just after lunch. Out I go.

Not far from our house is a little scrubby triangle of nothingness. Phone booth, telecoms junction boxes, a couple of anonymous, slender street trees, not getting in anyone's way. In the middle, a scrappy patch of grass and an unconvincing hebe, spreading its shrubbiness across the available space and flowering in a lacklustre kind of way when the time is right.

One of the anonymous trees is a good example of why you should never take anything for granted. For most of the year I walk past it without a second glance. And then autumn comes and it burps down its leaves, and it turns out they're all the colours and then some, a heady mix of gold and purple and red and even the odd bit of green along for the ride, and for a few days the pavement becomes a Jackson Pollock carpet, the variety of colours uplifting in their randomness. Thanks to a nifty app called TreeTalk, which maps London's street trees and constructs local walks so you can do a little tour of them, I now know that this is a Raywood ash, and the very act of looking it up and writing it down means that next year I'll remember it and be prepared. Probably.

A bit further on, a row of good old London plane trees, which have, at long last, decided to join the party. Tentatively at first, but with increasing confidence, they're shedding their leaves. On the pavement at the bottom of the hill, where the road floods when it properly rains, I find a leaf so big you could put a microchip in it and call it an iPad. It's not just huge, but beautiful too, a deep matt green, yellowing at one corner, the edges curling slightly. I walk past it, and then, on the basis that something that size deserves wider recognition, turn back, bend down and pick it up. I take it home, photograph it (with a pound coin for scale) and leave it on the kitchen table, where it will sit until we embark on one of our semi-regular tidy-ups. We'll decide that we really don't need a desiccated plane leaf any more, and we'll release it into the garden, where it will break down into the general mulch and do its bit for the next generation.

Two black-headed gulls squabble low overhead as I climb the hill. A robin hops up onto a bench as I walk past, not three feet away – it cocks its head, decides I'm not worth bothering about, and hops away again. Blue tits fossick, parakeets squeal, a starling whistles at me from the top of a flagpole.

A busy day out and about.

The air in the woods is still, and just about warm enough. A squirrel scampers up a tree trunk, along a high branch, and leaps to the next tree. It's a long branch, and flexible, and for a moment it looks as if the squirrel's made a horrific misjudgement and is about to be twanged up into the canopy. But it's either fearless or stupid or just really confident, and the trampolining action of the long branch barely disrupts its progress. It holds on briefly, waits for the upswing, and uses the momentum to jump further into the foliage and out of my sight.

An explosion of sound from a low bush. *Tsib-a-tsab-a-tsoo-diddy-dabble-iddy-wodda-tsipp-a-brrrrr-tsip-tsip-tsip-tsip-tsip-tsip-tsip—tjop-tsrrrrrrrrrrrrrrrr—ts'tjupp-tjupp-tjupp-tjupp.**

Wren. The first I've heard in weeks. And what a boon it is, not least because the sheer energy of the sound is enough to raise my walking speed by twenty paces per minute. The song of a wren is far louder than something the size of a satsuma has any right to produce. It's somehow both full and piercing at the same time, and while my preferred name for the bird, 'tiny shouter', implies something primal and basic, there's enough complexity in there to warrant a happy hour or two slowing it down and sorting out exactly what's going on with each of its various elements.

I'm OK with bird sounds. Not tip-top, but OK. As with most things, I'm happiest with the familiar ones, so if it makes a sound

---

* Transliteration of bird sounds is famously fraught with difficulty, but if we're going to do it, we're going in with all guns blazing.

and is on my local patch, I'm fairly comfortable with identifying it most of the time.

I make an exception for the variety of short, high-pitched *tsi* or *tsip* or *tsiy* sounds I encounter from time to time, usually from the impenetrable depths of a bush. What I want then is for the bird in question to present itself on a branch near me, preferably wearing a prominent lapel badge with its name written in block capitals with a bright red Sharpie.

And I make an exception for the sound that sprints towards me from the other side of the woods as I leave.

Khraik.

Something like that, anyway.

Krraaaarrrk.

There it is again, a bit longer.

Krrrraaaaaaaaiiirrk.

It's not a magpie. Or is it? No. Yes? No. Too high-pitched for a carrion crow. Could be a jay, but it doesn't have the same timbre. The jay's shriek can sound like the air being ripped apart – this is more like someone scraping a stick very quickly across a corrugated surface.

What I want to say is that it sounds like a corncrake, but that's ridiculous, because corncrakes, if they hang out anywhere – and by and large they don't much these days, what with a population crash and a 76 per cent contraction of their range since 1970 – do not hang out in small pockets of urban woodland. Remote grasslands in the northwest of Scotland, yes; downtown Streatham, no. They say anything can turn up anywhere, so you can't rule anything out, but . . . no.

Krraaaarrk.

'Good boy. Stay!'

Ah yes. All is clear. I am foolish and deluded and a bear of no brain at all.

The dog-walker comes towards me, her spaniel straining at the retractable dog lead that she has shortened so as not to cause passers-by any undue consternation.

'Hello!'

'Hello.'

She lets the lead spool out.

Krrraaark.

OK then. Let us never speak of this incident again.

52

SOGGINESS PREVAILS

23–27 October

Frost falls (*Sōkō,* 霜降)
First frost
(*Shimo hajimete furu,* 霜始降)

The clocks go back. Ten is nine and six is five and by the time you've got up it's getting dark and time to go to bed.

The wisdom of renaming the hours twice a year is often questioned. It doesn't actually give us more daylight in the summer – we're just programmed to associate the numbers of the clock with the rhythms of our day. The difference is purely a matter of collective psychosis. Sunrise yesterday was at 7.42 a.m., which for many people feels like 'getting-up' time. Today it's at 6.44, which for those same people feels like 'snuggling back under the duvet' time. Two minutes later, but also fifty-eight minutes earlier. Schrödinger's time-keeping.

Whether you're for or against this biannual temporal lurch, the suddenness of the change goes against our instincts. We're used to incremental adjustment, the hours of daylight increasing and decreasing almost unnoticed – in-breath and out-breath, like slow-motion lungs. And then, twice a year, we get a jolt.

The temptation is to ignore it and trust the rhythms of the body. Hungry? Eat. Thirsty? Drink. Tired? Sleep. Dark outside? Duvet, drink, book. Our oven, resolutely telling the wrong time since a power cut back in April, has the right idea. It's still wrong, but by a different amount.

I use the extra hour wisely – asleep. There's not much to get up for, in any case. Dull and cloudy with light rain moving in from the west. I can do without one more hour of that. If last season set the standard for changeable, blustery dampness, this one merely takes that as a benchmark and vows to beat it, like a long jumper whose deadliest rival has just set a new world record. The frost of the equivalent Japanese microseason is a distant prospect. I would, in fact, pay good money for some. Late October in Japan might historically be a time of burgeoning cold, but here we're treated to the kind of sogginess that gives England a bad name.

But when I do leave the house, the air is warm enough to make being outside a generally pleasant experience, and my slow lap of the cemetery is enhanced by an extended and intimate encounter with the cemetery fox – the male with the bushy tail and the small black mark on the left side of its mouth.

Maybe it's lonely. Maybe it yearns for human contact. Maybe I just exude a mixture of trustworthiness and magnetic charm.

Or maybe it's just hungry and knows humans are a soft touch.

Whatever the reason, it holds its ground. More than that, it approaches, albeit warily.

It's known to be tame, this fox. While my encounters with it have largely been conducted from a respectful distance, there are those – people armed with Tupperware tubs of food scraps and the patience to sit around for a while in the hope the fox will gravitate towards them – who entice it closer. A couple of days ago I saw a man sitting on a bench, the fox almost at his feet like a pet dog. It was a touching little scene, the barriers between the species broken down by the fulfilling of mutual needs – food for the fox, company for the human.

This intimacy would be unthinkable for anyone familiar with countryside foxes. The boldness of the urban fox is light years from the skulking behaviour of its country cousin. Their scavenging habits might make themselves unpopular in certain quarters – 'bastard's crapped in the border again' – and they present the same threat to chicken runs wherever they live, but the general attitude towards them in town seems to be one of benevolence. And while their lives aren't entirely free of danger, the one thing an urban fox doesn't have to worry about is that it will be chased down the A23 by a baying mob of hounds and red-jacketed humans on horseback.

No doubt that confidence has something to do with this fox's willingness to let me come close. There's a quietness to it as it stands on the path in front of me, an unconcerned patience. I'm not quite sure whether it's come towards me in expectation of food, but if so, it will be disappointed. What food I do have about my person – a KitKat and a packet of cheese and onion crisps – I have selfishly reserved for my own consumption. In any case, the KitKat's off the menu for the fox – like all chocolate, it contains theobromine, which is indigestible for canids, and therefore potentially dangerous.

Seconds pass, then minutes, and the fox shows no inclination to leave my company. I stay still, adopting a half-interested attitude to it. Yeah, you're nice enough, fox, but I'm not really that bothered.

This seems to work. It sits on the path next to me, does a bit of a stretchy yawn, stands, sits again.

This intimacy is a delicate privilege. Non-human animals have good reason to fear us. When they lower their guard and allow us into their sphere, it creates a bond – fragile, perhaps, and possibly perceived as such only by us, but a bond nonetheless. Sometimes these are brief moments, a mistake almost, and the animal is off before we've even registered them, the first sign of their presence the clatter of hooves, a rustling in the undergrowth, the clap of wings against foliage.

This close, no further.

But when they allow that invisible barrier to be breached, and when that breach is willingly maintained, specialness is in the air.

So I take it as the privilege it should be, and relish the time we spend in quiet acceptance of each other's company.

It can't last. After a couple of minutes the fox stirs itself, looks around, gives another stretchy yawn, and then, with the faint disappointment redolent of a dog that has just been denied walkies, but without the overacting, it trots quietly off down the path, hangs right into the trees, and disappears from my sight.

53

SPIDERS APPEAR IN SHEDS

28 October–1 November

Frost falls (*Sōkō*, 霜降)
Light rains sometimes fall
(*Kosame tokidoki furu*, 霎時施)

Yes, light rains do sometimes fall, as do heavy ones. And then there are the occasional torrential downpours, the kind that feel like some sort of endurance test.

I'm out when it hits, far enough from home to render futile any dash for safety. Whichever way you slice it, I'm going to get very wet. And then a bit wetter. And then wetter still.

My mind has to make a gear change to accommodate the idea, a feat it accomplishes with a fair amount of gear-grinding and clutch-slipping. But, once achieved, it's difficult to dissuade it from the feeling that wetness is an entirely desirable state of being. Aspirational even. It's such an effective tactic that even when the pharmacy, the focus of my expedition, turns out to be closed, the disappointment barely registers as a dent in my generally euphoric mood.

This embracing of discomfort is a neat trick if you can pull it off. I'm not always able to, which makes the semi-smug feeling when I do manage it all the more satisfying. As the damp seeps through my shoes and into my socks, and as my trousers cling to my legs like a needy toddler, I begin to understand what it must feel like to be an otter. But I nevertheless maintain a healthy pace and upbeat demeanour. Tempting as it might be, though, I don't burst into a song-and-dance routine. You have to draw the line somewhere.

In among it all, as I tramp the backstreets to the accompaniment of dripping sounds and squelchy feelings, a thin tinkling reaches my ears, so quiet and distant I at first take it for an audio mirage. I stop and listen. Definitely a tinkling sound, incongruously perky in the pervading gloom. Almost mindlessly so, you might say.

Somewhere up there is a goldfinch, and it doesn't give two tinkles about wetness. It's the mistle thrush that is known as the 'stormcock' for its habit of singing through the rain, but on this showing the goldfinch might give it a good run for its money. You could swear it was celebrating. In a person, this kind of oblivious optimism might be taken one of two ways – either as an energis-ing example of the power of simple-minded positive thought, or as an irritating grump-inducer. But the song of the goldfinch is so innocent I allow myself to be carried along by it. I could imagine it to be singing in defiance of the rain, a goldfinchy V-sign to dreich. But that kind of anthropomorphism sets a dangerous precedent, the logical endpoint of which is calling your garden robin 'floofles' and talking to woodlice.

Scanning a tree for a goldfinch in a downpour is like a soaking wet *Where's Wally?*, but somehow, for reasons that pass understand-ing, it's much more fun. It does carry with it one notable hazard, but the added stream of water the action induces is more than offset by the pleasure I feel when I finally locate the bird, distinguishing its miniature outline from the surrounding foliage by a kind of elimination process. Not a goldfinch, not a goldfinch, not a goldfinch – GOLDFINCH!

And just as I make that breakthrough, the tinkling stops and off it bounces, over my head and out of my life.

I wouldn't normally venture to the shed in the heaving rain, but the specific tool I need for a long-delayed household chore isn't to be found anywhere in the house, so to the shed I must go.

As I squelch my way down the garden, I note that the Race To Yellow has taken a dramatic turn. The robinia, whether as a concession to its opponent or as a premature declaration of victory, has decided to shed a good proportion of its leaves. So the garden is now festooned with a patchy yellow carpet, and none the less pretty for it.

The shed doesn't have the tool I want, but while I'm there I find myself looking in corners and nooks, curious to see what opportunistic creatures might have made their home there.

I don't have to look for long.

Nicely ensconced in an angle by the window is a tiny scuttler with slender dark legs protruding from a glossy two-tone body, the dark brown interlaced with beige lines. I don't know much about spiders, but my best guess for this one is that it's one of the six false widow spider species regularly seen in the UK.

Such loaded words, 'false widow spider'. Type them into an average Facebook group and prepare to be overwhelmed with hysterical comments. Type them into the Natural History Museum website's search engine, on the other hand, as I do later that day, and you might find a more balanced appraisal.

Yes, false widow spiders are venomous. Yes, they have been known to bite humans. But (and there is always a 'but') to leap from those two plain facts to frothing hysteria about 'DEADLY SPIDERS IN YOUR SHED' betrays a lack of even the most basic scrutiny. Because the actual danger of suffering anything worse than discomfort from a false widow spider is slim.

There are sound evolutionary reasons to be wary of spiders. Our ancestors were surrounded by them, and there was always the possibility that a bite would lead to serious illness or death. While this is no longer true to anything like the same extent (and particularly not in Britain, where the threat they pose to human health is so negligible as to be barely worth mentioning), their status as the most loathsome of creepy-crawlies is so deeply entrenched that there seems little hope of reversing it. The truth is that despite the insistence by arachnophiles that they're harmless little cutebundles, to arachnophobes they are – and will always remain – monsters.

And yes, just in case you were thinking I'm freakishly nonchalant about them, I do, just like anyone else, give a little start and possibly even a yelp when I come across one unexpectedly.

This one isn't yelpworthy, and seems quite content with my looming presence. I'm careful not to disturb it, while at the same time getting close enough to admire for a few seconds its cryptic colouring. Then we go about our respective businesses.

54

AUTUMN DAYS SOMETIMES ATTAIN PERFECTION

2–6 November

Frost falls (*Sōkō*, 霜降)

Maple leaves and ivy turn yellow
(*Momiji tsuta kibamu*, 楓蔦黄)

It's bletting season. Good word, bletting – I'd use it more often, given the chance. But it's a specialised term, and in use at only a certain time of year. This time of year, to be precise.

Bletting is what happens to certain kinds of fruit – medlars, quinces and persimmons among others – when they're left to ripen beyond what might seem good sense. Leave a pear to go squishy and you're best throwing it on the compost; let a quince do the same and you might want to grab a spoon and eat it. If, that is, you can get past its offputting appearance. A raw quince looks like an out-sized, slightly bulbous apple, and a fresh and sprightly one at that. You might even be tempted to take a bite. But only once. The tart astringency of a raw quince is enough to put off even the most daring of palates. Once bletted, though, it makes up for its unattractive appearance with a distinctive and alluring taste. Sweet and sticky, with a hint of dates. An epicure's delight.

There's a quincefall at the allotment. Rather than wait for the bletting to take hold, I opt for the quick fix. Heat, water, sugar, more heat. A bit of lemon juice. The deep rose colour of the resulting jelly is always a surprise, but one satisfying to the senses. And the process of making it brings calm, as any kitchen activity can when you have the luxury of regarding it as a pleasure rather than a chore. And, most important, by taking advantage of the fruit's seasonality I feel that little bit more connected to the world that produced it.

Excellent with cheese too.

The first two days of this season we consign to the bin. Cloud, wind, rain. Same old nonsense. But day three is the one. All those other 'perfect autumn days' turned out merely to be warm-up acts. Because this one, this cool, crisp genius of a day, is what it's all about.

It dawns bright and clear, and a sprinkling of frost on the shed roof – the merest dusting, but frost nonetheless – bears witness to the drop in temperature. As if to foreshadow the kind of day it's going to be, ten goldfinches bounce in as I wait for the tea to brew, landing in the top of the robinia, where they're clearly visible in its newly stripped branches. No, hang on, not ten. Twenty, at least. Thirty now. Make that thirty-five.

What I'm trying to say is that there are quite a few of them, arriving in straggly groups of five or so, then almost immediately flying off again the moment they've assembled. Perhaps they've come to reassure me that I'm not alone, that everything's going to be fine.

Whatever the reason, the tree is, however briefly, alive with gold-finches, and it's the best start to a day I've had in weeks.

The much-vaunted spectrum of autumnal leaf colours – all the browns, yellows, oranges and reds from gold to vermilion, mustard to carmine – has been impressive enough thus far, but dull skies have muted their vibrancy. Now, illuminated by a sun that never has a chance to get high in the sky, and which as a result produces a special kind of light for reasons that a scientist or a photographer will be able to explain better than me, they're shouting. WE ARE AUTUMN; BEHOLD OUR MAGNIFICENCE.

This energy is made all the more valuable for knowing you have less time to enjoy it. Those eternal summer days, when you feel as if you have all the time in the world to do whatever takes your fancy or nothing at all, are a distant memory now. And with that crucial hour gone – or at least apparently so – all the more reason to get up and out – come on, get off that phone, I'm not going to tell you twice – and soak up all that precious vitamin D.

This is definitely a day, once all the tedious business of life is taken care of, for a long walk. It'll be the kind of walk that brings a glow to the cheeks, and in among the background jibber-jabber there will be dashing starlings and insistent parakeets. Perhaps the shriek of a jay will rend the air. Perhaps it won't. But it will barely matter. Because it'll be enough just to be outside, energised by the crispness of the day, enjoying the sharp play of light and shade, the long slender shadows of trees backlit by a low sun. There might be the faint whiff of woodsmoke, because somebody, somewhere, probably in defiance of a couple of dozen statutes and by-laws, has lit a bonfire. And while of course we're all aware that woodsmoke, when taken in the context of its role in respiratory diseases, is a Bad Thing, it also feels like an Autumn Thing, so the faintest scent of it in the nostrils will, on this occasion, be welcome.

If I time it right, I will reach the cemetery just in time for the Golden Moment – the ten minutes or so shortly before sunset when the sun illuminates the trees and gravestones on the west-facing downslope in a way that could inspire symphonies, and the only reasonable response is to gasp quietly and then stand there and let it fill you like a mindfulness exercise. And there will be crumpets afterwards, leaving a pool of melted butter on the plate which I will scrape up with my index finger, and probably hot chocolate.

Later there will be stars, pinpricks on ink, and I will don layers and gloves and a comical hat and I will stand outside and get a crick in my neck as I peer up into the sky to see if I can find Orion and the Plough and possibly Mars (these are the ones I know) while, not for the first time, wishing I lived in a dark-sky area like Kielder National Park or the Orkneys or Antarctica or somewhere.

And if the reality can't live up to this imagined ideal, the amalgam of all great autumn days – how could it? – and if the walk is blighted by traffic and inconsiderate pedestrians and a dog that looks very much as if it's going to bite the bejesus out of me but thankfully veers away at the last minute, then that's all by the bye.

55

BRACKEN TURNS
TO BRONZE

7–11 November

Beginning of winter (*Rittō*, 立冬)
Camellias bloom
(*Tsubaki hajimete hiraku*, 山茶始開)

Slowly comes the change. Winter, according to *Game of Thrones*,* is coming. But this year, in this place, it is taking its time. The old Japanese calendar moves to a different rhythm, and while there have been times when the misalignment has been imperceptible, seeing the word 'winter' this early is a sign of how out of kilter it can be.

According to the meteorological seasons, winter isn't due until 1 December; follow the astronomical calendar and it's three weeks after that. And while average temperatures in November in this part of the world drop by about 4 degrees from relatively balmy October,

---

* I have never watched an episode of *Game of Thrones* – not to be perverse in the face of popular culture, just because I've had other things to do. But you pick things up.

the coldest months – the single-figure months – are December to February.

The air remains mild, temperatures hovering in the low teens during the day, and never threatening the zero mark at night. Medium-level cloud is the default, but day one is clear, and as I stand outside assessing the current state of things, a welcome visitor flies in.

I've thought of the Streatham mistle thrushes often. In the height of spring their breeding progress was one of my main pre-occupations, and the anticlimax of their failure cast a pall over the proceedings of that particular microseason.

It's impossible to know if this mistle thrush, upright and alert, is one of them, but regardless of its status in my avian back catalogue, I am at the very least glad to add it to the 'seen perching on the conifer two doors down' list.

That tree – a few feet taller than a three-storey house, and there-fore the tallest in the immediate vicinity – is a popular perch for birds of all sizes. In spring there's stiff competition between the songbirds for that top spot. Occasionally a carrion crow will barge in, give five rhythmic barks like a reversing truck, then fly off again. But I'll be pushed to top the prize sighting a couple of years ago, an itinerant sparrowhawk, all stillness and menace, surveying the neighbourhood with its yellow eye. For half an hour on that spring day, the habitual hubbub of small-bird chatter shut down entirely – the silence of terror.

The mistle thrush, not renowned as a gobbler of small birds, inspires no such reaction, although were it to fly down and start rootling around on the lawn, no doubt it would send tremors both literal and metaphorical through our thriving earthworm community.

It leaves after a couple of minutes. Birds tend to do that. I wish they wouldn't.

There's a little path in the cemetery, out of the way and easy to miss. It feels like my own little secret place. It winds its way down through the gravestones, narrow and unpaved, occasionally offering outstanding opportunities to slip and fall and bash my head. I accordingly watch my step, especially at this time of year, when, after the first flush of excitement, many of the autumn leaves are beyond the glamour stage and morphing into treacherous slime. A heavy leaf fall, combined with seasonal precipitation, turns walking down the slightest incline into a heady adventure, fraught with danger. And this path, plastered with leaves, is more than the slightest incline. My youthful surefootedness, all blithe and airy confidence that no matter what happens I'll stay upright, is a distant memory, so there's a strong case for arguing I shouldn't attempt it. But I do like this path. It offers a different view of the expanse of cemetery below, and as human traffic is relatively sporadic there's a good chance of getting friendly with a long-tailed tit or great spotted woodpecker – an outcome never to be scoffed at.

There are no tits; nor are there woodpeckers. But there is solace in the form of bracken. A good spreader, is bracken. Too good, really. It'll take over if you give it half a chance, and the enlightened folk at the cemetery, in this small patch where the graves are long past family visits, have done exactly that, its fractal fronds spreading copiously. The effect is especially attractive at this time of year, when the low ground cover turns from fresh green to burnished bronze, and the late-afternoon sun, choosing that exact moment to bless us with its watery presence, brings an added dimension.

I move on from the bracken, walking carefully, but no matter how measured my tread I can't avoid putting the wind up a wood pigeon. And one wood pigeon with the wind up it tends to start a chain reaction.

The first bird goes, its wings clattering as it bursts from the depths of a tree up ahead. It's immediately followed by a small covey of them from the same tree – about ten birds, of whose existence I had been blissfully unaware. And now there's an explosion, pigeons appearing from all parts of this little corner, and dispersing to some-where, anywhere, it doesn't matter as long as they're away from me and the unidentified danger I bring. They're not to know I come in peace. The noise they make is arresting, a brouhaha of wing claps and disturbed foliage not entirely dissimilar to a dozen brooms fall-ing out of a cupboard onto a parquet floor.

They do this deliberately. A wood pigeon is perfectly capable of flying up from a tree in silence. Admittedly, if you're close enough, you can discern the faint but distinct whistling of their wings – *wheeoo-wheeoo-wheeoo* – as they part the air, but this sound is of a different order. It's a handy way of telling any other wood pigeons in the vicinity that there's potential trouble afoot without going to the bother of shouting, 'There's potential trouble afoot!' And it has the added benefit that while warning their congeners to get the hell out of there, they are at the same time leading by example, and them-selves getting the hell out of there.

It's a sound to behold. Ten, then twenty, then apparently up to a hundred wood pigeons flying through a small wood of medium density. It could almost whizz me back in time a few decades to my childhood, if I weren't concentrating so hard on not coming a cropper on the Path of Treacherous Leaves.

Nostalgia ain't what it used to be.

56

STARLINGS WHIZZ AROUND IN GROUPS

12–16 November

Beginning of winter (*Rittō*, 立冬)
Land starts to freeze
(*Chi hajimete kōru*, 地始凍)

The land won't start to freeze any time soon.

Temperatures remain resolutely mild, to mutterings from the gardening and botany communities. It's not right, it's too warm, things are flowering when they shouldn't.

They have a point. Climate change shows its colours in different ways, and the erosion of the winters we used to know is just one of them. But take any single day's weather in isolation, away from the wider context, and it's possible – important, even – to appreciate it for what it is, to live in the moment. Climate is climate; weather is weather.

And this season the weather is Typically British, by which I mean predictably unpredictable. The rain, the wind, the sunny interludes. As so often, when planning excursions, timing is all, and it's in one of the interludes that I come across a pocket of house sparrows, out of sight behind a thick hedge, babbling exuberantly to themselves in sparrowese. I thought I knew all the sparrow pockets in the neighbourhood, but it's good to come across a new one. And even though I can't see them, that in its own way adds something to the encounter, as if I were eavesdropping on an important meeting through a closed door.

Sparrows are bringers of cheer, their constant chatter denoting a sense of community I'm sure we could learn from. They're local birds, seldom straying far from home, and forming loose colonies to which they are largely loyal. A sense of the hierarchy within these colonies can be gleaned from examining the plumage of the males – the larger and blacker their bib, the higher up the ladder they are.

As if prompted by the thought, a male sparrow pops up to the top of the hedge. To judge by the sparseness of its bib, it's an intern, chosen by the others to do the dirty work. I greet it with a breezy 'hello' – while some might blush with shame to confess this wilful anthropomorphising, I regard it merely as the most basic politeness. It chirps at me and is gone with a flick of the tail, no doubt delivering a favourable report about my manners and general presentation.

No sooner have I bid the sparrows a fond farewell than my attention is caught by the sound of eighty – I'm guessing – fast wings. I look round just in time to see a small flock of starlings swoosh past at roof height. They hold their shape, well coordinated. Movement within the flock is minimal, a matter of a small undulation within the general formation. But now there's a disruption. With a startled, angry outburst of outraged squawking, two birds tumble out of the pack, their momentum disrupted. Perhaps one of them, in a moment of un-starling-like behaviour, has clipped the wings of the other. Or maybe it said something uncomplimentary about the other's grand-mother. Whatever the reason, they engage in a brief, agitated mid-air scrap, rolling around in a manner reminiscent of a bar-room brawl, yet somehow managing not to plunge to the ground, before settling their differences and scurrying to catch up with the rest of the flock.

Another day, another walk.

Rain has been and gone. Wind, squally and petulant, has calmed, and now there's a vibrant energy in the air, enough to bring on an almost unconscious quickening of pace.

A principal contributor to this energy is sound, which after all is nothing more than vibrating air. A walk round the cemetery punctu-ated only by the muted mutters and chirps of a handful of songbirds has one kind of energy; throw in a bevy of parakeets and it's a differ-ent story. And today is all about the parakeets.

Wherever I go in the cemetery, there's a chance that these birds will be the dominant feature. Rare is the visit that isn't enlivened at some point by a low-level parakeet whizz-by or a protracted tree-top squabble. I can scan the canopy, uncertain whether there are great tits or blue tits or goldfinches up there until what I thought was a branch detaches itself from the tree and zips off with a *tseep*. But if there's a parakeet around, I generally know about it all along. They are obvious birds. And while their exotic colouring and brash squawking seems at odds with the understated British way of life, they've made themselves at home here, and in many areas are now part of the furniture.

Although I've seen them everywhere in the cemetery, their favoured haunt is the dying ash tree that dominates the main path. The massive bracket fungus, once large and stable enough for a squirrel to sit on, is withering and blackening. It now cuts a forlorn, shrivelled figure against the grey-green bark of the ash, and a stark contrast to the vivid green of the parakeet sitting on a branch just above it.

Afforded a close view, I realise there's a bit more to its appearance than first meets the eye. While the body of the bird, from domed crown to long, stiff tail, is a more or less uniform pale green, with the stark contrast of a short, hooked, bright red-pink beak, on closer examination you see that this colouring is matched by a delicate, slender eye ring, and, in the male, a paler echo across the nape. There's black too – a slender collar opening up to a denser bib, and the tiniest of threads running from eye to bill.

I catch this bird in contemplative mode. It seems to have completed its bombing-around duties for the day, or is at least taking a break. And while its three companions in the branches above it are continuing with their squabbling and general raucousness, it maintains a relatively calm demeanour.

This expression, 'relatively calm demeanour', comes with the caveat that parakeets don't seem to do calm. There's always something going on. As the other birds fly off for another lap, taking their shrieks with them, it becomes clear what the 'something' is.

This parakeet seems to be talking to itself. The familiar screeches are replaced with a soft burbling, a progression of quiet squeaks and mews and sighs – endearing, intimate sounds that serve to break down the impression of the bird as a hooligan and replace it with something softer, more sympathetic.

It breaks the spell with a piercing *squaaaarr*, and flies off over my head for another lap.

It's almost as if it heard me thinking.

57

PLANE TREES SPROUT SEED HEADS

17–21 November

Beginning of winter (*Rittō,* 立冬)
Daffodils bloom (*Kinsenka saku,* 金盞香)

The sky is greyer than a pencil lead convention. What with the mud and the slimy leaves and the subdued light, there's something a bit dispiriting about it all. The slow slide into winter can easily do that. No matter how much you cling to the knowledge that this time of regression is a necessary part of the annual cycle, that without retreat there can be no advance, it's the reality of it that bites. Autumn gave us the warmth of new colours, visible change to keep us interested. But now we enter the time of year when most things are drab. Nature is in recession. And when you crave colour to stimulate the senses and awaken the spirits, these can be difficult times.

There are exceptions. There always are.

In the garden, a cosmos has collapsed under the weight of its bright pink blooms and leans drunkenly across the lawn; nearer the house, appearing as if from nowhere, pert and pale green with the faintest hint of pink on one side, the first hazel catkins. Early they might be, but they're a sign that even in the depths of glum, with winter stretching ahead, something somewhere is growing.

The plane trees near the bus stop have shed their leaves, and now their dark seed heads are silhouetted against a dull sky. Christmas tree baubles, a few weeks early. The pavement is narrow here, and you could get all 'letters-to-the-council' about it, complain that the trees are misplaced, too big for the available space, cramping an already bottlenecked passageway, their roots constituting a trip hazard. But in truth the inconvenience here is slight, and the benefits they bring outweigh any potential downside. Street trees are an important part of any city landscape, and the London plane, staple of parks and thoroughfares since it was planted in great numbers in the late nineteenth century, is London's archetype.

Long-lived and resilient, they manage to combine height with elegance, their open canopies allowing light through and not stifling the street below. On smaller streets they've been pollarded to keep them in check, and the result, to my eyes, is rather stunted, especially at this time of year, when the stumps are denuded of their softening foliage. But given space to breathe, they're a magnificent tree, if so ubiquitous that Londoners tend to take them for granted. Whether the Victorians knew how long they'd last when they planted them with such enthusiasm is anyone's guess. But survive they have, and in such abundance that they've become a defining feature of London's cityscape.

Part of the secret to their success is the resilience born of hybridisation – they're a cross between two trees from opposite points of the compass, the occidental plane and the oriental plane. Their distinctive bark – overlapping plates in shades of grey, brown and khaki that give the trunk a hint of camouflage gear – makes identification much easier for the tree-illiterate, even in winter. It falls away in large flakes on a regular basis, taking with it any build-up of pollution.

I stop for a few seconds and look at the bark, almost consciously slowing myself down, determined all of a sudden not to be casual about it but to look a little more closely, no matter how strange it might seem to passers-by.

Am I the bird guy? Yes. But also, just occasionally, I'm the tree guy.

Another day, another walk. Bubble of goldfinch; squawk of parakeet; trot of fox. Reliable and welcome constants, touchstones of normality helping me through the winter.

For the first time for a few weeks, my cemetery walk is unaccompanied by the darting flight of redwings. Maybe they're off on a day trip, or maybe they're just lying low in another part of the cemetery.

By way of compensation, there is the faintest snatch of goldcrest song, one of those occasional winter treats that makes the ears perk up and induces prematurely optimistic thoughts of spring. It's the kind of sound you can easily miss – so high, so fleeting. I move closer to the suspected source, cock my head, and adopt a concentrating demeanour. At that moment, from a nearby garden, the piercing whine of an angle grinder starts up, obliterating any possibility of aural nature observation.

My irritation at the mechanical interruption is born of pure selfishness. These noises are part of life in the city. Silence is a pipe dream. But tranquillity is one of the benefits of this place. As I walk through the gates, leaving the high street behind me, I can feel the bustle recede, and my brisk pace slows, almost unconsciously, until I'm sauntering rather than walking. Most of the sounds I hear as I stroll round are sounds of nature, so the intrusion of the outside world is doubly unwelcome.

I leave it behind and continue. There's a nip in the air, and a hint of drizzle from uniform low grey cloud. By the crematorium, a group of mourners, hunched into their unglad rags, shivering, smoking, laughing. I always feel awkward when I stumble on such gatherings. This is an open, public space – but it's also a working crematorium. When my daily exercise intersects with the business of the place, I feel like an intruder, the crass tourist stumbling all over a sacred shrine. So I veer away, sidle off down through the trees, where a lone singing robin gives my detour a bittersweet, melancholy tinge, and leave them to it.

Another day, another walk.

What a difference the light makes. Yesterday all was drab; today the sun illuminates the same world, brings it to life. Yesterday, I wouldn't have noticed the golden-brown fungus squeezing out of a tiny gap in a tree trunk, crusty and chewy as a Yorkshire pudding; nor the little line of four mushrooms a bit further on, lined up like a band posing for an album cover, their bronze caps somehow triggering memories of the 'Tetley tea folk' advert from the 1970s;* nor would I have stopped in the woods just to be still and let myself be enveloped by the quiet energy of the place, the wind stirring the canopy just enough to provide a calming, gently undulating soundtrack.

Yesterday was a day for moving on; today is a day for lingering.

So I linger.

---

* You had to be there.

58

LEAVES LIE THICK
ON THE GRASS

22–26 November

Lesser snow (*Shōsetsu,* 小雪)
Rainbows hide
(*Niji kakurete miezu,* 虹蔵不見)

The sky is torn. It's a gentle breach – soft sheets of unthreatening, mid-level cloud, grey below, white above, separated by a streak of light blue. It's reminiscent of *kintsugi* – 'golden joinery' – the Japanese art of repair, using lacquer and powdered gold or silver to make a virtue of an honest repair rather than trying to cover it up.

Matching its benevolence, the day is mild and still. The peregrines are out, perched on the corner gargoyles high on the church tower, their outline clearly visible if you happen to be looking for them. I'm getting better at picking them out from a distance. I know the shape of the stonework now, where and how the shadows fall depending on the light and time of day. And if there's a disturbance in that particular matrix, it jumps out at me in a way unimaginable before I started this project of repeated observation.

They're still there, patient and motionless, as I begin my lap of the cemetery. Clockwise or anticlockwise? Clockwise, recently, for some reason. It soon brings me to Doulton Path, fringed by the tall trees where the wood pigeons roost, and it's along that path that I find today's greatest pleasure. Leaves, dense and floofy, carpet the full length of it. If there's anything better than a good shin-deep shruffle through fresh leaf-fall, then I'm not sure I want to know about it. It's the autumn equivalent of allowing your toes to sink wetly into the sand while paddling on the shoreline on a summer holiday. A simple, evocative pleasure, recalling the perfect moments of childhood, and acting, on this occasion, like a miniature time machine.

I'm accompanied as I go by the usual chitterings of the small birds in the branches above me, and, from afar, the mocking laughter of a green woodpecker.

I do two lengths, wading through the leaves and relishing the feel of them against my ankles, their flutteriness, the soothing quality of their yellows and oranges and browns. The light is soft, the air warm enough. All, for just a few minutes, is well.

Up at the woods the next morning, it's a different story. Freshness in the air, a light frost, a feeling of winter. About time.

And the light – crikey, the light. It renders everything spectacular. Instagram on a plate. You could take a photo of dog shit and it would look amazing.

I don't do that, but I do spend some time ogling the shafts of sunlight slanting through the trees, the way it lights up the bracken as if from within, the general peachiness of the whole ensemble. You know the routine.

And there's noise in the air. A nuthatch *p-pock-pock-puh-pock-pock-pop-ock*-ing from an unspecified branch above; jays, shrieking it up like fishwives from the far corner; the inevitable squadron of parakeets, trying to outdo them. And as I come around the corner, I hear a sound I haven't heard for months. Short, strident phrases, repeated for the hard of thinking.

That's the wise thrush.

For most birds November isn't a time for singing. Robins, which do it nearly all year round, are the main exception, and you might hear the machine-gun burst of a wren from the undergrowth at pretty much any time, but most birds sensibly save their energy for when they really need to catch the attention of their potential mates. The sounds of the nuthatch and the jays and the parakeets – these are warning sounds or contact calls or sometimes just an announcement to the world of some kind.

But this is song.

These bright and clear early winter days are just the kind of thing to prompt a song thrush into full voice. Not peak season, but getting ready for it.

It's a habit now. Hear the song, look for the bird. Fail to find the bird, cock the head, assume a perplexed air, look again. Walk back a few yards, realise the error of your ways, start looking again, but in a completely different tree. And there it is, obvious once you know.

The rewards of birding can seem elusive. To the layperson, it might seem as if a lot of time is spent freezing your nadgers off while peering into the depths of a bush in the hope that a small khaki-feathered arse will appear for a nanosecond – and it's easy to see that the appeal of such an activity might seem limited.

But when a bird decides to make itself really obvious, standing on a prominent perch and making a racket as if to say, 'Here! I'm here! And boy have I got something to tell the world' – well, it would take an act of will not to stop and allow yourself to be transported by it. And here we are, on the cusp of winter, after what might easily be described as A Bit of a Year. It's almost as if the song thrush was sent to deliver a boost just when we need it most – a sample of what we have in store once we get to the other side.

No doubt there are solid scientific reasons for the effect this sound has on me. Something to do with connections in the brain, the production of quantifiable amounts of certain chemicals. And no doubt for many people it's something they might not even be aware of, just a background sound that has, as far as they're concerned, nothing to do with their mood. But without getting too 'the stars are God's daisy chain' about it, all I can say is that after five minutes of simply standing still in the presence of this bird, I feel better.

Would I go so far as to say it sparks joy?

I would.

Home, then, to a sky as dramatic as the morning's was soft. Tinged by the setting sun, lurid streaks of orange, yellow and purple, with a topping of deep grey. The kind of sky it's impossible to ignore. As art, it would be laughable; in real life, it's spectacular. The voice of the song thrush in visual form.

59

EVENINGS DRAW IN

27 November–1 December

Lesser snow (*Shōsetsu,* 小雪)
North wind blows the leaves from the trees
(*Kitakaze konoha o harau,* 朔風払葉)

If autumnal melancholy has varying shades, this season's feels like the benevolent kind. It's as if the resistance to winter's onset has caved in, and now I can embrace it, allow it to be what it is. Perhaps it's the chill in the air on the first morning – proper chill, demanding hat and gloves – and its accompanying brightness. Reassurance that there will be winter, there will be cold, we won't be forever stuck in the mild damp of perpetual autumn.

And meanwhile the trees go about their business.

One of the advantages of the louring grey clouds, looming grumpy behind the house, is to show up the yellowness of the leaves. The silver birches out front have been turning for some time now, but the contrast against the 7B pencil sky highlights it dramatically. It's not entirely clear where the light is coming from, but the delicate leaves seem to glow highlighter-yellow from within.

In the back garden the hazel catkins play the same trick, their pale freshness lighting up their little patch. And the cemetery now resembles the combined aftermath of a ticker-tape parade and a particularly exuberant wedding. The leaves are everywhere, even the most recalcitrant of the deciduous trees throwing in their lot with the rest of them.

One tree won't be shedding its leaves any time soon. On the little triangle of pavement in front of the church, hemmed in by its own low white picket fence and adorned with symmetrically placed and uniform-coloured baubles, the West Norwood Community Christmas Tree has appeared from nowhere.

The picket fence makes all the difference. Without it, the tree might seem bare and rather bleak. It's lower than knee height, so looks slightly as if it's been stolen from a Hornby railway set, but while it's useless as a physical deterrent to vandalism, it does send a message to passers-by that the tree is to be respected, as well as lending it a certain small-town charm.

But mostly it's a reminder of where we are in the year. Nearly there. Nearly there.

Another visit to the shed, this time on a quest for an Important Box of Papers. I've searched in the house, knowing deep down that they're not there but not wanting to squelch my way down the garden before I've tried literally every other possibility at least four times. It would have been quicker and easier to go to the shed in the first place, but human behaviour is rarely logical.

The shed is not warm. But at least the energy I expend moving things around in my quest for the box keeps the worst chill at bay.

And sure enough I find it, exactly where I knew it would be. Relief is tempered by the prospect of dealing with it, because the papers, while Important, are also Extremely Tedious.

I delay the inevitable by having a rootle around. Maybe there'll be an overwintering butterfly, or another spider.

There are neither of those things. Instead, I find a nest.

It's papery, nestled in the rafters, about the size of a snooker ball, yellowish brown with a grey tinge – matching the bare wood of the shed ceiling. My instinct tells me that it's the nest of something buzzy. Probably a wasp. But my knowledge of this area is scant, so I take a photograph and throw myself on the mercy of Twitter, where people know everything, even when they don't.

The replies are a mixture of baldly factual ('wasps'), informative ('some kind of wasp, but whether they return to it and how aggressive they are depends entirely on the species'), hyperbolically comedic ('burn the place down and move to Antarctica'), and hostile ('anyone saying leave it alone is INSANE – the fuckers will sting you and your family – MULTIPLE TIMES').

People offering their opinions is nothing new. That's just human nature, and particularly Twitter nature. And I could get downhearted about the instinctive reaction of many people to destroy first and ask questions later, if at all. But I'm uplifted by one reply, which extols the beauty and symmetry of the nest's construction, while also emphasising the admirable 'live and let live' philosophy of most wasp species.

'Savour it. It's probably the most beautifully made thing in that shed, including the shed.'

I suspect it was written by a wasp.

✗

I've allowed the day to run away from me, and by the time I get myself together for a walk up to the common, dusk is making its presence felt. How easily it creeps up on us. Sunset is now before four, and the expression 'the evenings are drawing in' can safely be deployed. Late-afternoon buttered crumpets and hot chocolate will soon be a necessity rather than an optional extra.

There's a subdued bustle about the place. Dog-walkers, getting the last outing in before the light goes; the odd jogger.

I get myself away from street lights and sit. The bench has a slight dampness to it, but not enough to deter me. Hanging on the corner post, a child's navy blue bobble hat. If it were on the wearer's head, its angle would be described as 'jaunty', but here it's rather forlorn.

As the minutes pass, I find myself not moving. This is mildly unusual. My instinct is not to stop unless there's a pressing reason to, and a chilly November afternoon doesn't really constitute a pressing reason. But there's something about this spot, quiet and unpeopled, that makes me stay for just one more minute, then one more, then another still.

It's the light. Not only is it absolutely spectacular, it's changing by the minute as the sun sets. Purples, golds, yellows, reds, pinks. The works. Full sunset psychedelia, unfolding before me.

But even as the light show calms down and twilight unfolds in a more understated, less dramatic way, I stay there. Come for the fireworks; stay for the gloaming.

The whole process, through the three stages of twilight – civil, nautical and astronomical – takes around two hours. Most of the time it's like looking at the minute hand of a clock from a distance. Individual movements are imperceptible, but it still moves anyway. And then there's that moment, after a few minutes without apparent change, when you notice the light shifting, as if the hand controlling the dimmer switch has suffered a small spasm. And before I know it, shapes are indistinct, the nervous chippings of hidden robins have quietened, and I'm all alone in the London night.

Distant siren, roar of motorbike.

It would be nice to hear an owl.

I do not hear an owl.

But the air is damp and soft, and not as cold as I first imagined, and I head back home considerably calmed by the experience.

Recommended.

60

MUD ALL OVER
THE PLACE

2–6 December

Lesser snow (*Shōsetsu*, 小雪)
Tachibana citrus tree leaves start to turn yellow
(*Tachibana hajimete kibamu*, 橘始黄)

I'm in the woods. Behind me, mud. Lots of it. Each time I think we've reached peak mud, another half-day of rain comes along to churn it up a bit more, and access to the woods becomes that bit messier.

Today's rain was the squally kind, accompanied by wind strong enough to bring down some of the smaller, weaker branches. It's calmed down now, but there's still a backdrop of wind in the canopy. White noise of the tree-sea, shifting and swirling, never resting. The ground is fully carpeted with damp leaves in various hues of brown, breaking down in their own sweet time and joining the mulch. *Graw* of crow; *chip* of woodpecker; *snurfle* of labrador.

Nothing much happens in this place. And that's exactly as it should be.

Human perception is narrow. We see the obvious, the large, the in-your-face; we hear the loud, the insistent, the attention-seeking; we smell the pungent, the fragrant, the rancid. But that is a fraction of what is there. Our sensory system is tuned in to the merest slice of the universe's energy spectrum – about one ten-trillionth of it, to be precise.

We don't see the ultraviolet that enables the kestrel to follow a vole's urine trail. We don't hear the ultrasound of bat or the infra-sound of elephants. And if we smelled what a dog smells, the first hit would likely make us faint, overwhelmed by the intensity and variety of a thousand competing odours that go undetected by our comparatively puny olfactory system.

Even within what we can perceive, we all too often fail to do so, attracted only by the glamorous and showy, letting the quieter, hidden parts pass us by. And different people see different things. I walk round the cemetery and it's all about the birds; let a botanist loose in the same area and they would quickly show me a dozen plants I'd never noticed before.

It's in the spirit of this desire to examine the unexamined, to root out the apparently unexceptional and find interest in it, that I find myself squatting in front of a gravestone with my camera. The person it's commemorating 'fell asleep' on 12 May 1895, having attained the fine age of eighty-six. But their life, while no doubt full of interest, adventure and good works, isn't the focus of my attention.

Because on that gravestone is lichen. Loads of it. And lichens occupy a universe of their own. Even the question 'what is a lichen?' fills the layperson with a groping sense of wonder, because lichens aren't single organisms, but symbiotic partnerships. The protagonists: fungi and a partner called a photobiont, which will most often be algae, sometimes cyanobacteria, and sometimes both.

You had me at 'symbiotic'.

They are the easiest thing to ignore. Your eye might be caught by one of the brighter yellow specimens, but to many people, if noticed at all, they're a sign of neglect and decay, an indicator that someone needs to give this place a bit of a tidying up.

There are lichens everywhere, once you start looking. The back of that bench, the fence post on the corner, the railings by the zebra crossing. The top of our nearest postbox has a fine covering, yellow and grey on flaking red paint, like a satellite photograph of an alien planet.

It's estimated they cover about 7 per cent of Earth's land surface, which is one of those statistics that makes you think, 'Is that a lot?' And then you work it out and realise that yes, it is a lot.

A man approaches. He's just walking past, not coming up to me in a challenging way, but there is something questioning in his demeanour, a slowness of the kind you sometimes adopt when the people nearby are saying something juicy and fascinating, and you want to eavesdrop without making them curious.

I look up, our eyes meet, and we do that half-smile and a noise that is so non-committal it can't even be described as a grunt, and then we look away and he walks past.

But then I hear his voice behind me.

'Sorry, can I just ask . . . what are you photographing?'

Now there's a question.

I could go for the enigmatic 'Nothing . . . and everything.' Or I could spin a yarn about recording unusual gravestone names in the Magnificent Seven cemeteries.

Instead, I tell the boring, pragmatic truth.

'Oh, just this lichen.'

I should have left out the 'just'.

He gives a little upward double nod, with the accompanying 'ah' that pretends to signify enlightenment but does nothing of the kind. I can almost see the massive unanswered question hanging over his head like a cartoon bubble.

WHY?

Why indeed?

Because it's there – the obvious, hackneyed answer.

Because it's interesting – true, but bland.

Because I've developed a driving urge to look closely at things, and not just the obviously beautiful and striking things but the very stuff of a place, the aspects of it that, if they were taken away, you wouldn't notice, until the tipping point is reached, and so many of those tiny elements are stripped from your normal surroundings that one day you look around and realise that you're living in what seems to be a half-completed virtual-reality universe, and you say, 'Oh no wait, hang on, didn't there used to be a whole load of stuff here?', and by then it's too late, and you have a vague feeling of regret that you never appreciated it before it was gone.

It's happened to the natural world, of course. The now well-known phenomenon of Shifting Baseline Syndrome can be applied to any number of things. Birds, insects, fish, and much more besides.

But what I'm really getting at is the landscape, the background, the things that make up our world, whether they're man-made or 'natural', and how they affect our daily existence. The colour of brick, the texture of concrete, the shadows cast by railings on a pavement.

Almost by accident, this exercise in observation has made me see everything differently. It started with an idea to chart nature's gradual changes through a year of small increments. But it's impossible to do that without taking note of the man-made environment surrounding it and, for better or for worse, assessing it in some way. Which isn't to say, 'Ooh, let's celebrate the beauty of this slab of concrete.' Concrete has its uses, but give me a singing blackcap any day. It's just useful to acknowledge it. And if it has a patch of lichen on it, then so much the better.

I'd like to say all this to the man. But I'm English, and he's already gone, so I say it to myself instead.

The day ends with another of those sunsets, the lurid burning kind, colours shifting by the minute. The kind of sky you would organise a party to watch, if only you had enough notice.

This time I watch it from the comfortable warmth of my office. It's easy enough to be excited by it. Obvious, you might say, the stuff of cliché. But it's easy enough, too, to ignore it, or to glance up with a shrug and a 'whatever', and to continue on your way without letting these things impinge on your life.

I prefer my way. But then I would, wouldn't I?

61

WINTER CLOSES IN

7–11 December

Greater snow (*Taisetsu*, 大雪)
Cold sets in, winter begins
(*Sora samuku fuyu to naru,* 閉塞成冬)

The phone call from school comes late in the morning. My son is exhausted. He has developed a cough. At the same time, my wife shows some odd, almost random symptoms.

Covid tests come back positive.

Bollocks.

The rules are that we all have to stay at home for ten days. As I'm showing no symptoms, we also agree to stay well apart from each other for the duration.

We've been housebound once already this year. But that was back in spring, when the days were getting lighter, there was energy in the air, the natural world was burgeoning; now it's dark and darkening, short and shortening, hunkering down. The hibernation urge, already strong, is enhanced. You want to gather your loved ones close, snuggle under a blanket and do nothing more energetic than reach for the remote control from time to time.

There was also, for all the ghastliness surrounding it, something to find in the novelty of it all. But this time there is a pervading weariness, a sense that the road will be long, the journey slow. And with the disease in the house – a real thing rather than a vague danger, something that happens to other people – the stress intensifies. To the growing gloom of ever-shortening days and almost complete absence of sun, we add the contracting of horizons and the worry over an unknown future.

Lockdown 2: This time it's personal.

I'll miss the cemetery and the common and all the little nooks and crannies in between. I'll miss the routine I've built up, the exploring of my local area now part of the rhythm of my life. I'll even miss the parakeets.

It's tempting to think that I've become part of it all, that my removal from that little ecosystem, however temporary, will have its effect. How will the redwings manage without me there to observe them?

But this is a blatant delusion. Part of the joy of observing the natural world in a year of pandemic upheaval has come not just because it's 'something else to do', a distraction from The State of Everything, but also because in doing so I've noticed how little effect our travails have had on the natural world. It goes on its way, facing the same struggles it always did.

There's solace in the garden, not least the very fact of its existence. But it's not a place to linger. Temperatures hovering just above the

freezing mark, a quagmire for a lawn, seasonal abeyance of growth
– all conspire against garden-based activity. So the slow wander to
the shed and back, assessing and admiring the state of the plants,
allowing it to nourish and replenish, is an activity for another time.

But rather than looking out at it and seeing only the dark brown,
the wilted, the desperately bedraggled, I play a different game. It's
one that has stood me in good stead as a conductor, encouraging
orchestras to inject some freshness into a performance. It is simply
to remember that no matter how familiar – wearisome, even – a
piece of music might be to the performer, there is always the possibility that someone in the audience will be hearing it for the very
first time.

The same goes for birds. Bored of robins? For someone, it's a
miracle. And so it is for all the rest of us too.

That ability to see the world anew time and time again, to experience its freshness and wonder, isn't just a case of walking round in
a trance of unquestioning awe, exclaiming, 'Oh wow!' at the tiniest
thing, like Forrest Gump. It's more a question of curiosity, of going
out in the morning, asking, 'What will I see today?', and not taking
the results for granted.

And so I try to pull the same trick on myself, appropriating the
skin of an alien, newly landed in this small suburban garden. What
curiosities will I find?

A cat turd.

Try again.

Mint, still hanging on in the gap at the bottom of the garden
steps, bedraggled, straggly, beyond culinary use, but still showing
signs of life. The hazel, on the cusp, leaves going, catkins coming, the
balance between them about 50/50. Snapdragons, their bubble-gum

colours offering a dose of freshness among the drab. At the bottom, by the compost heap, the juneberry – a small shrubby tree no taller than head high – throws out a single puckered yellow bud from the tip of its bare, spindly, dark maroon branches. Underneath the acer, a tight clump of heather, bristling with purple energy.

There's plenty there if you look.

I wake to fog, both mental and actual. The mental fuzziness is the result of interrupted sleep; the fog outside reminiscent of Victorian television dramas. A dense shroud, home to probing headlights. Even when it clears, around elevenses, its aura hangs about, muffling the day. The sun is a distant memory, like the neighbour who moved away ten years ago whose name you were never quite certain you knew.

From somewhere behind the garden, a jay shrieks, ripping the air. Again. And once more. Something has irked it. Perhaps a rival, perhaps a perceived threat.

And then the rain arrives, light at first, intensifying through the afternoon until it comes with a relentless, glum inevitability. I do the washing up, allowing myself to be soothed by the rhythm of the falling water. It spills out of the gutter above the kitchen window, and drips down onto the water butt, the drops beating a regular rhythm on the thick plastic. *Thubb thubb thubb thubb*. Ninety-six beats per minute, with an occasional syncopation – a five-eight bar then a triplet then back to the regular *thubb thubb thubb*.

An unexpected movement from the hazel. Flit flit land. A blue tit, braving the wet, somehow weaving between the raindrops to the feeder.

I remember my own exhortation. Imagine I'm seeing this bird for the very first time.

I can't help myself.

'Oh wow.'

62

GREY SKIES
ARE UNREMITTING

12–16 December

Greater snow (*Taisetsu*, 大雪)
Bears start hibernating in their dens
(*Kuma ana ni komoru*, 熊蟄穴)

There are some seasons you savour because they give a hint of what's in store round the corner. Others you relish because of what they are. And others you can't wait to get rid of because they seem to offer nothing of use to man nor beast.

Hello, Season 62.

The absolute grimness of the rain and the grey. There is barely any awareness of the sun rising. It's nowhere to be seen, the sullen cloud hanging uniform and low, casting its deathly pall over everything.

A day to consign to the bin the moment it starts.

Bears start hibernating in their dens, do they?

Bears have very much got the right idea.

𝓍

Let's try again, shall we? Day two dawns bright and clear. Sun! Blue skies! Cheeriness on a plate! I'll definitely go out later and see what's happening in the garden. Just have to send this email first, and then make a cup of tea, and then breakfast, and just a bit of Twitt— Oh, just look it's gone grey again.

It's the stealth of it that's so annoying. Sneaking up on me while I was otherwise engaged. If only I'd taken the opportunity to enjoy the blue sky while it was still there.

Carpe bloody diem.

We're lucky. We have enough space to isolate effectively and without massive inconvenience. Besides, the potency of the disease means that even into the second week the patients show little desire to leave their rooms. But for all that I talk a good game – 'oh yes, we're managing fine, all things considered' – a positive outlook can take me only so far.

I find myself willing the sun to come out. The stress of our situation is exacerbated by the relentless grey, the shortening of the hours of daylight, the lack of colour or growth or anything in the way of a pick-me-up from the world I can see through the kitchen window. It would all be a lot easier in spring.

There's only one thing for it. Another cup of tea. It's not the answer to all ills, but it is at least an answer. There's the ritual, the air of ceremony. I'm not going to get dressed up for it, but I do appreciate each stage of the routine. Floomph go the old leaves into the compost, then the measuring out of the new – one spoon, two, and a half for the pot – while the kettle boils. Water straight on to leaves, a stir, allowing them to circulate. And then patience. Count to a hundred, then count again.

Those minutes of waiting test my patience like few other things. Only the prospect of a piss-awful cup of tea (and I have made many of those in my time) keeps me staring out of the window. There's nothing going on in the garden. It looks subdued, the colours drab and lifeless, the clouds set in for the day.

Whirr, whizz, whoosh.

Action.

They come in from nowhere, their energy lighting up everything around them.

The simple uplift of a gang of starlings.

There's no time to count them, but I'm guessing at twenty or so. Twenty manic starlings in a single small tree is enough to make it fizz. They have the energy of a group of children on an adventure, over-excited and way past their bedtime. Little squawky shrieks bounce back and forth among them as they chase each other round the garden and up over the shed and away.

It might be my overwrought state, but I could swear they were sent by the universe as emissaries specifically to perk me up.

Social media has its downsides, but at times like this it really comes into its own. Tendrils of human contact. The warmth and friendship of strangers.

A post on the local Facebook page catches my eye. It's a photograph of flowers. Not the usual, Instagram-style perfection of a single pink bloom at the height of its florescence in crisp focus against a blurred backdrop, but a messy, wonky snap, taken on the hoof. A mixed bunch of flowers in cellophane – pinks and reds and yellows. Bright and blowsy and commonplace. Tesco's finest. Someone has tied them to a lamppost, and now they're leaning slightly to one side, the string not quite doing the job as intended, but doing it well enough for the purpose. Parked cars behind, a row of houses. An average West Norwood street. They could easily be an impromptu shrine to a loved one.

On a normal day I might scroll past with barely a glance, or just incline my head with a nod and a smile and a raised eyebrow. But this isn't a normal day. Isolation, illness, stress, worry. They all build up. And I'm as susceptible to schmaltz as the next person.

There's a note attached to the cellophane. It's a message to anyone who might happen across it. A real-world gift, given a wider audience by a much maligned and abused medium, which sometimes, just sometimes, has its uses.

'May these brighten your day in a bit of a dark year.'

Sometimes it's the simplest things that break you.

The weather pulls itself together late in the afternoon for just long enough to make a difference. The sun pokes its way through the clouds for a few minutes and treats anyone who might be interested to that glowing angled wintry light.

I'm drawn to the splashes of colour in the garden. Pale bright purple of the clump of heather by the swing chair, Battenberg yellow and pink of snapdragon, obvious orange of marigold.

Hazel leaf count: eight yellow discs, hanging on. Plenty more on the ground.

The sun disappears, the light goes, dusk gathers. Just as I'm about to go back inside, a robin starts singing. Silvery ribbon, fluttery warblings – the usual routine. Something – perhaps the stillness of the air, perhaps the particular angle of delivery – makes the sound more than usually resonant. It's enough to keep me out there, hanging on its every warble, until darkness descends and it calls it a night.

In times of need, send birds.

63

GULLS GATHER IN FLOCKS

17–21 December

Greater snow (*Taisetsu,* 大雪)
Salmons gather and swim upstream
(*Sake no uo muragaru,* 鰄魚群)

I open the folding doors, step onto the terrace and take a deep breath. There will be sun today. I can smell it in the air. Or maybe I just believe the Met Office.

The robin starts singing, resonant and sweet. In among the silvery flutings, two notes – *tseeee woooo* – suddenly ring out loud and clear, and I'm slithering down a wormhole to spring last year when this bird – this very bird – announced its descent to the feeder with this exact phrase, like a vocal calling card.

But it won't get on the feeder for a bit. There's a squirrel there, executing a feat of gymnastics worthy of a 10 from the Canadian judge. On the one hand, I admire its inventiveness and audacity. On the other hand, that's bird food, not squirrel food.

'Fuck off.'

It scrabbles down the pole in a frenzy, leaving the feeder swinging above it. But we both know the ceasefire is brief. It will return, I will tell it to fuck off, it will leave. Return, fuck off, leave. The cycle of life.

I like squirrels, really. I'm in awe of their acrobatic and problem-solving abilities. They have endearing little puffy cheeks, and can often be seen in the kind of 'rubbing their hands together with malevolent glee' pose that makes them look as if they're plotting the downfall of mankind. Besides, weasels, deer and dolphins are in short supply round here, so they're our most easily seen wild mammal, and not to be sniffed at.

Just as long as they stay off the bird feeders.

This bias, this division of nature into 'things we like' and 'things we don't like', is ubiquitous. No matter how much we want to adopt an egalitarian attitude, to say 'we must love it all equally', this utopian ideal goes against human nature. However unconsciously, we all have our favourites, and for a lot of people they fall into the broad categories of cute, cuddly or majestic. It helps if something has a face we can identify with, preferably one with a potentially winsome expression. Anthropomorphism looms large.

We also like an underdog, a plucky survivor fighting against the odds. In this department, the grey squirrel suffers in the public imagination for the perception of it as an invasive bully. It doesn't help that the red squirrel, the species it has supplanted, is more delicate, shyer, its russet colouring somehow more appealing than the workaday grey of its cousin. Throw in the cuteness of its little tufty ears and you have a recipe for 'aww, look'. But if the relative abundance of the two species were reversed, it might be a different story.

The reasons for their contrasting fortunes in the UK is a matter for hot debate. The straightforward narrative of the more robust grey squirrels supplanting their red cousins by being more aggressive is widely accepted. But there is a counterargument, which posits that greys were simply taking advantage of the decline in reds caused by the squirrel pox virus. Whatever the true cause or causes, the grey is now far more widespread and abundant, leading to the aforementioned ill feeling. Their habit of stripping the bark from trees, often leaving it hanging in loose spirals from the trunk, adds to the perception of them as rough and brutish vandals.

But they're only doing what they need to do to survive. The universal story.

I stay on the terrace for a few minutes. Somewhere, an energetic great tit sings. The squirrel reappears on the fence right on cue, eyes me warily, then scoots down, bounces across the steps and scampers irrepressibly up the pole. It clings to it with its hind legs and stretches effortlessly across to the feeder.

9.8 – 9.8 – 9.9.

I could tell it to fuck off again, but somehow, this time, I don't have the heart.

Our period of isolation comes to an end on day four. The patients have made good enough progress to ease my worries about hospital stays and bedside vigils. I recognise this landmark with an extended walk, like a prolonged out-breath. I have 471 minutes of daylight on this pre-solstice day, and I intend to make the most of them.

Up the road, walking with the pent-up energy induced by ten days of isolation. Through the estate. Hello to the sparrows, chirping bundles of delight. Hello, trees! Hello, sky!

I nearly hug a pigeon.

By the path, the forlornest of sights – a battered and deflated football, greenish-yellow, sitting half submerged in the mud. It might be seasonal associations talking, but it reminds me of an unwanted Brussels sprout sitting in a pool of gravy.

Past the woods, onto the broad expanse of common leading down to the A23. The weather has behaved. There's a faint wind, the tops of the trees doing a token wave at the blue sky. Mild and clear. But I'd go out in a blizzard, just because I can.

In a fit of enthusiasm for the glamorous world of Streatham Common denied me this last fortnight, I count the birds. Each and every last one of them. Starlings – 133, streaming in a fluttering ribbon from the top of the plane trees down the side onto the grass, where they stay obligingly still for a bit, snuffling around for leatherjackets while I do a headcount. They're fast eaters though, probing with their pointed bills, swivelling their eyes forward to see if there's anything there, then moving on a few feet to repeat the process. Just beyond them, a loose gaggle of carrion crows (fifty-two), with a couple of jackdaws mingling.

But really it's all about the gulls – eighty-four black-headed, four common, two herring. This place hums with gulls in winter. It's less of a draw in summer, when the soil is drier, but in winter there are bugs and schmugs and little wrigglers galore, just waiting to be plucked from the damp earth. No need for the gulls to do their rain dance, stamping on the ground to trick the worms into thinking it's raining so they'll come to the surface and present themselves on a platter. The food is there, just below the surface.

A dog scampers towards them – they're too tempting a target – and up they get, scattering loosely, unhurried but knowing they have to do it, like office staff leaving a building for a fire drill. Dogs are part of the territory, and they know they will never be caught.

The starlings join them, but following their own trajectory and flight pattern. And then the corvids go too, doing the bare minimum, saving energy and taking the first opportunity to resume their probing.

Between them, the birds create a brief aerial ballet, the likes of which would set you back thirty quid in the West End. I watch them circle for a couple of minutes, then they come back down to earth on a different patch and renew the fossicking.

They are all – and I say this with the exaggerated enthusiasm of one released from torment – bloody marvellous.

64

MAGNOLIA SHOWS FIRST BUDS

22–26 December

Winter solstice (*Tōji*, 冬至)
Self-heal sprouts
(*Natsukarekusa shōzu,* 乃東生)

The shortest day dawns grey and stays grey, upgrading to drab only shortly before dusk. It throws in, for good measure, an undistinguished mizzle of the kind that loses nine consecutive by-elections.

Just as well the day is so short. It can only get better from here.

Despite the gloom of the weather, the optimism engendered by the year's hinge is palpable. From here the pendulum begins the long swing back, accruing extra light bit by tiny bit. Even though the shift is imperceptible, the date's position in the calendar has its significance, signalling the end of one thing, the beginning of another.

The beginning of hope.

Something is different. I just don't know what it is. I stop and look around, trying as hard as I can to emulate the great detectives. But

I can't help feeling I'm doing it wrong, that the difference I've noticed isn't what I think it is.

I look round the entrance area to the cemetery one more time. Ah yes. There it is. A distinct difference in one very familiar tree.

The magnolia is budding.

This tree, sentinel of the cemetery gates, is a habitual early bloomer, at least three weeks ahead of the smaller specimen in our front drive, and I'd lay even money on it pulling the same trick again this year. Maybe it's something to do with the variety, or perhaps its positioning, sheltered but not enclosed, so well placed to gather every last ray of sun. Or maybe the soil is particularly fertile here. It's not a large tree, but sturdy enough. Out of season it sits quietly, minding its own business, giving no hint of the glories to come.

It's only by walking directly underneath it and examining the silhouette of its upturned branches that I can detect the buds. Small pointed triangles with curved sides, the tiniest extensions of the spiky winter stalks, showing the way to growth.

Zoom in with the camera and I can detect that pale colour, so fresh in nature but carrying with it a marker of blandness, giving its name to the white of rented flats up and down the land.

The mildness has brought it on. For weeks now we've been waiting for temperatures to drop, but they've stayed resolutely in the high single figures Celsius. Today, the second day of this season, is no exception, delivering a familiar pattern – rain early doors, clearing to mild and pleasant in the afternoon.

The sight of the buds is a boon. This winter, still relatively early in its unfolding, has pulled off a neat trick: it has simultaneously never really got going while also being relentless and interminable. The damp and lack of light have been compounded by the background stress of the pandemic to make it draining and exhausting. What it needs is a proper cold snap, a series of crisp days to wake us up. Sharp frosts, zinging blue skies, brittle air. Ice on the ponds, snow swirling in flurries, icicles hanging from branches. Enough snow to make a snowman and go sledging would be good, but I'd settle for the components necessary for a series of proper winter walks.

The magnolia might not welcome it, but I would.

On the Doulton Path, the leaves underfoot still have their shruff-lable quality, but they're soggy now, and the descent into treacherous sludge can't be far away. A coal tit (*pit-chew! pit-chew!*) and a gold-finch (*tickly-tockly-tackly-tibbly-scradooby*) swap riffs, each going at its own pace, but somehow in almost perfect synchronisation, the goldfinch leaving the perfect gap in its festive tinkling for the coal tit to insert its pithy commentary. In the middle distance, parakeets and jays perform a more strident duet, and the whole is underpinned by a flickering chorus of small-bird chuntering.

I reach the end of the path and turn left up the hill, past the crematorium. A thin plume of smoke comes out of the chimney. As I crest the rise, the peace is interrupted by a sound that simultan-eously shocks me and takes me instantly back to 1970s Oxfordshire. I could swear it's a shotgun. It has the same crack, the same echo, and the same aftermath. It's more likely to be a backfiring car but, from a distance, the effect is the same. It reverberates towards me, close enough to shock, not so close as to deafen.

But it's the follow-up that is truly evocative. After the initial impact comes a panicked flurry of wings clapping and slapping against foliage. Wood pigeons and carrion crows rise as one, a feathered ripple spreading across the sky. It's only when they're disturbed that you get an idea of how many birds there are here. Hundreds of them, living largely unnoticed lives in the urban sprawl.

The cemetery fox appears, something in his mouth. A bone perhaps. He cocks his leg on a gravestone – part of me wishes he wouldn't – and trots on, quietly purposeful, showing no sign that the noise has in any way disturbed him.

Christmas morning, as is only right, brings a slice of the winter I craved. The temperature drops to just above freezing, the skies clear, and there is a fresh, invigorating chill in the air.

My morning walk is short but upbeat. There's food to be cooked, presents to be unwrapped. Christmas in a pandemic is undoubtedly strange – the country has been kept going by the prospect of a return to normality, but reality had other ideas, and gatherings have been forbidden – and there will be an air of melancholy to it. Memories of Christmases past and all that. But I've nipped up to the allotment to gather some cabbage and a couple of heads of lettuce for Boxing Day healthiness, stopped on my way back to admire the zinging colour of a stretch of pyracantha, the tight clusters of red and orange berries brazenly festive in the seasonal manner and bringing a smile to the face whether you want it or not, and all in all there is much to be thankful for.

And we look forward. Always forward.

65

STORMS SOMETIMES BLOW

27–31 December

Winter solstice (*Tōji*, 冬至)
Deer shed antlers
(*Sawashika no tsuno otsuru*, 麋角解)

The nuthatch is an endearing bird. Classy blue-grey on top, peach and white underneath, all enhanced by a long black eye stripe running from pointed bill to nape. The 'masked bandit bird'.

Of all the things to like about a nuthatch – its pastel plumage, its restlessness, its ability to climb head first down a tree – the one that impresses me the most is its DIY prowess.

The nuthatch will identify a hole in a tree as potentially suitable for nesting, then, using only its pointed beak and a great deal of ingenuity, will fill the hole with mud until it's just the right size for them and too small for any potential predators.

I have two hands, a tool kit, opposable thumbs and a second-hand copy of the *Reader's Digest Complete Book of DIY*. Yet charge me with the same task, and I would be certain to leave behind a shabby mess of Polyfilla that would collapse into the hole within

a week, no doubt endangering the lives of any birds foolish enough
to have nested there.

Nuthatches aren't uncommon birds, but any visit to the woods
is enhanced by an encounter. This is just such a visit.

There's been a storm, big enough to warrant a name. The naming of the storms resets at the beginning of September, when the
likelihood of their occurrence increases, so this one, the second of
the season, is called Bella. She swept across from the North Atlantic
on Boxing Day, reaching London early on the morning of the 27th.
The Met Office, with characteristic understatement, calls the rain
'heavy and persistent' – meteorologist-speak for 'absolutely heaving
it'. It's intense enough to wake me up in the middle of the night, but
come mid-morning it's cleared, leaving an aftermath of a briskish
wind and an optimistic blue sky. Just right for a restorative walk to
the common.

The *pock-pock*ing of the nuthatch is audible from outside the
wood, so I'm already in 'scanning the canopy' mode. And it's not long
before it makes itself visible, shuffling along a lowish branch, calling
as it goes. The sunshine seems to have injected it with a busy energy,
and the irregular rhythm has a manic quality, presumably spelling
out a secret message in Morse code. The chipping of a great spotted
woodpecker offers a syncopated counterpoint. But no sooner have
I found both birds by tracking their sounds than they shut up and
are replaced by two great tits, which choose that moment to strike
up in duet.

Try as I might, I can't turn off my inner musician. In defiance of
decades of birding folklore, neither of them chooses the famed *tea-*
cher tea-cher that is supposed to be so helpful when identifying the
song. The first bird, somewhere not far behind me, opts for a variant,

adding a note. *Tea-chacha tea-chacha*, if you must. The second, ahead of me and a bit further away, takes the first's theme and subverts it like a canny jazzer, turning the four-square rhythm into a triplet, and producing, absolutely by chance, a rhythmic effect to bring a smile to the face of any passing muso.

My listening is interrupted by a rustling from the depths of the bushes to my left. This kind of thing brings out the detective in me. What might be making the rustling? Will there be more of it? Will it stop as mysteriously as it began, or will the perpetrator emerge to assuage my curiosity?

On this occasion, the last.

A redwing pops up to the edge of the bush, stands still for the merest instant, then darts off away from me. As it leaves my sightline I become aware of another darting movement, then another, and another, and soon the air is full of motion, none of which I can quite get a proper view of before being drawn to another one.

This ability redwings have to materialise from nowhere remains mysterious to me. I regard myself as reasonably observant, and am aware that even under close scrutiny birds often go undetected. But redwings seem to be able to shape-shift at will, assuming the form of a patch of grass or the branches of a tree or the leaves of a bush before manifesting in their true form and zipping out of your sight.

But these redwings are hungry, so feeding takes priority over human-baiting. As I follow the path of the nearest bird, I see three more, then another small group of indeterminate number. They're descending on a sprawling holly bush off to my right. It is laden with red berries, but all the evidence points to this state of affairs being short-lived. They look in a plundering mood. A flock of winter thrushes can strip a bush of red berries as efficiently as piranhas can supposedly strip a carcass.

I catch one in the binoculars. It lowers its head, comes up with a berry in its mouth. With the merest flick, the berry is gone, and off it flies, on to the next.

They've had it relatively easy so far this winter. The weather has been mild, food plentiful. If a cold snap hits, things will get more difficult, and people will be more likely to see them in their gardens as they widen the search for food. And then, some time in March and without so much as a backward glance, they'll be gone, and we'll know winter is well and truly done.

It's hard to remember other times. When you're baking in the second week of 30-degree heat, the idea of sledging seems as remote as Alpha Centauri; the tables are turned when there's frost on the shed roof and you catch a glimpse of a photograph of a beach scene.

Nine months of a pandemic have a similar effect. Normal scenes from the Before Times stand out.

In the cemetery. On the left of the path, three young women, rigorously observing distancing protocols, gather round a bench. They're dressed appropriately for the weather – woolly hats, thick coats, sturdy boots. One of them is holding a bottle of Prosecco. As I pass, she eases the cork out with understated expertise and fills the three proffered plastic mugs. It is 10.49 in the morning. I want to applaud them. But their very presence here, on a cold and blustery late December day, hunched into their coats, smiles fixed on their faces, finding pleasure where and when they can, tells its own story.

66

CHRISTMAS TREES ARE
RELEASED INTO THE WILD

1–4 January

Winter solstice (*Tōji*, 冬至)
Wheat sprouts under snow
(*Yuki watarite mugi nobiru*, 雪下出麦)

The tedium of the sky. The Tupperware blandness of it, featureless, purposeless, pointless.

Hello, 2021.

I'm not one for resolutions. Not really. I've been bitten too often. But very quietly, and noting to myself that I am just doing it because I want to and definitely not making a commitment beyond today, I start counting the birds in the cemetery. Not just the species, but every individual bird I see. I log them in an app and upload the results to the British Trust for Ornithology's BirdTrack website. The benefits of this activity are many: I'm doing my bit for citizen science, ensuring that I get out of the house every day, and instilling a soft discipline to my daily routine.

It might seem, on the face of it, a matter of insignificance how many blue tits I encounter on my daily walk. But each record is a tiny piece in the big picture, and the information enables the BTO to chart patterns of growth and decline, helping it understand what drives these fluctuations.

Besides, it's not much of a jump from what I do already. Just a bit more structured. I notice the birds everywhere, but this takes it to the extra level, and requires that bit more rigour. The difference between 'some carrion crows' and 'twelve carrion crows' is a matter of concentration and close observation.

So I note them as I go round: six goldfinches, ten feral pigeons, three great tits, forty wood pigeons or more.

I'll do the same again tomorrow, but, as I say, it's not a resolution.

There's a feeling about the garden. Nothing specific, nothing tangible. Just the faintest hint in its general demeanour that things are possibly on the cusp of thinking about the idea of maybe doing some growing. If pressed to provide concrete evidence in a court of law, I would be unable to do so. It's just a hunch. But that doesn't make it any less real.

Maybe it's just that the hazel catkins are showing some mid-season form, especially the ones furthest away from the fence on the outer branches, a real indicator of the effect of light on growth. On the inside, tucked away in the shade of the fence, they're darker, more shrivelled, but on the outer branches the dangling worms show the yellow of rude health. Watchers of nascent spring rejoice. All we need now is a flower or two.

✕

It starts with a trail of needles, thin green pointers scattered sparsely on the pavement. Just a few at first, but thickening as I walk down the hill, and reaching peak density just in front of the telecoms junction box with the banner proclaiming, 'Fibre broadband is coming.'

The Christmas trees are being released into the wild.

The intensifying trail of pine needles leading to the abandoned tree reminds me of a wounded movie hero – not the main protagonist, obviously, but the expendable best friend left behind to stave off the enemy for as long as he can – dragging himself heroically, leaving a trail of blood, until he can go no further.

The trees will litter the streets over the next few days, left there by people who aren't aware that the council will pick them up. And some will remain, somehow having fallen through the gaps, gradually shedding their needles and going brown, the forlornest of all forlorn sights. The latest I've seen one was in mid-May, abandoned in a neglected front garden, a desiccated brown skeleton of almost infinite melancholy. But no matter what time of year you encounter them, they're a reminder of the bizarre and brutal life cycle of these trees, farmed specially so we can make them look pretty for, at best, a few weeks, then cast aside with barely a flicker of anguish.

What a strange species we are.

It might, just about, be asleep. But not even the most confident of urban foxes is going to snuggle down for a kip in a backstreet gutter.

There are no signs of external injury, no blood sullying its russet fur. I can't repress the thought that it might suddenly spring up, full of life, and trot away, all casual like, the way urban foxes do. But the angle of the head, lolling against the kerb, tells a different story.

It has, I assume, been hit by a car. But someone has moved it to the side of the road, perhaps to spare it further indignity, or perhaps just to get it out of the way so they can carry on with their journey.

It isn't the cemetery fox. This is some way off its patch, and I know its appearance well enough by now to be confident I'd recognise it in death as I do in life.

Death is all around. You don't have to look far to find it. But the sight of this fox gives me a jolt. Perhaps it's the size of it, or its fresh appearance, or just that I can't remember when I last saw a dead fox. Whatever the reasons, this isn't something you walk past without noticing.

It's impossible, no matter how much empathy you have, to allow yourself to be affected by every single death. Overload would quickly set in. And we find it easier to empathise with a fox, with its resemblance to Man's Best Friend, than, for example, a midge or a wasp or a gnat.

But I allow myself a small moment nevertheless. I will remember it.

Somehow, even though there hasn't been any more rain, the entrance to the woods has become muddier. A neat trick if you can pull it off.

The worst of it is by the fallen oak, a place I'm usually fond of. But the surrounding area is a quagmire, churned almost beyond passability, so I give it a miss.

It fell, this oak, in March 2019, victim of a spring storm. It broke low down and measured its length across the path. The inside of the trunk, violently exposed, had a freshness to it, the internal workings of the tree laid bare for all to see. They could have removed it, sawing it up and taking it away and leaving the trunk as the only evidence that this majestic thing had ever existed. But they didn't. It was given a trim so the straggly branches wouldn't inconvenience path users, and left there to act as an impromptu climbing frame for passing children of any age. Hat-tip to the people who made that enlightened decision.

67

HELLEBORES FLOWER

5–9 January

Lesser cold (*Shōkan,* 小寒)
Parsley flourishes
(*Seri sunawachi sakau,* 芹乃栄)

Life, as has often been noted by parents of indignant children, is not fair.

Fully aware of the massive, wider injustices at play all over the world since the dawn of history, I nevertheless observe, with the whining lilt of a five-year-old, that it's not fair. If it's this cold, the very least the weather could do would be to snow.

Yes, it's my fault for coming out without gloves. Again.

No, the world doesn't exist solely for my whimsical pleasure.

Yes, there are far more pressing and important issues in the world.

But still. I want snow.

Cheek-stinging rain, biting wind. With dusk rapidly descending, the only way to stave off the misery is to walk quickly. I stride up the hill, hunched into my coat, hood pulled over my head, looking neither to left nor right. Exercise, today, feels like a chore.

My spirits are momentarily lifted by the cemetery fox, alive and kicking. Well, trotting, at least. He shows his usual lack of concern at my presence, merely casting me a glance as he saunters across the rain-gleamed path, as if to say, 'Oh, you again. God, you look miserable.'

There's a funeral. A few mourners huddle under a large and colourful umbrella, its gaudiness at odds with the grim solemnity of their mood. Bad enough to have a funeral in a pandemic; even worse to have it in this kind of weather. I give them a wide berth and head down the hill.

The instinct kicks in. Look up. Don't know why, just look up.

Always obey the instinct.

It's a peregrine, flying so close that the barring on its chest presents as individual streaks rather than a general impression. A peregrine, flying so fast that without the instinct to look up I would have missed it altogether – three, four seconds at most. A peregrine, flying so low that for the first time ever I get a true impression of the bird with the naked eye, can feel its size, its energy, its spirit.

Falco peregrinus – the wandering falcon. Miracle bird.

Still bloody horrible out though.

Feral pigeons. A lot of them. A hundred, maybe more. They're scurrying around, pecking at the ground, a seething mass of activity that does nothing to counter any thoughts that they might just be idiots.

The reason for their agitation is simple. A man is scattering seed from a bag. It bounces off their backs and rains gently on the tarmac.

Some birds always seem to be in the right place to snap up the seeds, almost before they hit the ground; others are locked in a perpetual loop of seed-chasing, condemned to failure like a League Two defender marking Lionel Messi. To the left, a jackdaw, beady-eyed and alert, plays a canny game. Rather than join the pigeon melee, where competition is so fierce that most of the birds go hungry, it hangs off the pack like a wing three-quarter, waits for the inevitable seed ricochet, and reaps plentiful reward with minimum effort.

And then, responding to some unseen stimulus, up they go, a billowing sheet of pigeon, dispersing to escape whatever it was that spooked them. My instinct is to scan the skies for a predator – a kestrel or sparrowhawk perhaps, often the cause of the sudden flight of a flock. But there's nothing. Not that I can see, anyway.

A boy next to me – ten? eleven? – is open-mouthed.

'Look at them!'

The birds fly up and round, flocking loosely, but broadly unanimous in direction. The boy watches them, smiling at the spectacle, then laughing as they swoop low overhead. You can hear their wings, feel the air move. And I can feel the boy's thrill, infectious as people nearby crane round to look. This is how enthusiasms are born.

It's difficult to pinpoint the moment they collectively decide to come back down, but bit by bit they return, fewer in number as offshoots of the flock decide they'd be better off elsewhere for the time being, and soon things are back to normal and it's as if nothing had happened at all.

Another day, another sunset. This one is mostly yellow. The light burnishes the bellies of the wood pigeons roosting in the tall trees.

It kisses the rooftops. It filters through into the Rookery, lending it a golden hue. It imbues the place with the usual magic. There's been a glut of these sunsets this winter, each one different, each one inviting you to watch it until the last drop of molten light disappears over the horizon. I accept the invitation, to the accompaniment of a robin's song, then wander back up through the wood. A lone gorse flower sits, both perky and lonely, on the bush.

Gorse never feels to me like a city plant. In my mind it belongs on heaths and in forests – not to mention in the pages of *Winnie-the-Pooh* – but it turns up in woods like this from time to time, and the possibility that at any time of year you might find a curled yellow bloom in among the prickly thorns or catch a whiff of its coconut scent is a cheering one.

This little patch, near the fenced-off area in the wood, is lit by the setting sun. Stand in the right place and it's illuminated with a halo, and you can see gnats dancing a dance of magnificent, repetitive complexity. I stand in the right place, but within a minute or two the light has changed and it's time to go home, where I catch a glimpse of soft pink in the browns and greens of the front-of-house border.

The hellebores, furled and drooping, are gracing us with their presence, and very welcome they are too.

68

RAIN REVIVES MOSSES

10–14 January

Lesser cold (*Shōkan,* 小寒)
Springs thaw
(*Shimizu atataka o fukumu,* 水泉動)

I'm face to face with the most elusive bird in the cemetery and I daren't move.

More often than not I'm aware of the green woodpecker only from its distant laughter, like the hysterical mockings of a triumphant villain. Occasionally I'll be given a glimpse of its backside disappearing into the trees. But today it's come down to the grass just ten yards away, and I've frozen like a statue.

This question of encroachment plagues conscientious birders. The idea is that we go about our business – which essentially boils down to spying on them – while causing them minimum disturbance. Any disruption causes stress and makes them expend energy they might put to better use in the pursuit of survival. The distance at which such disturbance occurs varies from bird to bird, and naturally the more used to humans birds are, the closer they're likely to let us get.

And so it is with the green woodpecker.

To be fair, it has decided to land this close, so presumably it would be happy enough to maintain the status quo. So, tempting though it is, I don't try to get any closer. I know what's good for me.

It gives the appearance of being busy fossicking around in the grass, apparently unaware of my presence, but I know different. It's clocking me, for sure. At one point it looks up and I could swear our eyes meet. The markings on a green woodpecker's face – black around the eye, red moustachial stripe giving it the appearance of a scowl – make it seem, to my eyes, slightly crazed, an impression only enhanced by its mocking call, as mentioned above.

You could scrutinise this grass and not know the woodpecker was there, so closely does the green of its plumage match its surroundings. And, even better, the red of its crown is exactly the same shade as the faded plastic flowers sitting disconsolately on the grave behind it.

It gives me five minutes of its time. Then, before it has the chance to reject me, I tiptoe away, leaving it to its fossicking.

It's pissing it down. All day long. But I'm determined. I have sworn to take exercise, so exercise I shall take. And it will be in the form of a Deliberately Wet Walk, the kind where you know you're going to get drenched but you set your mood to 'don't care' and adopt a defiantly sprightly demeanour. The physical gait I adopt on these occasions is an important part of the psychological trick I'm playing on myself.

No hunching, no slouching, no hangdog expression. I will be brisk, I will stand up straight, I will be irritatingly jaunty.

It works a charm.*

There are fewer birds about the place than usual, which is natural and understandable given the weather, but the black-headed gulls are in residence on the common, standing stolidly on what resembles grass but is 95 per cent squelch.

They look mightily pissed off, but then that's par for the course with black-headed gulls. 'Mightily pissed off' is their default state of mind. As if to prove my point, a fracas breaks out between three of them for no apparent reason, the sound of their aggrieved squawkings piercing through the relentless drip drip drip of the rain.

My pace has flagged, and I give myself a little reminder. Brisk, straight, jaunty.

My mood is enhanced by the most apparently mundane thing. Moss on a wall. It catches my eye, this moss, not least because it's almost at eye level. And it has, to match my own deliberately generated mood, a sort of perkiness about it. In the midst of the rain, where everything else is subdued and cowed and just plain sodden, it gives the impression that all it needed was a good solid drenching to come alive.

Like lichen, mosses are ubiquitous, easy to overlook, and full of hidden wonders. They will make their homes out of nothing – a bit of bark, a denuded patch of soil, bare stone, the cracks in the pavement. Their chemical composition includes a kind of antifreeze to keep them going in winter, and unpalatable compounds to deter

* This is not always the case. The management accepts no responsibility, etc.

pests and protect them from disease. Dependent for their survival on humidity, they absorb pollution and provide habitat for small insects. Humble organisms, they require little and give much.

The importance of mosses for feelings of general well-being and contentment is well understood by the Japanese. Their use as a symbol of harmony and tradition spans the centuries, and they're regarded as essential elements of Japanese gardens. For anyone whose lawn has been denuded by what some gardeners regard as an invasive pest, this might seem counter-intuitive. But a minute spent contemplating the smooth satisfaction of a moss-covered stone will persuade anyone of the wisdom of the Japanese. Perhaps the solution is to accept that your lawn will never be perfect, and allow the moss to take over.

This little clump – soft and velvety, its pert fronds glistening with tiny droplets – reminds me of the post-storm clump that caught my eye way back in Season 2. This circularity does wonders for my mood and I make my way back home without needing to remind myself not to slouch.

Then, as I swing back down the hill below the estate, past the bush where the house sparrows live and underneath the starling tree, a miracle occurs. It's a minor miracle in the grand scheme of things, but I kid myself that my actions brought it on.

The rain eases off just a bit, and a flash of movement catches my eye up ahead. It streaks across my sightline, does a double jink, then up and across and over the house to the left. Nimble, fast, gone.

Kestrel.

I'd like to think it's the same bird I saw perched at the top of the cedar of Lebanon in the Rookery all those months ago; the one that darted across my garden in pursuit of a blue tit while I was on the phone; the one I saw being escorted to city limits by a carrion crow that time. It seems likely, given that this is an urban environment and that a kestrel's territory is between two and ten square kilometres.

And so, lacking any evidence to the contrary, I decide that it is.

69

SNOWDROPS POKE
THROUGH SOIL

15–19 January

Lesser cold (*Shōkan,* 小寒)

Pheasants start to call (*Kiji hajimete naku,* 雉始雊)

I know some things.

I know that a peregrine returning to the perch with a pigeon in its talons does not take kindly to the attentions of a herring gull intent on stealing said pigeon, and that in any ensuing fracas you probably don't want to be the herring gull. Or the pigeon, for that matter.

I know that the dunnock in the empty lot over the road is gagging for it, singing its scrabbly, indeterminate song from the top of a bush as if summoning dunnockdom to prayer.

I know that bit by bit, almost imperceptibly, the birds are making more noise.

I know that the sight of the willow near the cemetery wall, bright yellow in the gloom, its cascading tendrils like a waterfall captured in stillness, lifts my mood on a dank day.

I know that no matter how close the cemetery fox lets me get, no matter how submissive he seems, no matter how much I get used to his appearance and way of being and start to think of him almost as a pet dog, this is a stupid and dangerous assumption – he remains a wild animal, and if I were to try to put a lead on him or get him to walk to heel I would soon regret it.

I know that everything, this season, feels just round the corner: the snowdrops, poking green columns through the soil, the faintest of white piping just visible through the cracks; the winter heliotrope in the cemetery, beginning to carpet the small area to the left of the path up the hill; the hellebores in the front garden, heads bowed, hiding in the shadows. Soon. Soon.

I know that a watched snowdrop never blooms.

I know that when snow is forecast overnight but rain comes instead – and heavy, sopping rain at that, such that you can hear it through double glazing when you wake up – the disappointment I feel is not really appropriate for a grown man. I also know that I can't help it.

I know that if I want cheering up on a grey and blustery day, all I have to do is find a carrion crow and watch it trying to fly, its wings folding in on themselves, loose and floppy like a handkerchief, allowing the wind to take it just so far, waiting for the slight lull and then, with a couple of deceptively lazy beats, drawing itself up and through and away.

I know that despite the entertainment value of the carrion crow, I'm happier when the wind drops.

I know – while we're on the subject of carrion crows – that when there are thirty or more of them on a large patch of grass with exten- sive lying water, and you want to get closer to get a good look, it's probably a better idea to stay on the paved path rather than step onto the apparently benign but really very squelchy patch of grass just off it.

I know that I'm going to need a new pair of walking shoes before too long.

I know that as the cycle approaches its end I'm beginning to notice familiar sights from the beginning of the year – rowan berries, hazel catkins, the two greens of euphorbia, Day-Glo stems of dogwood, patches of cyclamen brightening up the borders – and that this gives a pleasing circularity to proceedings.

I know that ten years ago I couldn't tell the difference between all the various kinds of pigeon, and that while I'd jogged along quite happily for the last few decades without that particular piece of arcane knowledge, possession of it is officially a Good Thing, so that now, when I'm scanning the trees in the cemetery and there are fifteen roosting wood pigeons and among them one stock dove, I can recognise the stock dove from its smaller size, the lack of white on its neck, and its little black button eye, and this little bit of knowledge makes my life a tiny bit better in strange and unfathomable ways.

I know that when I'm doing the washing up and three redwings fly into the tree at the bottom of the garden I will always think, 'Ooh, redwings', and sometimes I will even say it out loud, and these are the little things that keep us going. In fact they're not little things at all, but the very stuff of life.

I know that there are days when I have the urge to stop and look at the bark of a tree, to examine it in detail and take in its crevices and angles and texture, and that to spend time doing this can be the best therapy.

I know that there are days when that seems a ridiculous thing to do.

I know – oh, yes, *now* I know – not to worry too much about the difference between those two kinds of day.

I know that I have got so used to being 'always on', noticing the little changes, the odd plants in strange corners, the pigeons nesting in the crevice above the local primary school, the number of redwings in the tree by the crematorium, that it would now take an act of will to stop being like that.

I know that without all this – the focus on small things, the conscious paying attention, the birds and the flowers and the trees and the bees and the dragonflies and spiders and fungi and the mosses and lichens and the weeds growing in the cracks on the pavements, and yes, even the bastard squirrels – my year would have been substantially less bearable.

I know that I might in fact have gone very slightly mad anyway without realising it, but that if this is the case, then it feels like a positive development, and not much removed from my natural state.

I know that snow is forecast.

I do not know if it will come, but I am prepared for disappointment.

70

SNOW SOMETIMES FALLS

20–24 January

Greater cold (*Daikan*, 大寒)
Butterburs bud (*Fuki no hana saku*, 款冬華)

The snow comes.

I am a mature adult, nearly fifty-six years on the planet. I pay taxes, can engage in at least partially informed discussions of world affairs. I have hung pictures without swearing, can change a plug, and know what to do in a power cut. I am able to be in a room with serious people for up to an hour without saying the word 'fart'. I have, and sometimes even understand, insurance.

I am, to all outward appearances – or most of them, at least – a 'grown-up'.

But show me even the prospect of snowfall and my inner eight-year-old bursts out in a giddy cloud of excitement and starts shouting 'SNOW SNOW SNOW' at the top of his voice while dancing a manic happy dance.*

---

* Less manic nowadays because of dodgy knees, but definitely very happy.

For a child growing up in low-lying Oxfordshire, snow was a noteworthy occurrence, eagerly anticipated but not often experienced. It wasn't just the possibility of a day off school that made it so enticing. There was the extreme prettiness of it all. The sheer perfection of a newly laid blanket of snow, assembled flake by painstaking flake until the lawn had disappeared, and just waiting for me, and only me, to be the first to disturb it.

And those childhood feelings run strong still.

Had snow been a more regular occurrence in my formative years, perhaps even to the point of banality and possibly hardship, my adult attitude might be different. I suspect that in places where it is routine, starting some time in autumn and ever-present until spring, there is a more mature, balanced attitude towards it. Probably it is regarded as a drudge, a tiresome and unavoidable fact of life. Certainly for anyone whose life is negatively impacted by snow and ice, it is understandably viewed with dismay. But even though the chances of my falling over* on a treacherous patch are greater than they were even ten years ago, I'm still in the grip of that excitable eight-year-old. The half-eye I keep on the weather forecast in normal circumstances develops into a full-on gaze, charting the evolving situation with the same rapt attention I lavished on the lightning radar back in the summer.

Perhaps all I want is a bit of drama.

When it does come, I stand by the window, nursing a cup of coffee and nibbling on a biscuit,† and watch it fall. A simple, calming

---

* I haven't quite reached the age where the expression morphs into 'having a fall'.

† Yes, OK, two biscuits.

meditation exercise. There's a bare sprinkling at first, dandruff flakes. The advance guard dissolves feebly on the ground, but bit by bit the flurries turn to billows and the billows turn to swathes and, as it thickens, the wind picks up and soon it's a swirling mass, most of it apparently flying upwards. And as they start to take hold on the ground, the dark brown of the terrace, pixel by pixel, turns white.

This is the kind of snow they write about in the old Japanese poetry. Soft, picturesque, benevolent. The reality, a lot of the time, was and is much harsher. Cold and inhospitable, making life a hardship.

Into all this excitement bursts a flurry of redwings – ten, twelve, fifteen – rising through the storm in a haphazard movement completely unlike their habitual direct flight, as if they've been temporarily disorientated. There's a friskiness to them that I anthropomorphically ascribe to excitement about the snow.

I go out. Of course I do. It's snow.

My tread is ginger as I go down the hill. I might be eight, but I'm also fifty-five. I almost come a cropper as my attention is distracted by a robin, putting on a similar display to the redwings but with more adrenalin. It occurs to me that, what with it being two years since the last snow in these parts, and the robin's life expectancy on average eighteen months,* it's most likely experiencing snow for the first time in its life. The poor bird seems to have simply no idea how to deal with it. Instead of its normal assured flight it scrambles first one way then the next, dipping down near the ground but apparently changing its mind about landing at the last minute, then swooping

---

* Yes, I know. That robin that's been coming to your feeder regularly for the last four years? Not the same bird. Sorry.

up again in a wild panic until finally it regains enough sangfroid to settle into a semblance of its usual behaviour.

In the cemetery, the mood-boosting quality of this snow is palpable. People have been worn down by the pandemic, the incessant rain and grey skies, and the apparently endless non-winter. And while what we really want is spring, the belated onset of something you really can call winter weather, however short-lived, is an undoubted boon to those susceptible to boonery.

The first thing I see as I enter the cemetery is a family. Two grinning adults and a slightly bemused toddler, no doubt experiencing the reality of snow for the first time. The father, with a quiet smile, is systematically making snowballs, scooping a handful of snow, patting it into shape in gloved hands, and placing each creation on the ground to form an orderly line.

There's a ritual to it, a soothing rhythm.

Scoop, pat, place. Scoop, pat, place.

He's done ten of them already. Whether they constitute the basis of an ambitious snow sculpture or the beginnings of a snowball arsenal isn't entirely clear. I walk on, just in case.

The snow intensifies as I walk round. Big fat flakes, wet splodges on my view of the world, falling and swirling and gradually accruing and engendering warm and vaguely benevolent feelings in the human heart.

It won't quite achieve the status of what I call a full snowfall – attained only when the white carpet covers the grass completely without even the hint of a spindly disturbance. But for a couple of hours it ticks all the necessary boxes.

Spring will come. The flowers will bloom. The birds will sing. But for now, we have the snow.

71

BIRDS EMERGE AFTER SNOW

25–29 January

Greater cold (*Daikan*, 大寒)

Ice thickens on streams
(*Sawamizu kōri tsumeru*, 水沢腹堅)

The day after snow, so often a time of dirty slush and ebbing euphoria. But this one's a cracker. Bright, cold, crisp and still.

I'm up early enough to usher in the dawn. Through the kitchen window the snow's luminescence lends an ethereal quality to the growing light. Faint flickerings, barely discernible, turn out to be unidentifiable birds flitting from tree to feeder. Probably great tits. They're usually the first.

As dawn's light spreads, muted colours become visible, as do cat tracks in the snow on next door's shed roof. And as the sun rises, it briefly casts a golden glow on the streets behind the house. With a bit of imagination, you could be in a Tuscan hill town.

OK, a lot of imagination.

The lawn looks threadbare, pockmarked where the snow has caved in slightly on the grass. If it had fallen for another hour or two, we might have had a covering worthy of the term 'carpet', but this is better than nothing.

Snow often brings birds. Cold times are tough times, and they need a lot of food to survive. And sure enough, the aftermath brings a flurry of activity to the feeders. I'm reassured by their very presence. It's when they're not there that I fear the worst.

As I watch, they scarper. Every last one of them. Not in the usual way, bird by bird, with a couple of stragglers hanging around, but in a blind panic. Cold sweat, no time to pick up your wallet, GO GO GO GET OUT SHUT UP JUST GO.

Sparrowhawk.

It's not even doing anything. It doesn't have to. All it did was fly in and perch on top of the tall conifer two doors down. A male. I can see the orange blush on its barred chest.

It sits there for a few minutes, presiding over the empty row of gardens in beady-eyed silence. Then it flies off to terrorise another neighbourhood.

I'm a quarter of the way round the cemetery, just past the memorial rose garden. The melt-off has only added to the saturation of the grass, and where the ground dips the water has gathered in a sizeable pool, which is attracting the attention of half a dozen carrion crows. The dynamics of the group could keep me occupied for a while. Two of them remain mostly still, jabbing sporadically at the ground near them without much energy, almost as if they know it's what's expected of them but are doing it only for appearance. Another is mobile, jumping around with that corvid bounce, like a two-footed canter. A fourth is in less of a hurry but catches the eye nevertheless, walking the jaunty wide-boy walk that carrion crows do better than any other bird.

Into this tableau, an intrusive sound. I've got so used to the aural canvas of the place that new sounds stick out like pink graffiti on Nelson's Column. It's reminiscent of a creaking gate, except that it's coming from directly overhead, where, as far as I know, there are no gates.

The bird making the sound is a carrion crow. This is no surprise. They have a wide vocabulary of grawks and squawks. A creaking gate would be well within their compass. But the thing that is making the crow make the creaking gate sound is more unusual.

It's a buzzard.

This might be the same buzzard I saw high over the garden all the way back in May. In fact, I'd lay good money on it. Carrion crows are two a penny around here; buzzards are not.

There is something incongruous about it, a bird so rough, so wild, so associated in my mind with countryside that an urban sighting takes me aback. But my image of them is rooted in my childhood, when they were only just beginning a recovery from the depredations of pesticide use in the 1950s, and a sighting in lowland Oxfordshire would have earned a gasp of wonder from an astonished eleven-year-old. Their range and population have grown immeasurably since then, and a London sighting is no longer cause for astonishment, but the eleven-year-old abides in me still, and he musters a gasp for old times' sake.

The choreography of the two birds follows a similar pattern to all the corvid–raptor encounters I've seen this year. The buzzard, apparently unconcerned, soars slowly in spiralling circles, wings splayed to conserve energy and catch what updraft it can. The crow is the agitated one, the geometry of its flight more haphazard and angular as it harries the buzzard, hoping to drive it away. The immediate effect seems minimal, but the larger bird does gradually spiral off, accompanied by the manic exertions of the crow. I watch them until they have disappeared completely from view, and continue gamely round the cemetery.

I read a feature about coping in a pandemic. Different people have different ways. Drawing, cooking, reading. Stargazing, cycling, binge-watching. Baking, card games, chutney-tasting.

My way has been local nature. Walk, observe, repeat. At some point in the last year I've visited every single street within a half-mile radius of my house. And while it's all become familiar to me, I've made a point of trying (although not always succeeding) to look at it all as if for the first time, taking in the whole of it, allowing its impression to settle, then at each individual thing, to see how it's made up. That goes there and that goes there and that other thing goes there. OK then. I see now.

I could evangelise about the importance of following this path, but it's not for everyone. More important than knowing all the names or counting all the birds or stopping to examine every leaf is something attainable to anyone. To become conversant – sometimes literally – with what's there. To acknowledge it, to include it in your daily routine, to notice it and say hello to it the way you would with the barman or the postman or the woman on the fruit-and-veg stall. Just a nod and a hello and occasionally a how are you. It's not too much to ask, surely?

72

JAYS RETRIEVE
ACORNS

30 January–3 February

Greater cold (*Daikan,* 大寒)
Hens start laying eggs
(*Niwatori hajimete toya ni tsuku,* 鶏始乳)

In Japan, 3 February is *setsubun* – the day before the beginning of spring. It's traditional to celebrate with the ritual of *mamemaki,* in which roasted soy beans are thrown out of the front door to drive out the evil of the previous year.

We're going to need a lot of beans.

When I had the idea of looking at my own patch for a year, I imagined that this local project would be incorporated into my normal birding activities. This would usually mean visits to wetlands, forests, heaths and occasionally the odd mountain or two. Maybe an island. I would have seen swans and plovers and terns and otters and deer and lizards and maybe – oh, please – a hare.

If given the opportunity I might have gone on a boat, as I did the previous year, and seen dolphins and eagles and what I'm pretty sure was a porpoise.

Variety, abundance, excitement.

The pandemic had other ideas.

This turned out to be a blessing in disguise. I developed a routine, a rhythm, grew increasingly attached to the little unexplored corners of my unexceptional local area. I saw bits of it I'd never thought of seeing, and I started noticing things I'd never thought of noticing. And this season is no different.

There is old man's beard, all straggly fluff, running rampant over a chain-link fence. There are lichens on a plane tree – different varieties, depending on which way they face and how much sun they get. There is a starling standing on a brick chimney, and when I look closely I see that its colouring – brown on the wings, metallic dark green with creamy white pips on the body, warm yellow bill morphing to black at the tip – is exactly mirrored by the brick it's standing on and the mosses and lichens adorning it. There are sparrows on the corner – the usual sparrows – present and correct and in good order. Eight of them in various states of visibility in the top half of the bush, with a few more no doubt sequestered in its depths. They have been an unending source of cheer, and the epitome of the uncelebrated lifeblood of local patch-watching.

There is more, much more. No matter how well you look, there will always be something else.

I continue with my little tour. Now the year is done, I will carry on exploring. Of course I will. It was a kind of habit before, even more ingrained now. And while circumstances have dictated that my explorations have been almost exclusively solitary, there is also

great pleasure to be had from shared experience. And so we come
to the highlight of the year, stumbled on in the last microseason. It
involves two men, two boys, and two extremely timely and oblig-
ing birds.

It started wet. It finishes wet. So much water.

The snow has melted, and there has been rain, and there are
graves submerged in great muddy pools.

A song thrush is singing, pelting it out from a handy perch. I
watch it through binoculars. I can see its mouth, synchronised with
the song. I can see the effort in its body as it produces the sound,
little twitches of wing tips, a shiver of the tail, a pulse in the torso.
I think of the energy it's expending in its efforts to procreate, the
primal, eternal urge to continue the species. It doesn't know why it
has to do it – it just does.

A jay flies in, and starts to behave in an officially Interesting
Way.

One of the things you discover when you read about jays is their
ability to remember where they've hidden their acorns. They're
famous for it. At it all the time. You can't heave a brick without
hitting a jay caching or retrieving an acorn from some hidey-hole
somewhere. The only thing is, I've never seen a jay in the process of
doing it. Not once.

Until now.

It flies in, unaccustomedly bold, and lands with a scowl on the
fine cherry tree to the right of the entrance path. There is hopping
about; there is mild agitation; there is adjustment of wings. And
then it reaches forward to a crevice in the tree, gives a little jiggle and

extracts a small item with its bill. It turns towards me, as if to present the object for my approval, and I can see clearly that it's an acorn. And then it's off, white rump flashing in the sunshine.

As it goes, I become aware of other people. Not just that, but other people with binoculars. Two men, two boys, all fully equipped for birding.

Lockdown has had its effect on my social skills, but I have retained residual memory of how to formulate an opening gambit.

'Hello!'

It's a successful gambit, reciprocated and developed. They are doing the Big Garden Birdwatch, an annual event that routinely ensures the absence of birds from people's gardens. In an attempt to foil them, they've come to the cemetery, where they figure the chances will be higher. As we chat, the boys look through their binoculars at anything and everything, naming birds.

'Have you seen the peregrines recently?'

'Great tit!'

'I have. Just yesterday, as a matter of fact.'

'Oh, excellent.'

'Robin!'

'Yes, they weren't around for a while, but they've been fairly regular for the last couple of weeks here and there.'

And at that moment, almost as if I'd trained it to react to the words 'here and there', a call comes from the church tower.

Kiii-ki-ki-ki-ki-ki-kiiii!

The sound pings towards us from a distance of a hundred metres. I turn and point.

'Up there. On the church tower. Peregrine.'

The boys are beyond excited. They train their binoculars on it, the younger one struggling just a bit with the focus. I do likewise. Clearly visible in silhouette, the female is hunched over a mass of something.

London's feral pigeon population has just taken a minor hit.

And as we watch, the male, visibly smaller in a way that isn't always apparent, swoops up to join its mate. They fuss around each other for a few seconds, then he leaves again, gliding down with grace and elegance before disappearing from view with a few shallow beats of his angular wings.

It's almost as if they knew they had an audience.

The activity of the birds is more than matched by the palpable excitement of the two boys. What with the jay and the song thrush and the peregrines, they've seen more avian activity in ten minutes than you might expect to see in a day. But most of all, they've seen it on their doorstep.

I resist the temptation to warn them that birding isn't always like this. Then we part ways and I leave them to discover more wonders on their local patch.

It would be too much to hope for a cormorant to round the year off. That single gronking flyover back in Season 1 was the only encounter I had with that species all year.

By way of compensation, shortly before sunset, I get four jays in the garden – *four* of them. They seem companionable enough at first, but then the squabbling begins and it becomes clear that this is not a happy family group so much as a territorial brawl. There is hopping about, a bit of frenzied squawking, a peck or two, and then there are three, then two, then none, and I'm left to contemplate the incoming sunset in peace. It's spectacular. Of course it is. I could take photographs and post them on Instagram. But just this once, I don't.

Onwards, and round again.

ACKNOWLEDGEMENTS

This book bears my name, but like all such endeavours it is the work of more than one person.

The people at Elliott & Thompson have developed a pleasing habit of letting me write the books I want to write. Simon Spanton's unremitting support and encouragement is indispensable. Sarah Rigby and Pippa Crane oversaw the book from idea to completion, and nudged me in the right direction at just the right moments. Alison Menzies is a one-person publicity machine, and Marianne Thorndahl makes things happen with the kind of understated efficiency it's all too easy to take for granted. Thank you all.

Thank you to Jill Burrows for impeccable copy editing, and not least for pointing out just how often I use the word 'pleasing' (too often). Thank you too to Clover Robin for another stunning cover design.

Laura Pritchard (as always) read early drafts, and (as always) made things better.

Thank you to the countless naturalists and writers whose work has expanded my knowledge (from, it has to be said, a very low base). There are far too many to mention here, but it's entirely possible you're one of them. Let's assume you are.

I undertook the observation of my patch almost entirely by myself – mostly for reasons of selfishness, but also because there was a pandemic on – but my thanks go to Helen Brownlie, fellow cemetery-stroller and keen fox-watcher, whose eyes and ears spotted things mine didn't.

Last but definitely not least, my enduring gratitude to my wife Tessa and son Oliver for all the usual things.